Twayne's United States Authors Series

Sylvia E. Bowman, *Editor*

INDIANA UNIVERSITY

Sinclair Lewis

(TUSAS) 14

SINCLAIR LEWIS

by SHELDON NORMAN GREBSTEIN

State University of New York

TWAYNE PUBLISHERS

A DIVISION OF G. K. HALL & CO., BOSTON

To Phyllis

Contents

About the Author

Sheldon Norman Grebstein was born in Providence, Rhode Island, and attended the public schools of that city. After two years at Providence College, he took his B.A. at the University of Southern California. He did his graduate work at Columbia, where he was awarded the M.A. in 1950, and at Michigan State University, receiving the Ph.D. in 1954.

Since 1953, when Mr. Grebstein completed his doctoral dissertation on Lewis as a social critic, he has published studies of various phases of Lewis's career in *Minnesota History, New England Quarterly, Philological Quarterly, Western Humanities Review*, and *Mississippi Quarterly*. In addition to his work on Lewis, he has contributed notes and articles to *English Journal, American Scholar*, and *The Humanist*. He has also edited a casebook on the Scopes trial, published by Houghton Mifflin in 1960 under the title *Monkey Trial*.

Mr. Grebstein is now at work on a study of John O'Hara, which will subsequently be published in Twayne's United States Authors Series. At present he is assistant professor of English at the University of Kentucky.

Preface

IN HIS LAST NOVEL, *World So Wide*, Sinclair Lewis made this prescient observation: "Americans want to see one movie star, one giraffe, one jet plane, one murder, but only one. They run up a skyscraper or the fame of generals and evangelists and playwrights in one week and tear them all down in an hour, and the mark of excellence everywhere is 'under new management.' " Lewis's intention here was to describe the behavior of Americans in Europe and to explain a few of our native attitudes.

But his comment could also serve as an apt description of the status of his own career, for no writer has ever risen higher in our critical esteem and then dropped more precipitately. In 1930 he was by far the most famous and among the two or three most respected American novelists. By the time of his death twenty years later, despite two best-sellers published just a few years before, the critics had written him off. Even now, as we begin to get perspective on his career and achievement, we tend to see him as a kind of literary phenomenon, an accident, a second-rate writer who by some miraculous conjunction of the times and his own special but small talents managed to capture our attention for a moment and then deservedly slid into oblivion. Or, as the editor of a respected scholarly journal put it, in his reply to an inquiry regarding his possible interest in an article on Lewis: "Why not leave Lewis in the corner into which he has so fairly been placed?"

The answer is that if Sinclair Lewis belongs in a corner, we must also find room in the same corner for a segment of American life. He was the conscience of his generation and he could well serve as the conscience of our own. His analysis of the America of the 1920's holds true for the America of today. His prophecies have become our truths and his fears our most crucial problems. *Middletown, The Lonely Crowd, White Collar, The Organization Man, The Status Seekers* are extended footnotes to Lewis's best work, and each day's headlines remind us bitterly of Lewis's repeated warning that if we have created only a high material culture without an equally high sense of beauty and decency and tolerance for individual differences, we have failed utterly.

If we can still read Sinclair Lewis with profit, why has he been so ignored and despised by those who determine literary reputations? There are several reasons. Some of them stem from the flaws in Lewis's own sensibility, talent, and attitude, and we must admit frankly to these flaws. First, Lewis was a man who could not firmly decide whether he was a satirist or a story-teller, a hard-boiled critic or a soft-boiled romancer, a novelist or a journalist, an artist or an entertainer. While in Lewis's best work these opposing tendencies achieved harmony and equilibrium, they too often collided. The result was a confusion in Lewis's thinking and an inevitable misdirection of his creative powers, an ambivalence toward his material and his craft which derived from an ambivalence within himself.

Second, Lewis was a keen and perceptive writer but not a profound writer, in the fullest sense of the word. He depicted love and death rarely; instead he wrote about romance and money. He was superbly a novelist of surfaces, of manners and mores, and only occasionally a novelist of morals and of the heights and depths of human experience.

Third, he failed to develop. Not one of his ten novels between 1930 and 1950 equalled his best work of the 1920's; and, although some of them deserve study and praise, too many are ephemeral. He undertook to defend what he had earlier attacked, or he repeated the same situations, characters, and satirical comments in a style somehow grown dated and stale.

Fourth, literary fashion moved away from Sinclair Lewis. The Marxist critics influential in the 1930's found his books no longer topical, and even hostile to their view. The Freudians found nothing in him which would support their commentary. The New Critics likewise ignored him. There were for them no problems of form in Sinclair Lewis, no experiments in style, no dilemmas, few complexities, no spatial or temporal disloca-tions, symbologies, obscurities. What could one say about a writer who claimed that he worked as hard on the frothiest tale as on the most serious novel, who rejected "style" as a generic concept, whose plots were mere strings of episodes, whose char-acters were flat, whose themes were announced forthrightly and

regularly at the beginning of each of his books? Only the reviewers continued to give him notice. The readers who continued to buy his books in substantial and at times staggering
quantities were represented by no voice in academic and literary
circles.

Part of my task in *Sinclair Lewis* is to argue against the injustice of Lewis's current status, in which his good books are
lumped together with the bad. He is a more important writer
than we now admit. In retrospect we discern that even one of
his greatest flaws—his ambivalence—lends dimension to his work
and enables us to feel that Gopher Prairie is, after all, worth
improving; that Babbitt is, essentially, a decent fellow; that we
must someday provide Arrowsmith the chance to work alone
and without pressure. We are now aware that Lewis's diatribes
against America were born of love, not hate; his intention was
not to defame us but to stir us from the dreadful torpor of
smugness and self-satisfaction—still the chief obstacle to our
highest fulfillment as a civilization.

This was Sinclair Lewis's purpose and glory. With that monstrous lack of self-knowledge peculiar to many artists, he claimed
at various moments in his career that he was not a reformer but
a diagnostician, or that he was not a realist or satirist but a
romantic medievalist. We know better. Like the hellfire-and-
damnation preachers whom he parodied but with whom he felt
a secret kinship, Lewis denounced us in novel after novel, essay
after essay, speech after speech. He was at his best in denunciation, and at his best he created an image of twentieth-century
American society which continues to haunt us in its essential
truth.

In this study I have focused, therefore, on his successes and
failures as a writer and as a social critic. Although *Sinclair Lewis*
is in no sense a biography (Mark Schorer's comprehensive biography of Lewis had just been announced for future publication
at the time of this writing), I have drawn upon the available
biographical material where it would illuminate Lewis's work.
The book is organized as follows. Chapter I establishes the
main lines of Lewis's work and sets forth what might be called
a "psychograph" of the writer. Chapter II deals with Lewis's
writing before 1920. Chapter III presents in chronological order
and with considerable detail each of the novels in Lewis's great

decade of 1920–1929; these are the works upon which his permanent reputation will rest. I have condensed other portions of my study so that this chapter would have the space it demanded. The remaining two chapters survey Lewis's melancholy career from 1930 to the end of his life.

SHELDON NORMAN GREBSTEIN

Lexington, Kentucky
July, 1961

Acknowledgments

I wish to express my gratitude to the executors of the estate of Sinclair Lewis for permission to examine the Yale collection of Lewis papers, and to Yale University for its courtesy in making those papers available to me. I am also grateful to the Research Fund of the University of Kentucky and to the Kentucky Research Foundation for grants used in the collection of material and the preparation of the manuscript.

I would like to make separate acknowledgment to the following for permission to quote from copyrighted material:

To the *Atlantic Monthly,* for permission to quote from Dorothy Thompson, "The Boy and Man from Sauk Centre" (Nov., 1960); Dorothy Thompson, "Sinclair Lewis: A Postscript" (June, 1951); and Perry Miller, "The Incorruptible Sinclair Lewis" (April, 1951).

To the *American Scholar,* for permission to quote from Frederick Manfred, "Sinclair Lewis: A Portrait" (Spring, 1954).

To Melville Cane, executor of the will of Sinclair Lewis, for permission to quote from Sinclair Lewis, *Our Mr. Wrenn* (1914), *The Trail of the Hawk* (1915), *The Job* (1917), and *The Innocents* (1917), all originally published by Harper and Brothers.

To the estate of David Cohn, for permission to quote from David Cohn, *The Good Old Days* (1940), published by Simon and Schuster, Inc.

To Doubleday and Co., for permission to quote from Sinclair Lewis, *Selected Short Stories* (1935), and *It Can't Happen Here* (1935).

To Harcourt, Brace and Co., for permission to quote from Sinclair Lewis, *Main Street* (1920), *Arrowsmith* (1925), and *The Man Who Knew Coolidge* (1928); from Grace Hegger Lewis, *With Love from Gracie* (1956); and from Harrison Smith, editor, *From Main Street to Stockholm* (1952).

To the Harvard University Press, for permission to quote from Monroe Engel, *The Maturity of Dickens* (1959).

To Alfred A. Knopf, Inc., for permission to quote from H. L. Mencken and George Jean Nathan, *The American Credo* (1920);

and George Jean Nathan, *The Intimate Notebooks of George Jean Nathan* (1932).

To the New York *Herald Tribune,* for permission to quote from Ramon Guthrie, "The Labor Novel Sinclair Lewis Never Wrote" (Feb. 10, 1952).

To the Oxford University Press, for permission to quote from James D. Hart, *The Popular Book* (1950).

To Random House, Inc., for permission to quote from Sinclair Lewis, *Gideon Planish* (1943), *Cass Timberlane* (1945), and *World So Wide* (1951).

To the *Saturday Evening Post,* for permission to quote from Christian Gauss, "Sinclair Lewis vs. His Education" (Dec. 26, 1931).

To the *Saturday Review,* for permission to quote from William Rose Benét, "The Earlier Lewis" (Jan. 20, 1934); and Charles Breasted, "The 'Sauk-Centricities' of Sinclair Lewis" (Aug. 14, 1954).

To Georges Schreiber, for permission to quote from his *Portraits and Self Portraits* (1936), published by the Houghton Mifflin Company.

To Charles Scribner's Sons, for permission to quote from Don Wharton, "Dorothy Thompson," *Scribner's Magazine* (May, 1937).

Chronology

1885   Harry Sinclair Lewis born February 7 at Sauk Centre, Minnesota, to Edwin J. Lewis and Emma Kermott Lewis. Two older brothers, Claude and Fred.

1891   Mother died. Father subsequently married Isabel Warner, 1892.

1890-
1902   Attended public schools in Sauk Centre. Read widely.

1898   Left home to enlist in Spanish-American War as drummer boy; apprehended by father in nearby town.

1901-
1903   Wrote minor social news, did odd jobs, worked as typesetter for Sauk Centre *Herald* and Sauk Centre *Avalanche*.

1902-
1903   Spent six months at Oberlin Academy, Oberlin, Ohio, preparing for Yale.

1903-
1906   At Yale. Contributed to Yale *Literary Magazine* and *Courant;* served as editor of *Literary Magazine*. To England on cattleboats during summers of 1904 and 1906. Summer of 1905 in Sauk Centre; conceived idea for novel to be called *The Village Virus*. While at Yale worked part-time for New Haven *Journal* and *Courier*.

1906   Left Yale, spent October–November at Helicon Hall, Upton Sinclair's utopian colony at Englewood, New Jersey, as man-of-all-work.

1906-
1907   Lived in New York, income from temporary jobs, editing, selling children's verses to magazines. November, 1907, to Panama by steerage in search of work on canal.

1907-
1908   Returned to Yale; received degree June, 1908.

1908-
1910   Roamed in United States. Held various jobs, including work as editor and reporter. Sold short-story plots to Jack London. Continued to write as free lance.

1910-
1915   Held a number of positions in New York City connected with publishing: manuscript reader, editor, advertising manager, reviewer.

1912   *Hike and the Aeroplane* published, under the pseudonym "Tom Graham."

1914   April, married Grace Livingstone Hegger in New York. *Our Mr. Wrenn* published.

1915   *The Trail of the Hawk* published. Resigned position with George H. Doran Company to devote full time to writing.

1915- Traveled with wife, temporary residence in several cities.
1920   Sold stories and serials to magazines. Summer of 1916 traveled by automobile across country from Sauk Centre to Seattle.

1917   *The Job* and *The Innocents* published. Son, Wells, born.

1919   *Free Air* published. *Hobohemia* (play) produced in Greenwich Village.

1920   *Main Street* published.

1921- Tried lecturing, gave it up, later returned to it, attracting
1922   sizable audiences and lively publicity throughout 1920's. To Europe to write *Babbitt.*

1922   *Babbitt* published.

1923   Traveled with Paul de Kruif, collecting material for *Arrowsmith. Arrowsmith* written in France, revised in London, 1923-24.

1924   Returned to United States. Summer in Canada with brother Claude.

1925   *Arrowsmith* published.

1926   *Mantrap* published. Spring, 1926, in Kansas City doing research for *Elmer Gantry.* May, 1926, refused Pulitzer Prize for *Arrowsmith.* Dr. Edwin J. Lewis died.

1927   *Elmer Gantry* published. To Europe, wandering. Winter, 1927-28, completed *The Man Who Knew Coolidge.*

1928   *The Man Who Knew Coolidge* published. April, divorced Grace Hegger Lewis; in May, married Dorothy Thompson. Returned to United States, bought farm in Barnard, Vermont, there finished *Dodsworth.*

1929   *Dodsworth* published. Began serious research on labor novel; never to be completed despite repeated efforts.

1930   Second son, Michael, born. December, awarded Nobel Prize for Literature. Traveled to Stockholm to accept award.

1931- Wrote *Ann Vickers* in New York and Barnard, Vermont.
1932

1933   *Ann Vickers* published.

1934   *Work of Art* published. Assisted Sidney Howard in dramatizing *Dodsworth. Jayhawker,* play written in collaboration with Lloyd Lewis, produced in New York.

1935   *Selected Short Stories* published. *It Can't Happen Here* published; later dramatized in collaboration with John C. Moffitt. Elected to membership in National Institute of Arts and Letters.

1936   Awarded honorary degree by Yale. *It Can't Happen Here* produced in fifteen cities by Federal Theater Project.

1936- Active in theater as actor, playwright, producer, and di
1942   rector. Made frequent lecture appearances during late 1930's and early 1940's.

1938   *The Prodigal Parents* published. October, 1937–April, 1938, contributed weekly book columns to *Newsweek.* Wrote play *Angela Is Twenty-Two;* subsequently acted in lead role of touring production.

1940   *Bethel Merriday* published. Fall, conducted writing class at University of Wisconsin.

1942   Divorced from Dorothy Thompson. Special lecturer in English at University of Minnesota.

1942- Intermittent residence in Minnesota, with extended trips
1946   to New York and elsewhere.

1943   *Gideon Planish* published.

1944   Lieutenant Wells Lewis killed by sniper in Alsace.

1945   *Cass Timberlane* published. Beginning in June contributed monthly book reviews to *Esquire* for several issues.

1946- When not traveling, resided at Thorvale Farm near Wil
1949   liamstown, Massachusetts.

1947   *Kingsblood Royal* published. Fall, in Minnesota doing research into state's early history.

1949   *The God-Seeker* published. September, sailed for Italy. Health failing.

1951   Died in Rome of heart disease, January 10. Ashes returned to Sauk Centre for burial. *World So Wide* published posthumously.

CHAPTER 1

The Two Sinclair Lewises

IN THE YEARS from 1914 to 1951 Sinclair Lewis, a flamboyant, driven, self-devouring genius from Sauk Centre, Minnesota, aspired in twenty-two novels to make all America his province. Although his star has now waned, he was in his time the best-known and most controversial of our writers; and, through a number of books remarkable for their satiric bite and for their ambivalent love and hatred of the land and people he took as his domain, he helped to make Americans known to themselves and to the world.

Lewis was a descendant of the line of Cooper, Emerson, Thoreau, Whitman, and Twain. Like them, he railed against the insidious effects of mass culture and the standardization of manners and ideas. Like his more immediate forebears, Bellamy and Henry George, he dreamed of a better America, and his vision moved him to hack at the weeds of mediocrity blighting what his contemporary Fitzgerald called "the bright green breast of the new world." In his best novels he turned the unblinking light of his critical gaze upon our most hallowed institutions: the small town, the businessman, medicine and science, religion, the American abroad; and in other books he focused upon social work and penology, hotel-keeping, native Fascism, fund-raising, marriage, racial hatred. Always his favorite targets were smugness, hypocrisy, dishonesty, conformity, snobbery, prejudice. For his zeal, his talent, his humor, he became the *first* American writer to win the Nobel Prize for Literature; but it was only one measure of the height of his reputation and his influence.

I *A Private War*

Perhaps the sharpest realization, as we survey the long career of Sinclair Lewis, with its more than a score of novels and hundreds of shorter pieces, is that as a writer he was constantly at war with himself. His novels are almost equally divided, each novel combining in itself these apparently hostile elements: half, the product of Lewis the satirist and realist; half, the work of the romancer and yea-sayer. Even in the great satirical novels of the 1920's there is this ambivalence.

The writer in America has almost always been faced with the dilemma of whether to be serious, poor, unread, and perhaps honored after death, or to be entertaining, rich, popular, and quickly forgotten. In Lewis's case this dilemma took a curious form, for he was honored only when he was being serious—when he was attacking or instructing Americans—and, when he became entertaining and affirmative, his work ceased to command attention. But it was much less a matter of choice for Lewis than it was for, say, Fitzgerald. For Lewis it was part of his nature, virtually a compulsion, to be at times a mere storyteller, an entertainer, a trickster or, to use the word most appropriate to him, a romancer.

As a boy in Sauk Centre he had read romances and had been deeply affected by Malory's Arthurian tales, by Sir Walter Scott and Dickens, and he soon became famous among the children of the town as a spinner of fabulous yarns.[1] Much of his college writing was verse in the Tennysonian vein; moreover, most of his short stories, as well as his first five novels, were romances. In the preface to his *Selected Short Stories* (New York, 1935), he wrote: "One of the things interesting to the author, though perhaps to no one else, in rereading these stories, is the discovery that he, who has been labeled a 'satirist' and a 'realist,' is actually a romantic medievalist of the most incurable sort. He realizes that, but for some mysterious trick of destiny, he might, instead of being properly classed with the subversive, the Communists who insist that most preachers are dull and most politicians are more afflicted by the gimmes than by righteousness, have gone on to be one of the really exemplary representatives of the Arts, men pure and traditional and frequently white-bearded. . . ."

However, as a romancer Lewis was not only a teller of amusing stories. He was also compelled to be affirmative, a solid citizen, a pillar of the community, and whatever moments of realism or satire he might include in his romances, he ultimately had to assert the enduring values of home, family, regular habits, the middle class, and sound business. Nor did Lewis disbelieve in these values. Like Whitman, he contained multitudes. He did love Main Street and Babbitt, even while he lashed them, but in his best books his hatred, not his love, lifted him far above the bog of popular fiction into which he too often tended to sink.

This split in Lewis's sensibility began very early in his life. In his father, his brothers, his neighbors, and the other boys of his age, he was confronted with virtues and qualities Sauk Centre admired: dependability, hard common sense, physical strength and coordination in sport and work, the ability to accumulate property and substance. They were not proud but contemptuous when he ran away at thirteen to enlist in the Spanish-American War and was apprehended at the railway station in a nearby town by his irritated father. They could not understand a boy who wanted to study foreign languages, who questioned his Sunday School teacher about the story of Jonah and the whale, who preferred books to sports, and who wanted to go away to an eastern college. One of his neighbors recalled that he knew Lewis was destined for great things when Lewis claimed (he was then about five years old) that he could eat grass, and forthwith gnawed off a square foot of lawn. Another good citizen of the town, a lady, said of him: "Nobody in Sauk Centre knows how Red heard all those things he had his people say because he never stopped talking long enough to listen to anyone." A third, who had known him well as a boy, remembered him as "a freak, all eyes and all energy, who had the uncommon trait of observing every minute detail upon merely walking through a room."[2]

Thus the two Sinclair Lewises were formed. A shy, sensitive, lonely boy, aware of his peculiarities yet hungry for the town's approbation, he developed—as such children often do—an overt perversity and hatred for what he secretly loved and in which he wished to share. He made a strength of what Sauk Centre termed weakness, and, as he grew up, he came to discover with increasing bitterness that these were no knights and no ruined castles in Minnesota. In his impulse toward revenge for these disappointments, Lewis the satirist was born.[3]

But there is another side to the story. Lewis's grandfather, father, uncle, and older brother Claude were all medical men; and, while Dr. E. J. Lewis put no specific pressure on his youngest son to follow in the family profession, Lewis carried a lifelong burden of guilt over not having been a physician.[4] He once told his second wife, Dorothy Thompson: "The only people I ever wanted to impress were my father and brother Claude. I never succeeded. . . ." Late in his life he confessed to an interviewer that he would most of all have liked to combine medicine with writing as his life's work.[5] He deeply admired his father and older brother and eventually he established a close relationship with Claude, but he never lost the conviction that they—and especially his father—despised writing as a career or that they could not take it seriously as fit employment for a grown man.

This feeling rankled in Lewis; inevitably his resentment broadened to include all America—and the inability of her lower and middle classes to understand or appreciate the artist, his creation, or, indeed, anything non-material. This reaction was one of the roots of his tormented and contradictory personality; it was basic, we also believe, to his satiric impulse. Just as he was torn by ambivalent attitudes toward his birthplace, so was he disturbed by his warring emotions toward his father, the stern, upright, competent, undemonstrative Dr. E. J., who was so regular in his habits that the town swore it could set its clocks by his routine movements.

Ramon Guthrie, who knew Lewis intimately, has asserted that Lewis's relationship with his father was vital in determining the course of his career. "All of his best books were an affirmation of the hard-won emancipation from being Harry Lewis of Main Street. Yet throughout his life, whenever Red stood on the verge of giving the true measure of himself and the forces that were in him, the shade of Dr. E. J., as Red always called him, snorted the phrase that never lost its power to bring him to heel: 'Harry, why can't you do like any other boy ought to do!' " In this way, Guthrie concludes, Lewis's worst books were the work of Harry of Main Street, written to please his father; his best books were the work of Red Lewis, the satirist, the artist, the rebel.[6] Further evidence comes from the memoir of Lewis's first wife, who describes Dr. Lewis as senselessly rigid and arbitrary, and writes: "I know nothing of psychoanalysis but even I can see that the influence of the father figure at this early age may have created the neuroses from which he later suffered."[7]

Lewis was again bitterly disappointed when he went to Yale; he expected it to share his burning enthusiasm for ideas, literature, knowledge. Except for the warm response from a few like-minded friends and the friendship of some of his professors, he found instead only general coolness and scorn. Driven by the sense of his own inferiority as a raw westerner amidst suave easterners, he announced himself a radical and an agnostic, and his classmates promptly dubbed him "Red" and "God-forbid"—both for his appearance and his opinions—and then snubbed him. Their pursuits—athletics, campus politics, social life—bored him, and they could not understand anyone who did not share these interests.[8] As a classmate recalled: "Lewis was as different from the correct young types around him as Sauk Center [sic] is from Tuxedo. He had none of their artificial constraints and far more real dignity of nature." Chauncy Brewster Tinker, one of those whose friendship and tolerance were essential to Lewis's survival at Yale, remembered him in this way: "The conventions and restrictions of good society—especially of collegiate society—were offensive to him. His abiding temptation was to undermine them and blow them at the moon." In fact, Lewis felt himself so out of place at Yale that he told an acquaintance he was tired of the derision he was suffering and intended to leave college.[9] His dissatisfaction with Yale, together with his already great restlessness and thirst for adventure, motivated him to leave school for a few months and join Upton Sinclair's Helicon Hall, a utopian colony in New Jersey. But his integrity and his sense of duty to his father brought him back to finish his studies.

We may judge with what spirit Lewis came to Yale from this entry in his diary, written the year before his entrance and on the occasion of checking some references on Macaulay, then one of his favorites: "All such work as looking up these references gives me a desire to be a master of some subject—say of ancient Egyptian religion or ancient Egyptian history or the geography of the Ancient World or Sanskrit or the History of Rome from 509 B.C. to Birth of Christ; or the History, Literature and Language of Phoenicia—touching especially or rather studying especially Astarte, a favorite topic of mine." Further on, this entry appears: "A boy—nay a child of eighteen, knowing or expecting to know anything. I must wait fifty years to begin to learn."[10]

Although his social experience at college was unhappy, he found satisfaction in intellectual activities. He indulged his "hydroptic thirst for knowledge" (Professor Tinker's phrase) in

wide but disorganized reading; "drawing more books from the
Yale library than, I believe, any undergraduate has before or
since," William Rose Benét later recalled.[11] Among the authors
he read were Hardy, Meredith, James, Howells, Austen, Brontë,
Shelley, Keats, Coleridge, Rossetti, Swinburne, Clough, Ibsen,
Tolstoy, Pushkin, Turgenev, Gogol, Flaubert, Zola, Huneker,
Pinero, Jones, Shaw, d'Annunzio, Sudermann, Yeats, George
Moore, Nietzsche, Haeckel, Huxley, Moody, Marx, Gorky, Blake,
Pater. Before he was graduated, he also read and was pro-
foundly influenced by H. G. Wells.

II *The "Knocker"*

Amidst the German drinking songs and pseudo-medieval
lyrics which constitute the bulk of Lewis's college writing, we
may also perceive an occasional hint of Lewis the reformer,
realist, and satirist. The essays written for a course in Seven-
teenth Century English Literature foreshadow, in their skillful
imitations of Butler, Burton, Earle and Overbury and in their
adeptness at mimicry, parody, and burlesque, the techniques
of his later satire. Some of Lewis's contributions to the *Courant*
and the *Yale Literary Magazine* also predict the later Lewis:
they reveal an eye for realistic detail, a keen sense of injustice,
a hatred of hypocrisy. One story ridicules a minister who steals
chickens in order to experience sin; another castigates a vain
pontiff; and an editorial defends "Unknown Undergraduates."
Another editorial remarks on the sight and sounds of New Haven
to be seen only when all good people have long been abed.
In short, it was while at Yale that Lewis began to grow as a
writer and to discover the fertility of his own imagination.

The later Lewis was also predicted in a series of editorials
which he wrote in the summer of 1908, during his employment
by the Waterloo, Iowa, *Daily Courier* (from which he was
abruptly discharged after several weeks for incompetence).
While most of these editorials on local and national issues were
staunch, sober, earnest, and even hortatory pieces on such subjects as the Standard Oil Company, nudity in art, and good
roads, two were especially significant. One was an editorial on
religious impostors and fraudulent evangelists; the other, still
more prescient, was called "Needful Knockers." These excerpts
speak for themselves: "It is well known to the philosopher that

the clear sighted pessimist is quite as often in the right as the optimist, who is likely to be blinded by enthusiasm. . . . The great reformers and martyrs have been knockers for the most part. . . . Yet it was these same knockers who saved the world. . . . The booster's enthusiasm is the motive force which builds up our American cities. Granted. But the hated knocker's jibes are the check necessary to guide that force."[12]

However, these were rare moments in Lewis's career. For the most part he was a hack, a popular romancer, who turned out light humorous verse and sentimental tales for the magazines and who worked in the meantime at a variety of writing and editing jobs. Then, as later, he had inexhaustible powers of invention. He conceived more plots and ideas than a writer could use in a lifetime; he even sold some of the excess to Jack London.[13] His stories, including those few with serious undertone, are indistinguishable from the potboiling fiction of the time in their optimism, cleverness, and superficiality; yet he apparently suffered neither difficulty nor pangs of conscience in doing them. Unlike Fitzgerald, he had no fear that he would suffer bankruptcy if he drew too heavily upon his resources. By 1911 he had published sixty-six poems, articles, and stories. By 1920 he had published some twenty-five additional stories and six novels. Of these novels, despite a number of passages or social criticism and some mild satire, only one, *The Job* (1917), could be called realism.

But the other Lewis waited behind the guise of hack writer and romancer. The other Lewis had already been struck with the idea for the novel later to make him famous, *Main Street* (1920). The other Lewis had read Wells, Veblen, and Shaw; had carried a membership card in the Socialist Party of New York for some fifteen months; and had written an article called "The Passing of Capitalism" in which he asserted: "And does it not by now seem that practically every writer—certainly in America and to some extent in England—who is gravely seeking to present the romance of actual life as it is to-day, must perforce show capitalism as a thing attacked, passing—whether the writer lament or rejoice or merely complain at that passing? Few of them have any very clear idea of how the passing is to occur; as to what is to take its place. . . . Yet there it is, in nearly every seeing writer of to-day—an attack on capitalism."[14] The Lewis who wrote popular fiction was motivated, at least in part, by the desire to break away from the routine of publishing work and to be a free lance; he then wished to accumulate enough money to put down on paper the big and honest novel growing within him.

With *Main Street*, Lewis became a celebrity. In fact, his fame and occasional notoriety as a public figure frequently overshadowed his fame as a writer. Somehow, whether or not he intended it, Sinclair Lewis was always news. One of his speeches, given in Stockholm on the occasion of receiving the Nobel Prize, heightened the argument already raging about the choice of Lewis for the award. Earlier, Lewis had made the headlines by his firm refusal of the Pulitzer Prize. He was news when he accused Dreiser of plagiarism at a public dinner and a scuffle occurred. He was news when he energetically supported La Follette against Coolidge in the 1924 presidential campaign. He was news when the Daughters of the American Revolution refused him the use of Constitution Hall, and he was news in dozens of other incidents. Each of his major novels of satire, especially *Main Street, Babbitt, Elmer Gantry, It Can't Happen Here, Kingsblood Royal,* aroused a storm of comment and controversy, the furor around each settling just in time to be stirred up by the next. Certainly no American novels of the twentieth century have aroused more discussion than did *Main Street, Babbitt,* and *Elmer Gantry* in their time.

III *A Tormented Personality*

But success and fame are never free to those who gain them, and they seem to have exacted an unusually heavy price from Sinclair Lewis. He was from the outset a strange and contradictory personality, a dynamo of energy, ideas, words, yet shy, lonely, insecure. Professor Tinker wrote of Lewis in college: "Associating with him was no quieting experience. He wanted in return as much as he gave, and this was of course a staggering demand." William Rose Benét recalls the Lewis of 1909: "There were . . . the almost endless monologues in which he suddenly took on a character part, and the fantastic imaginings that would be worked out in the most intricate detail, till one almost screamed for surcease from the spate of words. From intense hilarity the man would also, at times, turn as grave and didactic as a Baptist minister and proceed to lay down the moral law, according to his own highly individual ideas, with an almost snarling earnestness that seemed to bode hell-fire for the unbeliever."[15]

Lewis did not become more stable as he grew older. His success as a writer fed his vanity and increased his self-indulgence. As a man of international prominence he expected people to put up with his oddities. He grew ever more petulant and difficult and was subject to sudden moods and whims sometimes lasting for hours, sometimes days. He could be the most convivial of companions, warm, friendly, generous, then fly into towering rages, wound his hearer or a roomful of people with his razor-edged tongue, or abruptly walk out. In one moment he would make the most elaborate plans for some activity or project, then abandon them in the next. Always his enormous surface egotism demanded that others recognize his talent and importance; he resented any intrusion upon the monologues he could carry on interminably. The Nobel Prize made him even more difficult. Yet, paradoxically, no one could be more kind and encouraging to young writers. Like Poe's tormented Man of the Crowd Lewis surrounded himself with all types of people, striking up instant friendships, always searching for new talk, new places, new acquaintances—and becoming quickly bored with each. He traveled incessantly. His drinking became an increasingly troublesome problem, eventually damaging his health, although apparently affecting him little while he was working on a novel.

Not surprisingly, Lewis was neither a model husband nor father, although, if we may take his wives' memoirs at face value, he inspired in both Grace Hegger and Dorothy Thompson a tenderness which lasted long after the marriages had dissolved. With some sense of the irony of it, we observe that Lewis, who had himself suffered because he felt unloved by his father, was remote to his own two sons. He was proud of his older son, Wells, who gave promise of becoming a talented novelist in his own right; however, though deeply grieved at his son's death in World War II, he kept his feelings largely to himself. The younger son, Michael, when asked about his father, replied, "I hardly know the man."[16] It was thus a fate partly of Lewis's own making when he died in Rome with no members of his family or close friends near; all his life achingly lonely, he had by the end of it outraced all his loved ones.

All who have heard Lewis's talk and recorded their reminiscences in print vouch for his brilliance. Rebecca West once said that after a number of hours of conversation with Lewis one forgot that he was a person and began to think of him "as a great natural force, like the aurora borealis."[17] Clifton Fadiman called him "a Mercutio from the prairies." Essential to his conversation was his amazing power of mimicry, a verbal agility so great he could instantly and on the spot compose verse in the manner of any poet his listeners would name.[18] While he often used his mimetic gift as a mere parlor trick, it was much more important to him both as a means of literary composition and as a way of testing his creation upon an audience. Later, his dazzled hearers might discover that they had been exposed to entire chapters of Lewis's most recent novel months before its publication.[19]

Undoubtedly some of his peculiar behavior originated from his secret grief and sensitivity over his appearance. W. E. Woodward, who first met Lewis in 1912, described him as "a lanky, blue-eyed, red-haired fellow with a rough face and as homely as a rail fence"; this is not a flattering picture but it is hardly repelling. However, Lewis's face became increasingly disfigured by a type of skin cancer and by the radium and electric-needle treatments for it. Dorothy Thompson has given us this graphic sketch of Lewis at their initial meeting in 1927:

> He seemed to bring in with him a disturbing atmospheric tension such as that which precedes an electric storm. I saw a narrow, ravaged face, roughened, red, and scarred . . . less of the face below the hawkish nose than above it, where it broadened into a massive frontal skull . . . reddish but almost colorless eyebrows above round, cavernously set, remarkably brilliant eyes, transparent as aquamarines and in them a strange, shy, imploring look . . . a small and narrow mouth, almost lipless . . . and which in the course of a few minutes could smile a dozen ways. The face of a man who had walked through flame throwers. An elegance about the figure, slim, narrow, long-boned, very tall. . . . Very well dressed in clothes obviously from Savile Row. And an immediate aura of greatness, large, torrential, tortured, and palpitatingly sensitive.

Frederick Manfred (Feike Feikema), a Minnesota writer who visited Lewis in 1946, describes him thus: "The face I saw was a face to haunt one in dreams. It was a face that looked as if it were being slowly ravaged by a fire, by an emotional fire, by a fire that was already fading a little and that was leaving a slowly contracting lump of gray-red cinder." And others have testified that Lewis's appearance added to his sense of inferiority, creating a "psychic trauma"; that it made him avoid people and intensified his loneliness.[20]

Lewis's appearance was more than a personal tragedy and more significant than as a cause for his exasperating behavior. I believe it got into his books. When we are not at ease within ourselves, when we have some cause, real or imagined, to feel that others do not admire and love us—as Lewis had cause to feel in Sauk Centre, at college, and in his appearance—we may react in a number of ways. One of the classic modes of reaction is to turn upon oneself and in some manner injure oneself, as Lewis may have done with his drinking and his failure to control the fierce temper which drove others away. Another mode is to escape into a fantasy world, to project the wounded self and the circumstances of the wound into a larger, more satisfying world, where the unresolved problems of reality can be resolved in the imagination. Lewis perhaps did that with his fictional romances. Another reaction is to turn against the world, to nag and pick and tear at it, to hurt it and degrade it as the self has been hurt and degraded. Finally, one can try, in the attempt to make the world better, to make the self better. These were the impulses behind Lewis's satire. It all stems from love, or rather the failure of love. "I think one of the most tragic facets of his nature was his disbelief in his own capacity to evoke love from others. He hurt others, very often out of this frustration," the second Mrs. Lewis wrote shortly after his death.[21] We may conclude that this is one of the keys to the paradoxical Sinclair Lewis, the man and the writer.

IV *The American Dickens*

But in dealing with Lewis as a *writer* and in order to see his work in its largest perspective, we must forgive and forget his personal quirks and shortcomings, as we forget Coleridge's addiction to opium, Marlowe's homosexuality, Pope's petty vindictiveness, and Pound's collaboration with the Fascists. The books loom larger than the man; ultimately only the books endure. Taine has demonstrated that the man can help us to understand the books, but Poe has also shown that the work has a meaning and existence apart from the creator.

In what tradition, then, does Sinclair Lewis belong and with what illumination may we see him? Constance Rourke has mapped out one wide avenue of inquiry by placing Lewis in the highroad of American humor. To her, Lewis is basically a teller of tall stories, a fabulist, a legend-maker, who in *Main Street* and *Babbitt* originated national archetypes. In his derision, in his use of homely metaphors, in his technique of combining biting understatement with exaggeration, in his gift for comic mimicry, in his passion for the monologue, he moves with the grain of native humor, as typically American in the mode and personality of his work as is his audience's fascination with Lewis's images of them. Rourke concludes that because of the verisimilitude of his portrayal of American life Lewis may assume the same importance in the development of the American novel as did Defoe in England. Already, she says, we have been changed by what we saw of ourselves in Lewis's mirror.[22]

Rourke's analysis is especially important in that it focuses on an aspect of Lewis's work we tend increasingly to overlook, his humor. Significantly, the official citation for the Nobel Prize read: "The 1930 Nobel Prize in Literature is awarded to Sinclair Lewis for his powerful and vivid art of description and *his ability to use wit and humor* [my italics] in the creation of original characters." Considering the events of our time, it is no longer a novelty that European observers should perceive important truths about us.

However, there is more to Lewis than native humorist. He is also a realist. In a sense he fulfilled Howells's plea for writers who could take the commonplace and familiar in American life and make of it durable literary material. Herein Lewis follows not only Howells but also Garland, Fuller, Herrick, and others; in fact, Lewis more than once credited Garland with teaching him that life was more than samite and roses, and he noted that *Main-Travelled Roads* and *Rose of Dutcher's Coolly* were much undervalued books. He also greatly admired Edith Wharton, dedicating *Babbitt* to her (with her permission).[23]

Both Wharton and Lewis are superlatively novelists of manners, each of the manners of his class. Furthermore, it was as a realist that Lewis studied the surface detail of American life, its speech, its houses, its gadgets, its caste marks, with a thoroughness and accuracy which have never been surpassed, not even by Dreiser, Lewis's closest competitor in this respect. "A Cameraman" E. M. Forster once titled an essay on Lewis, and it is as a cameraman, a photographic realist, that the majority of the critics of the 1920's tended to see him.[24]

As a realist, or critical realist, Lewis has had considerable influence on the modern American novel. While he has attracted no close imitators and founded no schools, as have Hemingway and Faulkner, he is at least partly responsible for the continuing vogue of the "debunking" novel and for the continuously close scrutiny which our writers have paid to the nation's manners, morals, and institutions. Marquand is the mid-century novelist who most nearly resembles him, although Lewis is of far greater importance. Both were deeply conscious of social and class traits and highly skilled in their portrayal: Lewis the laureate of the middle midwesterner, Marquand of the upper easterner. Both were effective because of the tension caused by the basic affection which underlay Lewis's satire and Marquand's irony. Both were irascible men who responded quickly to irritants. Both had long and prolific careers. Both had a sensitive ear for the speech of their class and region. Both had humor and compassion. They also shared some of the same faults: both tended to write copies of their own best books; both were too often writers only of the surface; both were reticent, even prudish, about sex.[25]

But we must resist filing Lewis away so neatly, for he was also an idealist and a reformer. As a boy Lewis had been deeply affected by Thoreau's *Walden*. It was for him an early vision of Mecca, and it became Arrowsmith's final solution—retreat to the woods. Like Emerson and Thoreau, Lewis hated conformity, materialism, hypocrisy, pretentiousness. Like them, despite his surface congeniality, he tended to be an *isolato*. Like them he loved man more than he loved men. Lewis's utterances, which caused the same stir in his audience as did Emerson's, even attacked the same sacred cows: "proper" behavior, traditional religion, the worship of the golden calf. Like Emerson, Lewis made part of his living by lecturing. Like him he admired nature and saw it as a balm and retreat, but never learned to know it intimately or love it truly.

Like Emerson and Thoreau, he saw the individual as the measure of all things, and like them he was unhappy with the government of his day and its policies. Emerson's entry in his *Journals*, Florence, May 21, 1833, "I like the sayers of No better than the sayers of Yes," reminds us of Lewis's early essay "The Needful Knockers." Another excerpt from the *Journals* (June, 1847), could well have been written by Lewis; in fact, it recalls Lewis's early plan for *Main Street* which he titled "The Village Virus": "America seems to have immense resources, land, men, milk, butter, cheese, timber, and iron, but it is a village littleness; village squabble and rapacity characterize its policy. It is a great strength on the basis of weakness." Like Emerson and Thoreau, Lewis was dissatisfied with America and Americans, but he could offer no concrete and viable program of improvement. The crucial difference between Lewis and the transcendentalists, of course, is Lewis's irreligiosity, his lack of belief not only in an oversoul but in any spiritualization of human experience. He is said to have discussed these matters passionately in private, yet they do not get into his books other than in the form of a yearning for life to be somehow better than it is. Death is rare in his novels; and, in the few instances in which it appears, it belongs to plot rather than theme.

We cannot demand of a novelist that he affirm the existence of a soul, a deity, an afterlife, an immortal love, or any of the concepts and faiths to which most men cling. Too, Lewis had his own set of beliefs: in a wiser and more just social order, in individual fulfillment, in freedom, in personal integrity; nor are these to be derided. But we can demand of a writer that he confront love and death, as did Dreiser. For this reason we now value Dreiser above Lewis—although Lewis is in many ways a better writer—because in Dreiser we get the cosmic sense, the totality of vision, which does not exist in Lewis except for some moments in *Arrowsmith*.

These comparisons could be continued. Some critics have shown the similarities between Lewis and Twain; there are also a number of resemblances between Lewis and Whitman. But one further parallel will suffice. Whatever his faults, Sinclair Lewis will eventually occupy approximately the same position in American literature as does Dickens in English. As a number of critics and scholars have observed, there are very strong similarities between the two as men, as writers, as thinkers. Important as Thoreau, Garland, Wells, and others were to Lewis's development, it was Dickens who most fascinated him and to whom he constantly returned. Perry Miller, who became a close friend of Lewis in the last year of the novelist's life, writes: "He knew Dickens by heart. There was little to be gained by asking him about what had come in between, about realists and naturalists. . . . Most of them meant little to him, except for Shaw and Wells, who to him were primarily writers that showed what might be done with Dickensian exaggeration in a modern situation." Professor Miller continues: "He was in love with mythological and typological creations like Micawber and Gradgrind, and all his effort had been to evoke such genii out of the American bottle."[26] In an early essay which is still one of the most perceptive on Lewis, his friend and contemporary James Branch Cabell stated that many of Lewis's characters, such as Pickerbaugh, Gantry, and Chum Frink, were the "elvish" grandchildren of the Americans Dickens had created in *Martin Chuzzlewit*.[27]

True as these insights are, it is an error to emphasize only the fabulism and exaggeration Lewis and Dickens shared. There are other vital likenesses. Dickens believed that the writer ought to feel tenderness for his characters. Lewis, of course, often stated his affection for Babbitt, the citizens of Gopher Prairie, and even Gantry. Dickens believed that the writer's responsibility was to discover and reveal beauty in the commonplace. This was precisely Lewis's intention for much of his career; even in his satires he pursues it through the characters of Carol Kennicott, Babbitt, and others. Dickens used facts to support his imagination; for example, he got himself smuggled into court so he could observe a stern judge and thus create an authentic character in *Oliver Twist*, and he depended upon a doctor friend for medical information he needed in *Bleak House*. The accumulation of data was also essential to Lewis's method. It has been said that in his techniques of gathering information he was more the anthropologist than the novelist. He even used technical assistants: a clergyman for *Elmer Gantry*, a research scientist for *Arrowsmith*.

Dickens wanted his characters to be vivid and yet credible within their own possibilities. Although these characters have often been falled "flat" because of Dickens's heavy reliance upon their "humors"—his emphasis of a single idea or quality—the frequency with which these characters have passed into the common language ("Micawberish," "Pecksniffian") shows that such characters may be higher art than most current critics realize. Dickens's dramatic instincts, basic to his fiction, expressed themselves in his early attempts at acting before they were absorbed by his writing. Lewis, too, felt a great pull toward the theater; in fact, he worked in it for a number of years as playwright, actor, and director. More important, Lewis's habit of acting out his character creations, absorbing his own personality in them, closely resembles Dicken's imaginative mode. Lewis's characters are also typed and flat, yet "Babbitt" and "Gantry" have passed into the common speech. There is not much stronger evidence of the vividness and truth of a writer's conceptions.

Certainly both writers were convinced that the story should be lively and amusing. Both writers also ran to bulk in their work, a bulk deriving from largeness and looseness of creation rather than overwriting, although both were frequently guilty of that. Both operated by a method of accretion, making their points primarily through reiteration. Neither was distinguished by subtlety. Their tools, heavy and blunt, were swung with gusto.

Dickens had strong convictions about the professional and aesthetic responsibilities of the writer. He opposed the practice of the author directly addressing the reader, believing that the story and characters ought to carry the message. He held that the novelist should avoid imitation and dependence upon worn conventions. Withal, he was moved by a high moral seriousness and social concern. He never forgot the large size of his audience and he believed that it was part of the writer's duty to address himself to the masses. Fiction, he was convinced, must have a purpose; we recall that he told Carlyle *Hard Times* was intended to shake up the public. Always he retained his belief that art could change people's lives.

Lewis was as bitterly opposed to the imitativeness and conventionality of the fiction of his time as Dickens. Again and again he pauses to strike out at the popular writers of his day, Harold Bell Wright and others; yet Lewis, like Dickens, was neither wholly successful in rising above the conventions he mocked nor in avoiding thinly disguised sermons to the reader. Lewis had the same sense of audience as Dickens, a sense which may have also worked to Lewis's detriment. We feel this especially in some of Lewis's later books, in which he seems to be addressing himself to the same people who took him up in the 1920's and whom he presumes have now grown older and mellower with him. Dickens's sense of "truth," his moral purpose, was akin to that motivating Lewis in his satire and realism, even in such affirmative novels as *Work of Art,* although Lewis could not help claiming that he was at heart merely a storyteller.

The peculiar mixture of radicalism and orthodoxy in Dickens's political and social views was much like Lewis's. Dickens believed that the English system of representative government had become corrupt, but he urged no new or better one. Lewis, too, was always highly critical of the conduct of American politics although not of its structure. He once called himself an "agrarian radical," and his views range from a form of Fabian Socialism early in his career to a later independent and unspecific liberalism, with occasional flashes of conservatism.

Dickens, like Lewis, was greatly aware of class distinction and hated snobbery, although unlike Lewis he at first denied the existence of class conflict. Both men came to see the upper classes as aggressors and oppressors, with the popular classes fighting back in self-defense, yet both could admire and exalt individual aristocrats (in Lewis, Dodsworth and Cass Timberlane). Dickens's childhood poverty caused in him a lifelong consciousness of its evils and a deep sympathy for the poor, tempered with bursts of hatred for their filth and disease. Lewis, through his early struggles as a penurious free lance and editorial hack, shared Dickens's sympathetic attitude, although he was much less personally and consistently involved with the poor than Dickens.

Both writers were generally hostile to money and money values, at the same time enjoying great financial return from their work. Both attacked philanthropy, big business, finance, speculation, and those whose wealth put them above law and common standards of decency. However, the feelings of both writers toward industry and technology were mixed. Dickens attacked the machine's power to dehumanize but approved of the railroad and the telegraph because of their utility to man. Lewis, too, affirmed the technology itself as evidence of human genius and approved the manufactured device for its ability to ease discomfort, and at the same time he decried the social, business, and industrial system which inevitably grows from technology.

Both men continued to believe in the individual will as the source of all vice or virtue; both disbelieved that man was ultimately the victim of forces. This is not always clear in Lewis because of his concentration on social pressures, but the careful reader will observe that in his novels there are usually individuals who are strong enough to fight off all pressures. While both opposed extremist movements—Dickens, Chartism; and Lewis, Communism—both urged individual action; Dickens stressed *earnestness* as the *via regia*, Lewis *integrity*. The following passage, which appears in a recent study of Dickens, could with minor emendation be applied to Lewis and to his relationship with America: "Increasingly, he expressed this earnestness by pointing out to the English on every possible occasion the 'social evils and vices' which they did their best not to recognize, and by undermining the false values and prides by which they lived and destroyed life. He was a subversive who undermined the accepted principles of his time, whether those principles related to representative government, class structure, treatment of the poor, making of money, or other subjects."[28]

A few further parallels may be noted between Dickens and Lewis. Both writers were deeply marked by their boyhoods, later reproducing them in various ways in their books. While Dickens's was more traumatic than Lewis's, both he and Lewis had the same sense of not belonging. Dickens identified himself with the poor; Lewis always felt himself a raw country lad. Both got their training in journalism. Both had long careers, each roughly thirty-five years in length. Each wrote in great quantity, including much periodical work intended for popular consumption. Both were active as public figures and speakers once their writing had brought them fame. Both seemed to bask in social life, were gay companions, made many friends, although both remained inwardly lonely. (Dickens, however, kept his friends.) Both were restless, constant travelers, propelled by some inner turmoil and feverish energy.

In short, Dickens and Lewis are amazingly alike. Lewis will last as long in America and in the English language as has Dickens, although he will probably never command the respect paid to Dickens. In any case, literary reputation has a way of seeming more important to professional critics and students of literature than it does to the general reader, who has never given up either Dickens or Lewis.

CHAPTER 2

Romance and Affirmation:
The Early Novels

ALTHOUGH Sinclair Lewis's importance did not begin until 1920 and *Main Street*, it was not his first novel but his seventh. Between 1914 and 1919 he published in rapid succession *Our Mr. Wrenn, The Trail of the Hawk, The Job, The Innocents*, and *Free Air*. While these books have been forgotten, they do hold great interest for the student of American literature.[1] In them we may perceive many of the basic patterns of Lewis's later work; furthermore, they serve as reliable markers of some of the currents of popular fiction in the pre-World War I era.

Despite the appearance of the poems of Ezra Pound, Vachel Lindsay, Edgar Lee Masters, Carl Sandburg, Edwin Arlington Robinson, and Robert Frost; despite the fiction of Jack London, Frank Norris, Edith Wharton, Theodore Dreiser, and others; despite the Muckrakers and the voice of H. L. Mencken already rising in the land, most American readers continued to prefer writing which was traditional in its forms and which was affirmative, optimistic, and romantic in its tone. Booth Tarkington, Harold Bell Wright, Zane Grey were favorite authors; and, if the reader had a taste for realism, he turned not to Dreiser but to O. Henry and Winston Churchill. True, the defenses of the Genteel Tradition had been undermined and the cosy affirmations of popular fiction had grown desperate, but both persisted until the end of the First World War.

As James D. Hart has asserted, romance was the key to a book's success between 1900 and 1917; and, although it is irrefutable that romance has always been characteristic of American popular literature, this was of a particularly weak and diluted sort. Many different kinds of books captured the public's imagination, yet all depended upon romance. Hart has summarized it this way: "The only requisite for the popular book was that the writer possess a romantic view comforming to the prevailing genteel standards. Confronted by a complex culture, depressed, confused, or yearning for a life happier than sober actuality, the people needed myths and symbols to endow them with strength and joy, and these they often found in the idylls of the printed page."[2]

I *Education Through Experience*

It is precisely this idyllic romance, these comforting myths and symbols, which are dominant in the early novels of Sinclair Lewis, who was from the start remarkably sensitive to the attitudes of the mass audience. These books do contain flashes of satire, considerable authenticity of fact and detail, some realistic characters and situations, and even statements of indignation at social injustice—factors which all reveal Lewis's capacity for seriousness; but in the main they are the work of Lewis the romancer, cheerful, buoyant, reassuring.[3] A scrutiny of them should prove rewarding.

Our Mr. Wrenn, Lewis's first novel, was written in his spare time and completed while he was employed by the George H. Doran Company as editor and advertising manager. It took him two and a half years to finish. In many ways it contains the germ-cells of much of his later work; moreover, it was a deeply personal book. While it was not the true-life story of the Lewis who had struggled as a free lance and editorial hack in New York, it was the story of the sort of "little" person, lonely and searching for fulfillment, with whom Lewis could not help comparing himself at this stage of his career. Furthermore, the novel reflects several autobiographical parallels. Both the hero, William Wrenn, and Lewis had crossed to England on a cattle boat (Lewis did it twice during college summer vacations, once landing with but fifteen cents in his pocket). Both were lonely and longed for companionship. Both were fascinated by the faraway. Both were unhappy with the routine of their jobs and sought to break out of it, Wrenn into a position in which he could exercise some imagination and independence, Lewis into free-lance writing for the same reasons.[4] But most profoundly *Our Mr. Wrenn* is the expression of Lewis's simultaneous restlessness (a dissatisfaction with the status quo) and optimism, a conviction that going to new places somehow makes a better man, who, when he returns—as Lewis's heroes usually do—is wise and strong enough to overcome the forces which had earlier suppressed him.

The formula of *Our Mr. Wrenn*—the little man who grows bigger through revolt against the stuffiness of his environment and/or the tyranny of his job, becomes more aware through travel, and stronger through the tribulations of romance—was the formula which Lewis used in each of his first five novels as well as many of his later books. Put in currently fashionable critical terms, it is the quest for self-knowledge, the search for identity. We may also perceive in these novels Lewis's optimism and his belief in the democratic ideal in that his heroes do succeed in improving themselves; their strivings, their rebellions, do come to fruition.

Lewis's preference for the obscure proletarian or lower-middle-class hero holds true of his other novels of the period, with one exception. In his second book, *The Trail of the Hawk,* the protagonist leaps high above his village origins by dint of his skill as an aviator and becomes for a time a figure with national reputation. In temperament and tastes, however, he remains humble. The others all begin and end as simple and lowly folk. When they rise, as they all do, they ascend at most from proletarian to petty bourgeois or from petty bourgeois to bourgeois. Thus, Wrenn is promoted from humble clerk to clerk; Seth Appleby of *The Innocents* begins as a shoe clerk and ends as co-owner of a village shoe store; Uná Golden of *The Job* climbs from office girl to minor executive in a chain of small hotels; Milt Daggett of *Free Air* studies engineering after disposing of his tiny garage.

These characters illustrate, all together, a vision of American success which is predicated upon modest middle-class standards. Lewis's early heroes may and do gain self-confidence and poise, factual knowledge, the daring to strike out in new ventures, and compatible mates; but they must not (and do not) forget what they were and who they really are. They can become neither aristocrats nor intellectuals. In short, they represent in their origins and attainments those images cherished by the mass audience to which Lewis deliberately appealed and to which he himself was able to respond at this stage of his life. The matter may be developed further by examining one of the classic American modes of amelioration, the educational process.

From our beginnings as a nation we have had a passionate belief in the power of education as the way to a better life. We see it in the belief of the founding fathers, especially Jefferson, that a republican form of government could not survive without an educated electorate. At the same time we have always been suspicious of mere book learning, because knowledge for its own sake—"useless" knowledge—was associated with the aristocratic system. Consequently, our schools, our public institutions at least, have developed most rapidly either as specialized or technological institutions, or they have sought to justify their non-specialized and humanistic curricula as preparations for democratic living. It is also true that while we pay lip-service to the academic degree and now tend to judge a man by the number of years in his formal schooling, there has always been a strong counterstrain in American life which holds that the best education is received outside the classroom in the "school of hard knocks"; that a man is not truly educated until he has seen something of the world, come to know what different sorts of people there are, worked at a job, suffered privation. We still despise no one more than we do the "educated fool," and we continue to make the absent-minded professor a stock comic figure. Despite our seeming reverence for the academic letters inscribed after a name, he who has come up the hard way, the self-made man, continues to be an American folk hero.

We find these concepts profusely illustrated in the early novels of Sinclair Lewis. They are all, in fact, novels of and about education. The heroes and heroines are put through a learning process in which book learning has a strictly subordinate role. In this process they inevitably grow more sophisticated in their manners, improve their appearances and personal attractiveness, increase their practical or vocational skills, become keener observers of human nature and more adept at handling people, and develop a broader world-view. In short, Lewis's characters undergo the same experiences, with the same results, that the average reader could visualize for himself. Here we see the impact of the realistic movement, the distance between Lewis's romances and the Graustarkian; for, romantic as Lewis's early books are, they rarely reach above the limits of easy possibility. To reach too high would not permit the reader's personal projection into the hero's role. A detailed analysis of Lewis's first two novels, *Our Mr. Wrenn* (1914) and *The Trail of the Hawk* (1915), illustrates his use of the theme of education.

II *Our Mr. Wrenn*

The education of Willie Wrenn begins with his inheritance of just enough money to allow him temporary freedom from his job and to provide the means for a trip to Europe. Money, of course, in tidy rather than staggering sums, is inextricably interwoven with our notions of self-improvement through education; it is the way, the path of escape from routine, the length of the voyage on which we will travel and learn (just as money was the means for Lewis to escape routine drudgery so that he could write novels). This money, a mere $940.00, is also the first impulse toward Wrenn's regeneration, for it begins to change him even before he goes abroad. It gives him the courage to invite people out for a drink, to date for the first time, to talk back to the boss. But his deeper education does not begin until he travels. He not only meets rough types ready to fleece him or abuse him and is toughened by these episodes, but also encounters such persons as Morton, who enlarges his perspective by introducing him to socialism and to the radical Industrial Workers of the World, and who phophesies that socialism will someday replace religion as a force in human affairs. Morton tells him: "Brotherhood of man—real brotherhood. My idea of religion. One that is because it's got to be, not just because it always has been. Yessir, me for a religion of guys working together to make things easier for each other" (p. 42).

Some book learning is usually a part of the experience of the Lewisian hero (all of Lewis's novels mention books and authors, ranging from a few to scores); accordingly, Wrenn forms in England an acquaintanceship with Dr. Mittyford, a Stanford professor, who is for a while his travel companion and guide. Mittyford is the prototype of one of Lewis's favorite targets for satire, the stuffy and pompous academician, yet the satire comes not at the expense of Mittyford's learning, which Wrenn and Lewis admire, but at the supercilious way he wears it. Having brushed with radicalism, the hard life, and the bookish,

Wrenn is now ready for the great experience, the *sturm und drang* of romantic love and the meeting with a mode of behavior utterly new to him. Enter Istra Nash.

Istra Nash is actually a dual prototype. She represents not only Lewis's dislike for the bohemian (the "hobohemian" he called it), but also his rejection of the beautiful, clever, alluring, intellectual, yet emotionally shallow and destructive woman, a species culminating in Fran Dodsworth. To Wrenn, whose experience with women has been virtually nil, Istra Nash is the apotheosis of romance, adventure, learning, and passion. She is imperious, affected, selfish; but she is also daring, imaginative, free. From her Wrenn hears his first clever talk for cleverness's sake, sees something of elegance in manners, and is introduced to the salons where the expatriates gather and chat knowingly about sex, art, and revolution. In a word, through Istra the hero learns about bohemia; and, like the average man he represents, he is both fascinated and repelled.

Inevitably, Wrenn's romance with Istra causes him pain, the sort of suffering essential to a true education in that it wounds but does not cripple. He emerges from it—as from his other experiences—a more aggressive and personable fellow who is successful at making friends and in his work. Above all, he has learned enough about life and himself to be able to conquer his dangerous feelings for Istra and to choose Nelly Croubel (note Lewis's use of characternyms, "Istra" as opposed to "Nelly"), the sweet and passive woman who will be good for him. True, Nelly is colorless and dull beside Istra, but she is the ideal wife for the average man. As the novel ends, Wrenn has passed all his examinations. He has traveled, learned, and returned to the best kind of life for which his education could have prepared him: success in his work, friends, and a comfórtable domesticity. It is a lower-middle-class utopia.

Lewis's style is here worthy of comment. While that style is not fully mature in *Our Mr. Wrenn*, it is already distinctive. Later, in the books appearing after 1920, he became a more adept and resourceful craftsman, his method more documentary, his tone more sober. However, his diction, dialogue, sentence types, narrative techniques (with the point of view usually third person-omniscient) remained essentially the same. The early books, as well as such later romances as *Mantrap* (1926) and *Bethel*

Merriday (1940), are generally characterized by a playful, deliberately facetious approach, including an occasional now-dear-reader passage. In Lewis's romances the reader is instantly made aware and kept aware that this is a *story* and that someone is telling it, which is typical of the psychology of popular fiction. Yet there is a leavening of realism, some harsh detail, a focus on the commonplace and ordinary. The cheerful voice, when Lewis describes his hero's tribulations or loneliness, sometimes begins to tremble; the sweet tones verge on the bittersweet.

Diction is the key to Lewis's style, early and late, especially the pivotal adjective or adverb, with the choice of verbs next in importance. Thus, Wrenn's mustache is "unsuccessful." He approaches a theater "primly." His landlady eats enormous heaps of food "slowly and resentfully." His room is "abjectly respectable." He plans "coyly improbable trips." Wrenn "trots" to the theater, "peers" at the ticket-taker, and "trembles" into the doorway. He "pranced" toward the building where he works, is "shot" out of his chair by the boss's buzzer, and "scampered" in to see him. "The manager dropped his fist on the desk, glared, smoothed his flowered prairie of waistcoat, and growled, his red jowls quivering" (p. 5).

Another basic technique is Lewis's employment of figurative language. He uses it a great deal, including a wide range of types and varieties: metaphor, personification, simile, metonymy and synecdoche, and others. Here is a sample:

> The April skies glowed with benevolence this Saturday morning. The Metropolitan Tower was singing, bright ivory tipped with gold, uplifted and intensely glad of the morning. The buildings walling in Madison Square were jubilant; the honest red-brick fronts radiant; the new marble, witty. The sparrows in the middle of Fifth Avenue were all talking at once, scandalously but cleverly. The polished brass of limousines threw off teethy smiles. At least so Mr. Wrenn fancied as he whisked up Fifth Avenue, the skirts of his small blue double-breasted coat wagging (pp. 4-5).

This passage also demonstrates Lewis's technique of using an external description of a city street, of a building or room, terrain, weather, to underscore or counterpoint plot, theme, or character. The technique is as typical of Lewis's best work as of his romances. For example, in *Main Street,* at every step of Carol's disillusionment by the town of Gopher Prairie, we are reminded of the beauty and grandeur of the Minnesota land itself.

The result of Lewis's style is to produce an impression of speed and color rather than depth and intensity, especially when the tone is one of self-conscious cleverness. Furthermore, Lewis rarely gets into the character's head, either in *Our Mr. Wrenn* or thereafter; he habitually describes experience from the outside. We do not learn enough about the character as an individual from what he thinks and feels; instead we are given what he says and does. We have too little chance to interpret him or see him develop. All too frequently the development is accomplished by Lewis's loaded diction, so that the character's words and deeds only confirm the reader's ready-made judgment. Again, the technique is that of slick fiction and is ever-present in Lewis's romances. In his best books, of course, Lewis surmounted many of these limitations. He always had difficulty maintaining consistent tone, but the strength of his feeling usually carried him through, while the accuracy and amount of his realistic detail compensated for the superficiality of his approach. Moreover, such creations as Babbitt, Gottlieb, and Sam and Fran Dodsworth prove that at his peak Lewis was capable of bringing to life subtle and complex characters. Istra Nash of *Our Mr. Wrenn* gave promise of that ability.

III   *The Trail of the Hawk*

The Trail of the Hawk, Lewis's second novel, was like the first written in his spare hours. In style and tone, however, it is much closer to the later Lewis than *Our Mr. Wrenn* and its hero is a far more formidable personage. While it is always obvious in *Our Mr. Wrenn* that the hero could never become more than a clerk, Carl Ericson is quite another story; for Lewis makes it very clear that he intends Carl, the son of Scandinavian immigrants, to stand as a representative of the new American pioneer. In fact, as Lewis later remarked with great pride, Carl Ericson was a phophecy of Charles Lindbergh, another son of Scandinavian immigrants, who came out of the same Minnesota backland to win fame as a flyer.[5] Considering his loftier destiny, Carl's education must of necessity be more varied and strenuous.

It begins during his village boyhood, which is reminiscent of Lewis's own. Carl is a lonely lad, yet imaginative and friendly. His first vision of a better life comes from Bone Stillman, the village atheist (another stock character type in Lewis's work) and a reader of Ingersoll and Marx. Bone Stillman preaches to Carl the message of ambition, the same message that fired Lewis's life. This passage is virtually a diagram of Lewis's conduct:

> "Life is just a little old checker game played by the alfalfa contingent at the country store unless you've got an ambition that's too big to ever quite lasso it. You want to know that there's something ahead that's bigger and more beautiful than anything you've ever seen, and never stop till—well, till you can't follow the road any more. And anything or anybody that doesn't pack any surprises—get that?—*surprises* for you, is dead, and you want to slough it like a snake does its skin" (p. 50).

Carl's education continues, now in the formal sense, at Plato College. Here he meets Professor Frazer, who introduces Carl both to literature and to a utopian socialism. As Frazer explains it, socialism—especially of the sort advocated by Bellamy and Shaw and Wells—sees men as brothers, advancing toward the goals of an increasing lifespan, a shortened work-week, work for the love of craft and not money, and the common good. In other words, Carl Ericson is an idealized projection of the young Lewis, and his "education" is a vehicle for Lewis's ideas. So far his training has been rather a happy one; now he must begin to suffer. He does, when his mentor Professor Frazer is dismissed from the college for his heresies, and Carl, disillusioned by this expression of the village mind, leaves college also.

Like the restless Lewis rebel he is, Carl wanders, caught by the excitement of travel, captivated (like Lewis) by the size and multiplicity of America. He wanders to New York but is repelled (like Lewis) by its hugeness and crowds, by the poverty and strangeness of the city's masses. Like Lewis, he even goes to Panama to work on the canal. Travel for Carl thus replaces his college education and teaches him much more than he could have learned in the classroom. Undoubtedly this was another projection of what Lewis himself had concluded from his own experience, in which his formal education had been heightened by two trips across the ocean; a stay at a utopian colony;

and, after college, other trips to Iowa, California, Panama, Washington, D. C., and elsewhere.[6]

But Carl as yet has attained no practical skills, an essential part of the education of the Lewis hero, as it is, we believe, in the education of every American youth. It may also be interpreted as Lewis's way of compensating in his books for what he lacked in reality. Accordingly, Carl turns to aviation (one of Lewis's early enthusiasms), which not only fulfils the practical requirement but permits the expression of the pioneer impulse, for these are the trail-blazing days of American aviation. Through flying, Carl, now known as "Hawk," climbs to fame, completing the dream, both Lewisian and American, of becoming the successful man of action.

At this point Carl must again broaden his skills. There is nothing left for him to accomplish in flying, and he has already brushed with death. Therefore, he takes a job in industry, but according to his character and the terms of his education, it must not be a routine job. It must be creative. Just such a job is the development of a new kind of automobile, a "Touricar," a vehicle fully equipped for camping and one of the many original ideas for devices, products, and business practices scattered throughout Lewis's books. Lewis's touricar is just now being marketed. It, and other of Lewis's ideas, suggest that could he have tolerated the life, he would have become a highly successful businessman or manufacturer solely on the basis of his originality and his attention to detail. Moreover, this aspect of Lewis was helpful to him in gathering material for his later books and making it seem authentic, especially in such novels as *Dodsworth* and *Work of Art*.

In any case, Hawk Ericson is now ready for the final phase of his training, love, and it is precisely this experience which occupies the last third of the novel. Indeed, as we survey the entire novel we realize that it is neatly structured according to Lewis's formula. The first section deals with the hero's early life in a small town and includes the formation of his ambitions. The second portion narrates his travels and adventures, which bring him maturity and self-confidence. The final third records his romance and marriage, in this instance complicated by problems of adjustment and business success. Since the love interest in Lewis's early novels will be discussed below and from another point of view, suffice it to say here that the hero, already mildly interested in a comfortable home-town girl, becomes enamored of the fashionable, beautiful, but at the same time warm and responsive Ruth Winslow of New York. After a courtship made difficult by differences in class and attitude, they marry, only to find their marriage threatened by quarrels arising from the pressures of big city life, the heavy demands of work and domesticity, and a general restraint of their freedom.

At this stage Lewis provides his hero and the reader with what he cherished as a basic truth, the end product of education—escape. It is also at this point that Lewis the rebel, who is only occasionally present in these affirmative novels, breaks through. Consequently, the end of *The Trail of the Hawk* departs sharply from middle-class values and becomes a diatribe against society for punishing those who marry and have children. In fact, Lewis urges us to flee this fate. Carl says, "People don't run away from slavery often enough. And so they don't ever get to do real work either." And, "Perhaps if enough of us run away from nice normal grinding, we'll start people wondering just why they should go on toiling to produce a lot of booze and clothes and things that nobody needs" (p. 407).

This is, of course, one of Lewis's standard solutions, run, go to new places. We now know that he was running from himself, and only ostensibly from the routine which he feared would stultify his work. He never stopped running, and if we may accept the evidence in Grace Hegger Lewis's memoirs, his restlessness eventually brought disaster to his own marriage. Philosophically, the message seems to follow Thoreau, only it is debased, for Thoreau did not offer it as a permanent solution. Although we can sympathize with Lewis's desire to keep the fun in life and the romance in marriage by a change of scene and the avoidance of routine, he apparently did not know that variety comes ultimately from within.

The ending of *The Trail of the Hawk* might also be justified, without biographical application, as a suitably romantic conclusion to a romantic novel. But this does not satisfy us for two reasons. First, the novel is one of the two early Lewis books *not* essentially whimsical and frivolous. Second, Lewis's tone in the passages urging flight is not playful; it is deadly earnest. Furthermore, Hawk Ericson, as I have indicated, contains a good deal of Sinclair Lewis.

IV *Love as Education*

It would be unprofitable to trace in detail the theme of education in the other novels of the period, for *The Innocents, The Job,* and *Free Air* could also be read in this fashion. In *The Innocents* (1917) two old people learn self-sufficiency and attain success by doing the unexpected and embarking on a walking trip West. In *The Job* (1917) the heroine, a working girl, becomes more and more highly skilled and more and more cosmopolitan through her experiences in various jobs, her encounters with various human types, and the bitterness of a bad marriage. *Free Air* (1919) is the tale of a cross-country courtship of an upper-class eastern girl by an automobile mechanic from the West: during it the girl learns democracy, the boy learns the value of social polish and knowledge, and both learn about love.

We have suggested that the education of Lewis's heroes, the process of self-fulfillment, almost always includes romantic love and, in fact, depends heavily upon it. Closer scrutiny reveals a consistent pattern in these love relationships, for in three of the five novels the heroes are irresistibly attracted to girls who are more sophisticated, better educated (in the formal sense), and from older, richer families. Furthermore, two of these heroes are raw westerners and their beloved are finished easterners. Maxwell Geismar, in his fine chapter on Lewis in *The Last of the Provincials,* asserts that the dominant theme of Lewis's early books is this contrast and conflict between the East, with its elegance and clearly defined class structure, and the West, drab, immense, and egalitarian.[7] While Geismar's thesis is challenged by the simple fact that the East–West theme is true only for two of the five novels Lewis wrote in this period—*The Trail of the Hawk* and *Free Air*—the entire matter of romantic love does need additional exploration.

To put it succinctly, most of the romantic love in Lewis's early novels is abstracted from his own courtship and marriage of Grace Livingston Hegger. She herself has written that she is the basis for the chief female characters in *The Trail of the Hawk* and *Free Air;* we also know that Lewis used some of her experiences and characteristics in his portrayal of Una Golden in *The Job.*[8] In short, Lewis's sophisticated eastern heroines are based on his first wife, who was a stylish dresser, who had a British accent which by her own admission varied in degree with the company she was in, whose father was the proprietor of an art gallery, whose family had kept servants, and who, we may infer, was a snob on more than one occasion.

Lewis's western heroes are Lewis himself, the unpolished country boy—or so he thought himself—who felt doubly awkward in the presence of such a lady and was yet drawn to her. As Lewis once wrote in a letter to a friend, "She's accustomed to elegance, and polite society, and when I'm with her I feel always I'll do the wrong thing." In their real-life courtship Lewis insisted on playing the lowly courtier to Grace's noble lady. He took her not to dine nor to fashionable places, but for picnics in New Jersey, proudly displaying his camping skill, or for long walks in New York, seeking out little-known spots. The reticence about sex, the courtly romance, the lovers' talks, the tenderness and simultaneous fear which Lewis's men feel for their women are thus all projections of his own experience. Nowhere is this protection more obvious than in *The Trail of the Hawk*. Elizabeth Jordan, Lewis's editor at Harper's, wrote: "Hal himself was at heart a hawk, wild and untamed. Notwithstanding his devotion to Grace, it was hard for him to accept responsibility and the routine of domestic life." And Lewis inscribed his wife's copy of the novel as follows: "'Youth bubbles in every line' says the blurb on the jacket. It is true, in the sense that you are in every line, and you are youth. This is not so much a novel, dear, as a record of our games and talks and thoughts and journeys. Without you none of it could have been written."[9]

There is also autobiographical material in the relationship of Walter Babson and Una Golden in *The Job*. Babson is much like Sinclair Lewis; an ambitious young writer trying to make his mark in a country full of ambitious young writers, he is lonely, confused, a dreamer, half-bitter, and in search of a cause and a way to happiness. Of Babson's attempts to write stories and filler for the commercial market, as Lewis did, Lewis says, "Pathos there was in all of this; the infinitely little men and women daring to buy and sell 'short, snappy stuff' in this somber and terribly beautiful world of Balzac and Wells and Turgenieff" (p. 62). Babson brings romance into Una's life. Through him, and here we see again the fusion of education and romantic love, Una becomes aware that love is not the lofty and spiritual affair portrayed in genteel novels, but earthy and physical. She also learns something about radicalism from him; for he is a socialist, a believer in union labor, an advocate of the single tax, and a skeptic in religion. Thus Babson is one of the agencies of the educational experience which befalls the Lewis hero, an experience always including a questioning of the accepted. Una herself is another of Lewis's "little" people, perhaps closer to Wrenn than any other early Lewis hero and certainly not one of the eastern types; however, in her job as an office worker in New York, in her support of a widowed mother, she also parallels Grace Lewis.

Finally, on this particular matter, we note that *Free Air*, the novel immediately preceding *Main Street*, fuses the elements of education, romance, autobiography, and the conflict between eastern hauteur and western folksiness. Milt Daggett is, like Hawk Ericson, from Minnesota; Claire Boltwood is, like Ruth Winslow, from New York. Just as Hawk wins Ruth, Milt wins Claire by his practical skill and by his conduct of nature expeditions. Both men must pry the girl away from her background, loosen her up, get her to roughing it; but, at the same time, the heroes must have or learn enough poise and dignity to face polite society. The focus of the hero's education in *Free Air* is much more upon the social—manners—rather than upon the cultural or intellectual. The heroine is already well instructed in all but the practical truths of democracy, and these she learns from her suitor and from the West through which they travel. As regards the trip itself, traveling by automobile from Minnesota to the West Coast, Lewis and his wife made just such a trip in the summer of 1916.

V *Romances of the Commonplace*

It has been obvious throughout this discussion how affirmative and how close to the popular taste and the popular ideals Lewis's early novels were. Without exception they could be placed in that category which has been labeled "The Romance of the Commonplace." Moreover, it was specifically Lewis's intention that these novels be romances of the commonplace, for each of the five books contains one or more passages openly declaring this intention. Nowhere is this more patent than in *The Innocents*, Lewis's fourth novel of the period, which is at the same time a shockingly bad book—a strong piece of evidence as to how maudlin Lewis could be when he let his sentimental impulses go unchecked—and an excellent example of the romance of the commonplace. The novel's "Dedicatory Introduction" makes this plain, and it also indicates what some of Lewis's sources were:

> If this were a ponderous work of realism, such as the author has attempted to write, and will doubtless essay again, it would be perilous to dedicate it to the splendid assembly of young British writers, lest the critics search for Influences and Imitations. But since this is a flagrant excursion, a tale for people who still read Dickens and clip out spring poetry and love old people and children, it may safely confess the writer's strident admiration for Compton MacKenzie, J. P. Beresford, Gilbert Cannan, Patrick MacGill, and their peers, whose novels are the histories of our Contemporaneous Golden Age. Nor may these be mentioned without a yet more enthusiastic tribute to their master and teacher (he probably abominates being called either a master or a teacher), H. G. Wells.

A detailed explanation of the romance of the commonplace is unnecessary here. We are already too familiar with it in our radio and television dramas, in our motion pictures, in our popular magazines, and most notably in the pages of the *Saturday Evening Post*. It is one of the dominant forms in contemporary mass culture, and it depends upon two elements: (1) a surface realism, or a realistic description of places, clothing, furniture, etc.; (2) an unquenchably affirmative view of human nature which may permit people to be nasty and difficult but never depraved or atavistic. Thus, the romance of the commonplace perfectly suits the taste of the American popular audience because it avoids the fairylandish and vaguely aristocratic subjects and situations of high romance, while it still satisfies the urge for vicarious experience by permitting audience projection into one or more approved categories of success, most usually success in love and success in business. It has conflict, of course, and problems, but the conflict is never such that it cannot be resolved and the problems are never insurmountable. The matter was expressed perfectly by an important voice in one of the mass media (I do not recall whether he was the producer of a series of television dramas or the editor of one of the larger magazines) who said, "We want stories about happy people with happy problems" (this is a close paraphrase, if not an exact quotation).

Even were there no "Dedicatory Introduction," we would know from the start that *The Innocents* will be just such a romance. Its characters, Mr. and Mrs. Seth Appleby, are stock types, folks who have been married forty years but still have enough spirit and active affection to nag each other. They are also familiar early Lewis characters, little people in the big city, whose lives contain the ingredients for considerable drama once the ingredients are properly agitated. The action in the novel centers around three episodes. First, the Applebys risk their life savings in a small restaurant on Cape Cod, which subsequently fails because of competition from an arty tearoom which opens nearby. This provides Lewis the opportunity for some satire on "hobohemians." Next, they struggle for survival in New York, gradually losing the fight and even attempting suicide. This permits Lewis some passages of O. Henry pathos. Finally, they escape from the patronizing care of their daughter (whose home and marriage is a prelude to a good deal in *Babbitt*), and set off on a walking trip across the entire United States. This allows Lewis to include one of his favorite romantic themes and a staple of the romance of the commonplace: the revolt of the parents against the children, or more simply, the revolt of those least likely to revolt. Although the Applebys get only as far as Indiana, they attain on this trip self-respect and success.

A prime factor in the romance of the commonplace is the regeneration of character. Accordingly, we see in *The Innocents* two sweet, timid, and downtrodden old people become staunch and assured, virtually executive types. Mother grows quickly enough and large enough to face down a sheriff's posse, while Father evolves from shoe clerk to entrepreneur in his world-view and demeanor. The change in character is, of course, of paramount importance to the novelist, but the serious writer must work with it as Darwin describes a change in species, through successive slight variations, or else he must indicate that the factors producing the change have long been at work beneath the character's still-familiar surface behavior. We cannot believe in characters who suddenly act, as Mother Appleby does, in a manner totally new to her.

But why continue? This kind of behavior is characteristic not only of Lewis's romances but also of the corpus of popular fiction. After all, what could be more comforting to the fireside reader than to will a change and see it happen, suddenly, painlessly, permanently? Furthermore, *The Innocents* utilizes some of the materials of the American myth. It is the Horatio Alger story, only with elderly heroes, and it includes the movement West. Finally, in its idyllic ending, one whose sweetness render it indigestible, the novel asserts the beneficence of the American village, for where else but in a place like Lippittsville, Indiana, could two old people at last find happiness, success, and security? Once again dynamic democracy and benevolent capitalism have emerged triumphant.

Free Air, Lewis's last novel of the period, also illustrates Lewis's weaknesses—at times his near-fatal weakness—for the romance of the commonplace. It is not quite so syrupy as *The Innocents* (which was even rejected by the *Saturday Evening Post* as too sentimental!), nor so self-consciously cute, but with very little alteration it would still make a Grade B movie or *Post* serial. In fact, *Free Air* is a kind of summation of the popular fiction of Lewis's early period; for it has travel, adventure, romance, colorful characters, "problems," an upbeat philosophy, twists and turns of plot, and the necessary revisions of personality and attitude without hard struggle. The book's surface realism is provided by the narrative of driving across the country, when such a trip was still an adventure and the automobile still new enough to be fascinating. Without the bits of driving-lore and automobile mechanics, without the panorama of American terrain, the book would be totally shapeless and unconvincing.

VI *Foreshadowings*

But it would not be fair to Lewis to leave the impression that his first five novels had nothing of merit or seriousness in them. Actually, they do contain character types, satirical passages, situations, and themes which foreshadow his later novels. For example, Istra Nash, Ruth Winslow, and Claire Boltwood are all ancestors of Joyce Lanyon (in *Arrowsmith*), Fran Dodsworth, and others. Hawk Ericson is in some ways a younger Sam Dodsworth. The escape from a stultifying environment which we find in each of the early books is also recurrent in the later ones, although the tone has grown much harsher and the escape becomes a rejection of the entire social system. The concern with class and caste conflict remains constant throughout Lewis's career, although nowhere else is it so easily resolved as in the early romances.

Each of these novels has, also, a number of satirical passages, with the satire usually directed at characters rather than institutions—a pompous professor, a stuffy suburban couple, the president of a provincial college, a salesman. But because the satire is scattered and without a frame of reference, it generally lacks the corrosiveness of the later Lewis. Lewis the iconoclast and critic is, however, noticeably present in two books, *The Trail of the Hawk* and especially in *The Job*. In *The Trail of the Hawk* we may observe the writer's dissatisfaction with the social system in such declarations as this (the speaker is Professor Frazer):

> "Do you realize that I am not suggesting that there might possibly some day be a revolution in America, but rather that now I am stating that there is, this minute, and for some years has been, an actual state of warfare between capital and labor? Do you know that daily more people are saying openly and violently that we starve our poor, we stuff our children with useless bookishness, and work the children of others in mills and let them sell papers on the streets in red-light districts at night, and thereby prove our state nothing short of insane? If you tell me there is no revolution because there are no barricades, I point to actual battles at Homestead, Pullman, and the rest" (p. 91).

The same novel also contains this passage:

> The East Side of New York. A whirlwind of noise and smell and hovering shadows. The jargon of Jewish matrons in brown shawls and orthodox wigs, chaffering for cabbages and black cotton stockings and gray woolen undershirts with excitable push-cart proprietors who had beards so prophetic that it was startling to see a frivolous cigarette amid the reverend mane. The scent of fried fish and decaying bits of kosher meat, and hallways as damnably rotten of floor as they were profitable to New York's nicest circles. The tall gloom of six-story tenements that made a prison wall of dulled yellow, bristling with bedding-piled fire-escapes and the curious heads of frowsy women. A potpourri of Russian signs, Yiddish newspapers, synagogues with six-pointed gilt stars, bakeries with piles of rye bread crawling with caraway seeds, shops for renting wedding finery that looked as if it would never fit any one, second-hand furniture-shops with folding iron beds, a filthy baby holding a baby slightly

younger and filthier, mangy cats slinking from pile to pile of
rubbish, and a withered geranium in a tin can whose label was
hanging loose and showed rust-stains amid the dry paste on its
back. Everywhere crowds of voluble Jews in dark clothes, and
noisily playing children that catapulted into your legs. The
lunger-blocks in which we train the victims of Russian tyranny
to appreciate our freedom. A whirlwind of alien ugliness and
foul smells and incessant roar and the deathless ambition of
young Jews to know Ibsen and syndicalism. It swamped the
courage of the hungry Carl as he roamed through Rivington
Street and Essex and Hester, vainly seeking jobs from shop-
keepers too poor to be able to bathe (p. 148).

This kind of writing is the work of the other Lewis—the
realist, social critic, keen-eyed observer of his civilization's sins—
already fully developed in his second novel, *The Trail of the
Hawk*. The tone of the passage is interesting and tells us a
good deal about its writer. It mingles fascination, revulsion,
sympathy, fear, and anger. The fascination is that of the strangeness of all this to the son of a Minnesota doctor. The revulsion
is at the smell, dirt, vulgarity. The anger, which comes from
the fact that such conditions exist in America, is directed at the
exploitative system which makes slums and keeps people in
them. The sympathy is with the poverty, which Lewis had shared
while living in this very neighborhood. The fear stems from the
fecundity and drive of these people, their challenge to the middle-class world of Lewis's origin. The passage is nearly Dreiserian, but it lacks Dreiser's cosmic sense—the sense that this is
played on a pathetically tiny stage at the behest of unknown
gods. Furthermore, Carl Ericson cannot identify himself with
these people; he cannot, as Dreiser did, feel shame, or fear that
he would never rise above the lower classes, as would the
Dreiser hero. Lewis can describe the scene more objectively
because he was never more than a temporary part of it.

The Job (1917) has an even greater quantity of realism,
enough to make it stand as a striking phophecy of the later
Lewis, although it too is ultimately affirmative in its tone and
conclusion. It opens with a mildly acidulous portrait of small-
town types and with a slightly ironic statement about the effects
of the small-town environment. It proceeds to suggest that
widowed mothers are like vampires to the children charged with
their sustenance; and, after a brief tribute to the power and

necessity of business, the novel concentrates on the grinding routine of the white-collar worker in the large city.

In *The Job* Lewis specifically rejects what he has elsewhere asserted, that business is a modern form of high romance; he treats it instead as an enslaving force. Even the bosses, its priests, do not understand the religion they serve. "Efficiency of production they have learned; efficiency of life they still consider an effeminate hobby. An unreasonable world, sacrificing birdsong and tranquil dusk and high golden noons to selling junk— yet it rules us" (p. 43). In passage after passage Lewis reminds the reader how business has driven beauty and passion out of life. There are dozens of pages which stress the dreariness of the heroine's job and daily routine, the ugliness and crush of the subway, the loneliness of the working girl's empty flat. Such descriptions manifest Lewis's special gifts: his solid grasp on materiality and his ability to suggest the spiritual poverty of modern life by conveying both the meretriciousness of its exterior and the inner pathos of its inhabitants. Nor does he hesitate to drop the mask of reportorial realist and speak out passionately against injustice, as in this comment on the subway: "The engineers had done their work well, made a great thought in steel and cement. And then the businessmen and bureaucrats had made the great thought a curse" (p. 134).

Another aspect of Lewis's departure from sweet sentimentalism is his straightforward portrayal of Una Golden's private life. Although *The Job* is hardly a landmark of sexual realism, Lewis does dare to give his heroine an active libido and to devote a considerable portion of the novel to the depiction of Una's unhappy marriage to Eddie Schwirtz, a salesman, of whom one contemporary reviewer commented, "Mr. Lewis has put all the banality of all the American drummers into this one genial swine. . . . He is the composite of all the complacent American barbarians who ever guzzled prosperity and bragged generosity and whined affliction at the first flick of nature's whip."[10]

Schwirtz is the only character of the scores in these early novels whom Lewis can be said to hate; he is an ancestor of Babbitt, although without Babbitt's essential kindliness, and he is a direct predecessor of Lowell Schmaltz of *The Man Who Knew Coolidge*. Moreover, Lewis's rendition of Schwirtz's speech, a conjunction of catch phrases, clichés, slang, and pet words, indicates that his skill in the satirical monologue was already mature. This is a sample (the subject is Womanhood): "Not that I want to knock The Sex, y'understand, but you know yourself, bein' a shemale, that there's an awful lot of cats among the ladies—God bless 'em—that wouldn't admit another lady was beautiful, not if she was as good-looking as Lillian Russell, corking figger and the swellest dresser in town" (p. 194). Schwirtz derides culture, prefers music with "some *melody* to it," scoffs at those who attempt to improve taste, and ridicules the critics of the American businessman, boasting that he earns more than the critics. For inspiration Schwirtz reads Henry Van Dyke and Billy Sunday; rejects "nasty realistic stories" about unhappy marriage and poverty; and prefers such material as detective tales or a "nice, bright, clean love-story."

Lewis's portrayal of another character, S. Herbert Ross, an advertising manager, is a pioneer treatment of what has become a stereotype in the fiction of midcentury, the Madison Avenue man. And his descriptions of the cold war in a business office— the castes, conflicts, ambitions, treacheries—anticipate the sort of thing now popular in middlebrow realism. The whole account of Pemberton's, a drug and patent medicine house where the heroine works, is also valuable social documentary and cultural history. Here the office girls break into unaccountable fits of hysterical weeping; the young women grow "dry and stringy"; the old, "catty and tragic." Pemberton's is a modern business and uses machines, but Una observes that the system is faulty because the machines save time only for the owners.

In short, the dominant tone and detail of *The Job* is realistic, so realistic that it was hailed in its time as one of the most candid and authentic American novels dealing with the life of the working girl. Even today, with a handicap of nearly fifty years, it reads surprisingly well. Unfortunately, *The Job* is given a happy ending (according to Grace Hegger Lewis, the ending was prettified to please Lewis's publisher), in which the heroine has resolved the problems of career and romance and in which Lewis is forced to reassert that the business life is a good life.[11]

Despite everything he has said about capitalism and the daily grind, despite his obvious preference for socialism, he at last defends the system and the employer. His defense is based on what W. H. Whyte in *The Organization Man* calls the Protestant Ethic, the pride of accomplishment, the triumph of individual fulfillment through work and its just rewards: money, position, authority. If the system wears down the weak, at least it exalts the strong, the novel concludes. But, Lewis is still no believer in complete *laissez-faire;* business has a basic moral responsibility to make life better. Consequently, Una's success comes in a job where she will be a "creative" businesswoman, making hotels better, cleaner, friendlier places. Although her efforts will bring in larger profits, she will also serve the people by giving them what they want and appreciate—quality. Sinclair Lewis, even in these affirmative years, could only approve of business when it had tangible value. He was a writer, but he admired any work so long as it was well done and meaningful.

Ironically, in view of Lewis's final defense of the capitalistic system, *The Job* (like *Our Mr. Wrenn* and *The Trail of the Hawk*) exposes the protagonist to an education which includes an introduction to socialism. In fact, Una gets a more thorough indoctrination than either Wrenn or Ericson because she has two instructors, Walter Babson and Mamie Magen, a lame Jewess. For a time Una even thinks of herself as a Fabian socialist. In this socialism, as in some other matters, Lewis's early novels reveal the heavy influence of Wells, Shaw, Garland, and Veblen, especially upon *Our Mr. Wrenn, The Job,* and *The Trail of the Hawk.*

First, there is no doubt of Lewis's lifelong admiration for H. G. Wells; and, appropriately, Lewis's initial novel *Our Mr. Wrenn* bears strong similarities to Wells's *Kipps* (1905) and *The History of Mr. Polly* (1910).[12] These include parallels in subtitles, chapter headings, the personalities and adventures of the heroes, the narrative patterns, the emphasis on escape from routine, and romances with alluring upper-class women which end in disappointment. All three heroes, Kipps, Polly, and Wrenn, are Dickens's godchildren, and the prevailing atmosphere and humor of the books are Dickensian. Wells's attitudes toward life and society are also very influential in *Our Mr. Wrenn.* The distaste for the crushing demands of the job, the sympathy for the poorly educated little man beset by forces larger than himself and forced into a servile and sterile life-pattern, are Wellsian as much as they are Lewisian.

The Trail of the Hawk contains further evidence of the influence of Wells, and also that of Veblen and Shaw. Arthur Coleman, who has studied the genesis of Lewis's social ideas, has pointed out that the novel utilizes five basic themes of interest to Wells, Shaw, and, to some extent, Veblen. They are: (1) the barriers of provincialism; (2) the waste of mis-education; (3) the possibilities of socialism; (4) the promise of science and technology; (5) the precariousness of marriage in modern society, especially as it is affected by job security. The same themes appear in *The Job*, which also resembles some aspects of Garland's *Rose of Dutcher's Coolly*. Although the two heroines differ in their abilities and ambitions, they face the same problems: the difficult role of women in a changing society, the resistance to the development and fulfillment of the woman as a person, the pressures of life outside domesticity, the generally unsatisfactory status of the wife. Veblen's ideas are visible in *The Job* in the comments on business and money values. Indeed, it has been said that chapter fourteen of Lewis's novel is little more than a popularization of Veblen's *The Theory of Business Enterprise*.[13]

But if we can explain *some* of the patterns and concepts in Lewis's early books by a study of literary influences, we cannot explain the existence and character of the books themselves without returning to their author and his intentions (Sinclair Lewis was not aware of the "intentional fallacy"; he worked by design). First, there must be laid to rest the notion that all five novels were purely hackwork—at least insofar as the phrase suggests the writer's motives were solely commercial. Three of the novels, *Our Mr. Wrenn, The Trail of the Hawk,* and *The Job,* whatever their faults, were essentially honest books which strenuously exercised Lewis's powers. Lewis later testified to this himself.[14] Furthermore, the three novels were favorably reviewed, even attracting the notice of such men as Howells, who wrote to Lewis praising *The Trail of the Hawk,* and Garland, who complained that Lewis had treated the descendants of the pioneers too sharply. Some reviewers felt enough enthusiasm to speak of Lewis as the writer of the future great American novel.[15] Indeed, had *The Trail of the Hawk* and *The Job* been Lewis's only books of the period, the signposts to *Main Street* would have been very clearly visible.

However, we cannot ignore *The Innocents* (1917) and *Free Air* (1919), which have sometimes been justified as "interludes" (the word is Lewis's own); for if they are interludes, we must then ask why they needed to assume the flavor and substance of confectioners' sugar. In these books we see not only Lewis the romantic but a Lewis willing, unfortunately, to use his talent as a commodity. Therefore, any explanation of the significance of these two early novels must include the profit motive. Part of the truth, certainly, is that they were written for a market and for the money Lewis needed, first to begin married life, then to leave full-time publishing work to free-lance, and finally to stop free-lancing and write *Main Street*. Lewis had already decided that he could do slick work to support his serious work, and the publication of such dissimilar books as *The Innocents* and *The Job* in the same year seemed to bear him out. Furthermore, once Lewis saw money-making possibilities in a novel, he tried to take advantage of them all. This was especially the case with *Free Air*, which Lewis serialized in the *Saturday Evening Post;* he then delayed its publication as a novel so that he could run other installments in the same magazine.

In view of Lewis's ascendency after 1920 his attitude toward these early books is interesting. He seems all through his career to have wavered between the poles of humble apology and defiant defense. In the 1920's, especially once *Main Street* was in draft, he was usually ready to apologize for them. Even when he defended their serious intention, he did not argue for their quality. Later, in the confused 1930's, he again avowed the virtue and power of the romantic tendencies which produced them. His letters to Harcourt surely reveal his wonderful (or terrible) self-ignorance, ambition, and inconsistency. In one missive he declared that *Free Air* should be represented not as outdoor adventure-romance but "romance with dignity and realism"; in another he advised that Harcourt send *Free Air* to the Pulitzer Prize Committee as a serious and factual novel; and in yet other letters he asked that his publisher write the critics to urge them to overlook *The Innocents* and *Free Air,* and to assure them that *Main Street* would be the real thing.[16]

There is little else to say about Lewis's early books. They show us Lewis the optimistic rebel, the romancer, the money writer, and they provide a few glimpses of the realist and satirist. As the popular fiction they are, they now lie in the limbo of all popular fiction, justly so, with the possible exception of *The Job*. Having resurrected them for good reason, they should now be returned to their resting place. For the Lewis who matters is the Lewis of *Main Street* and after.

CHAPTER 3

The Great Decade: The Twenties

I *Main Street*

BY 1920 the American small town had already entered the period of decline which was to continue and accelerate until the mid-century. Both a symptom and a cause of the weakening of its strength can be observed in the migration of its young people to the city, which attracted them with brighter lights, better jobs, and greater personal freedom. Further, the displacement of farm labor by machinery, the increasing hardship of the independent farmer in making a living under the conditions imposed by buyer–shipper combinations (a factor which had earlier been turned into literary capital by Frank Norris), the advent of the automobile, the supermarket, the shopping center, and the mail-order house—all these contributed to the deterioration of the insularity and economic self-containment which had been vital to the small town's good health.[1]

But even as the town declined materially, it continued to prosper in our national mythology, which celebrated it as the home of the purest democracy, the friendliest people, the largest happiness, the sturdiest freedom. This mythology especially favored the midwestern small town. Meredith Nicholson's *The Valley of Democracy,* published in 1918, perhaps marked the culmination of the happy village tradition. Nicholson's book was a hymn of praise to the Midwest, to its folksiness, energy, and liberty. Even where Nicholson conceded the existence of flaws in the region and its settlements, his tone was so reassuring that the reader could not be convinced that anything was seriously wrong. If the Midwest was somewhat uninterested in culture, the writer admitted, its lack of class distinctions, its ambition and progressive impulses would soon rectify all shortcomings. He wrote: "The people of the Valley of Democracy . . . do a great deal of thinking and talking; they brood over the world's affairs with a peculiar intensity; and beyond question, they exchange opinions with a greater freedom than their fellow citizens in other parts of America." And, "One is struck by the remarkable individuality of the States, towns, and cities of the West." And also, "In the smaller Western towns, especially where the American stock is dominant, lines of social demarcation are usually obscure to the vanishing point. Schools and churches are here a democratizing factor, and a woman who 'keeps help' is very likely to be apologetic about it."[2] In short, whatever was wrong elsewhere in the world, there was little to worry about in regard to the midwestern American town. To this dogma we paid homage in 1920—until Sinclair Lewis and *Main Street*.

The novel which, with *Babbitt*, was to make Lewis the most timely American novelist since Harriet Beecher Stowe, according to one literary historian, had been gestating in Lewis's consciousness for fifteen years.[3] He, too, had been reared in the belief that the small town was paradise; but he had changed his mind in the summer of 1905 when, home from Yale on vacation, he had overheard a number of the good citizens of Sauk Centre ask again and again, "Why don't Doc Lewis make Harry get a job· on a farm instead of letting him sit around readin' and readin' a lot of fool histories and God knows what all?"

According to his own recollection of, the genesis of *Main Street*, the book was titled "The Village Virus" in its earliest conception. It was to be the story of Guy Pollock, a young lawyer who succumbs to small town mediocrity.[4] Lewis resolved to try again after a visit to Sauk Centre in 1916, when he was once more reminded of the village's narrowness by its shock at such radical behavior as his taking long walks to picnic with his wife on the prairie, and by its peeping, its rigid view of propriety, its dullness.[5] Grace Hegger Lewis recorded the result of this visit in her autobiographical novel *Half a Loaf*, when Timothy Hale (Lewis) says to his wife Susan: "This visit has re-created my boyhood so vividly that I've got to write about it or die. And having you along, a stranger to it all, has helped me to see the place through your eyes as well as mine. I'm sick to death of this romanticizing of the small town, the holding on to log-cabin tradition in an actuality of firebrick and arty bungalows. . . . Doggone it, it won't be a popular book but I got to write it all the same."[6]

Shortly afterward he made another start on the novel, now named "Main Street," and completed 30,000 words before he laid it aside. At last, having published *Free Air* as a two-part serial in the *Saturday Evening Post* and also sold it to the movies, he was able to take a year off to write the book which could no longer be denied. His apprenticeship, which had been long and demanding, had taxed his conscience as well as his imagination; and he told a friend, "I have been whoring long enough. I'm going to write a book this time *for·myself*."[7] Lewis had complete freedom from his publishers, the newly formed firm of Harcourt, Brace, and Howe, and he worked to the limits of his ability, without interference and for the first time without reverence for the popular idols. When he was finished, he knew he had written a good novel, although he had no way of knowing (despite his many suggestions to his publishers regarding the book's advertising and distribution to reviewers) that *Main Street* would become a runaway best seller.

With the forthrightness and lack of subtlety thereafter typical of Lewis's satires, the theme and purpose of *Main Street* is announced in its foreword. The rest of the novel proceeds to reiterate and illustrate what is said or implied in the foreword. It reads in full:

> *This is America—a town of a few thousand, in a region of wheat and corn and dairies and little groves.*
> *The town is, in our tale, called "Gopher Prairie, Minnesota." But its Main Street is the continuation of Main Streets everywhere. The story would be the same in Ohio or Montana, in Kansas or Kentucky or Illinois, and not very differently would it be told Up New York State or in the Carolina Hills.*
> *Main Street is the climax of civilization. That this Ford car might stand in front of the Bon Ton Store, Hannibal invaded Rome and Erasmus wrote in Oxford cloisters. What Ole Jensen the grocer says to Ezra Stowbody the banker is the new law for London, Prague, and the unprofitable isles of the sea; whatsoever Ezra does not know and sanction, that thing is heresy, worthless for knowing and wicked to consider.*
> *Our railway station is the final aspiration of architecture. Sam Clark's annual hardware turnover is the envy of the four counties which constitute God's Country. In the sensitive art of the Rosebud Movie Palace there is a message, and humor strictly moral.*
> *Such is our comfortable tradition and sure faith. Would he*

not betray himself an alien cynic who should otherwise portray
Main Street, or distress the citizens by speculating whether
there may not be other faiths?[8]

There can be no doubt that this is a different Lewis speaking;
he is now the realist and satirist and no longer the romancer.

Whereas the dominant theme of Lewis's early work and, in a
sense, of all romantic fiction is education—improvement, progress, finding the proper set of ideals and making them reality—
the theme of Lewis's serious books, beginning with *Main Street,*
is disillusionment. The protagonist cherishes lofty ideals or a
belief that he can fulfill himself by making the world a better
place, and he holds affirmative notions about people, manners,
and morals, only to see his illusions battered down one by one
and to come to the bitter realization that his ideals are incompatible with the reality he must endure. Thus, Carol Milford,
a former librarian and the book's heroine, who had decided,
"I'll get my hands on one of those prairie towns and make it
beautiful" (p. 5), undergoes a counter-education—an education
in disillusionment.

Her counter-education begins immediately after her marriage
to Dr. Will Kennicott, as she rides through the midwestern flat-
land en route to her new home in Gopher Prairie. She is overcome by the smell, dirt, and squalor of the train and its passen-
gers, appalled by the stolidity of the farmers and the ugliness
of the towns they pass. Her husband cannot see the ugliness
and sameness. To him they are "good, hustling burgs," and he
reminds Carol that only fifty years earlier this land had been
wilderness. But Lewis is concerned, as was Whitman in *Demo-*
cratic Vistas, with the future of the entire civilization of which
the rich fields and ugly hamlets are the beginning, although
he seems at this point much less sure of its final happy out-
come than was Whitman.

Carol's first hard look at Gopher Prairie, in which, building
by building and detail by detail, the town's shabbiness and
planlessness are dissected, sharpens her disillusionment. It is,
furthermore, one of the most effective passsages of its kind in
American fiction, equalled earlier in the mercilessness of its
scrutiny only by Sinclair's description of the meat-packing houses
in *The Jungle* and by a few of Dreiser's depictions. This tech-

nique, which Lewis was to use even more skillfully in *Babbitt,* is like that of the newsreel documentary; the slow relentless movement of the lens misses nothing but pauses to note details of special significance. The narrator, his voice presumably objective, speaks what the camera sees, hammering home point after point, remarking ugliness after ugliness: the cat sleeping on the vegetables in a grocery store window, the food-stained tablecloths in the hotel dining room, an unshaven farmer with a face like a newly dug potato. In such a setting the pseudo-Greek bank building and a clean display window in the department store become miracles.

The counter-education continues when Carol learns in various experiences and with varying amounts of chagrin that the town's social habits and behavior are as distressing as its architecture. Its idea of a successful party is to invite the same people who will at the same time arise to do the same "stunts," eat the same refreshments, talk about the same subjects with the same dullness or viciousness, keep firm to the same reactionary opinions about the farmers, labor, and politics, and arrive and depart at fixed hours. Her attempts to stimulate some gaiety are met with embarrassment and ridicule, and killed by an unshakable preference for things as usual.

But Carol's most important and painful lesson, and one which carries the greatest weight of Lewis's indignation, deals with the pettiness and narrowness of human beings. The lesson is that constriction of habits and imagination makes for constriction of the soul; in short, small towns mold small people. She is educated at the Jolly Seventeen club, where the women snipe at her, act defensively proud of Gopher Prairie, and even more emphatically than their husbands express the same biases toward the Scandinavian farmers upon whom the town depends for most of its business. The lesson continues when she learns from Vida Sherwin, one of her few friends, that the townsfolk are watching her and gossiping about her, criticizing her every movement, from her attempt to stage bright and original parties to the way she treats her hired girl. She learns that even the town's adolescent boys discuss her in overfamiliar terms. Carol, who has been misled by the town's surface cordiality into the belief that her activities are free and unimpaired and that people like her, is crushed by these revelations. She never fully recovers from her disillusionment nor does she ever fully forgive Gopher Prairie for it—just as Lewis never forgave Sauk Centre for its criticism of him.

Another stage in Carol's counter-education is her attempt to improve the town by working through its main cultural force, the Thanatopsis Club, which is composed of Gopher Prairie's most eminent ladies. She finds herself stopped at every point by private interests: the wife of the school superintendent thinks reform should begin with a brand new school building and the minister's wife wants a new and larger church. That plan of Carol's dies like all the rest, along with her good intentions and part of her spirit.

And so it goes in episode after episode, in which Lewis demonstrates the provincialism, the hypocrisy, the narrowness, and at last the cruelty of small town life. Guy Pollock, once talented and ambitious, sits like a tired old man in his musty office, a victim of the "Village Virus"—the fear of meeting the competition and energy of the larger world outside. The town's professional men harbor petty jealousies and hostilities, one undercutting the other. A young teacher is discharged from her job and driven from the town in disgrace, even though the school board does not truly believe she is guilty of the misconduct with which she has been charged. Her crime has been her youth and high spirits. The town's only other rebel, Miles Bjornstam, atheist, socialist, and thoroughly decent human being, leaves Gopher Prairie a broken man when his wife and child die of typhoid and it is rumored that he has killed them with mistreatment. Finally, Carol herself must leave when the combination of Gopher Prairie's war-inspired hatred of all things German and its booster spirit becomes more than she can endure. Her education in disillusionment has been so complete it threatens to rob her of all dignity and identity, of the very urge to live. By this time Lewis has also convinced the reader that, as Twain concluded about Pap Finn, the only way to reform Gopher Prairie is with a shotgun.

However, Lewis's concern is broader than Gopher Prairie, and Carol's differences with the ladies of the Jolly Seventeen over the status and wages of their housemaids extend beyond the town. To Lewis this quarrel whether the hired help are to be treated as chattels or friends is merely a local instance of political and economic changes taking place throughout the world. Carol's rebellion is thus allied to the growing discontent of the dissatisfied and downtrodden everywhere, a rebellion which Lewis correctly predicted a generation before it occurred. Again and again Lewis reminds us that Gopher Prairie is a microcosm, that it merely reflects universal events, that it influences these events and is influenced by them. In this way Lewis is a synecdochist in *Main Street*. He makes of his Minnesota what Frost does of New Hampshire, a part standing for the whole, the particular representing the general. Moreover, Lewis's greatest fear stems from the possibility that Gopher Prairie's philosophy of dull safety shall conquer all America and then the world, and that it will drive the variety and beauty out of other cultures just as it has, within two generations, standardized the Scandinavian and German settlers and made them ashamed of the Old World ways which are actually the richest aspects of their lives.

So far we have observed in *Main Street* only Lewis the satirist and social critic. Lewis the storyteller is also in evidence, however; without story the novel of opinion becomes a tract. The story here concerns Carol's personal life, and it records Carol's experiences as a woman, wife, and mother. But even in this there is a crucial difference between the Lewis of *Main Street* and the earlier Lewis. In *Main Street* the focus is directed at the environment rather than at the individual, at what the protagonist sees and suffers rather than what he is, whereas in the novels from *Our Mr. Wrenn* to *Free Air* (with the possible exception of *The Job*), environment had been subordinate. Furthermore, Lewis's approach to complication and conflict are much more serious and realistic. In any case, the merger of story and social criticism is successful in *Main Street*, for it not only provides welcome intervals in the heavy barrage upon the small town's vices (Lewis often balances chapters of satire or attack with chapters describing some development in Carol's private life), but also gives another dimension to the novel's thesis.

The exterior conflict, Carol's war with Gopher Prairie, has counterpoint in the interior conflict, Carol's war with her husband, Will, who is also the representative of many of Gopher Prairie's best and worst qualities. Where Carol is for change, any change, Will claims to believe in progress but is really suspicious of anything new. Where Carol tends to be stand-offish but is basically democratic, Will displays spontaneous good-fellowship yet harbors deep prejudices about caste, class, and nationality. Where Carol yearns for the beautiful, Will is scornful of all that smacks of the arty or aesthetic. Where Carol is flighty and unpredictable, Will is a willing slave to routine. Where Carol is moody, Will is stable. Where she is given to fantasy, he is utterly pragmatic. Where she is fastidious, he is indifferent to personal appearance and habits. Where she is guilty of crimes against propriety, he is guilty of crimes against morality. In short, in the marriage of Carol and Will, and in the contrast of their values and personalities, Lewis the story-teller illustrates and reinforces what Lewis the social critic has asserted. It is an effective combination and one crucial to the success or failure of Lewis's books. While one element is never present without the other—even in such romantic concoctions as *The Innocents* and in such wholesale indictments as *Gideon Planish*—only where there is balance and conjunction, point and counterpoint, message fused with plot, is Lewis worthy of serious consideration as a *novelist*.

With all its virtues, *Main Street* is not a flawless book. While it remains, after forty years, a solid achievement and is still an effective attack on the small town and its state of mind, there are imperfections. The novel is over-long, although Lewis cut 20,000 words from it before it went to press.[9] This length, together with the lack of variety in Lewis's style, produce some monotony. Characters tend to be flat and to be subordinated to theme—they become puppets rather than performers. The very anger which gives the book its impetus occasionally lapses into mere shrillness.

When we consider the charges which some critics advanced against *Main Street* (and other of Lewis's books), we find the complaint that he was not being fair in his criticism, and that he failed to provide a program of reform for the errors he exposed. Although there is some validity in these charges, it could be said in regard to the first simply that satirists are never fair; one of the secrets of effective satire is the very selectivity which produces a recognizable but incomplete picture. As for the second, at least as it applies to *Main Street*, Lewis had in an early draft of the book included a good deal of constructive suggestion, which he deleted on the shrewd advice of James Branch Cabell, for such material would have blunted the book's edge. Cabell also persuaded Lewis to keep Bea Sorenson, Carol's housemaid, a minor character, whereas Lewis had originally intended to make her a full-scale figure and to contrast her with Carol in order to show how Bea's assets and humbler ambitions let her find happiness in Gopher Prairie (a bit of this remains, for at the same time that Carol surveys Gopher Prairie and finds it hell, Bea gazes at it and thinks it heaven).[10] Even in the book's final form, with the focus on Carol, Lewis's ambivalent attitude toward his main characters leads to what most critics consider the novel's basic weakness, a weakness present to greater or lesser degree in much of Lewis's work.

To put the matter plainly, Lewis cannot, despite his obvious hostility toward the town, seem to be consistent about who is the hero, who is the villain, and who is the fool. First, we are given the notion that Carol's dreams of reforming a whole town are rather vague and silly; yet there is nothing silly about her when she perceives Gopher Prairie's ugliness and narrowness. Then, in contrasting Carol with Vida Sherwin, who also wants to improve the town, Lewis appears to demonstrate that Vida's plan for gradual reform through compromise is more realistic and sensible (although in her yearning for beauty *now*, Carol has the higher right; she may be impractical but she is hardly ridiculous). Again, we are made to wonder where Lewis stands when, in a number of passages which are among the best in the novel, Lewis describes the hard life of the country doctor. All of Carol's grand schemes pale beside Will Kennicott's quiet heroism and competence in an episode in which he amputates a man's arm under primitive surgical conditions, as part of a routine day's work. Further, in the arguments between Carol and Will we often see Carol through his (and the town's) eyes as a difficult, shallow, temperamental girl who is looking for trouble; and we are forced to concede the truth in Will's viewpoint. As Maxwell Geismar has noted, *Main Street* is also the story of Gopher Prairie's revolt against Carol Kennicott.[11] She deserves some of its scorn because of the clumsiness and naiveté of many of her reform attempts.

Finally, in the last third of the novel, when Lewis shifts emphasis from Carol's conflict with the town to that with her husband, his tone definitely mellows, and while the book may gain somewhat in poignancy, its tonic effect is weakened. In her separation from Will and from Minnesota Carol learns that there are many worse towns. She also learns poise, objectivity, and what Lewis tells us is the best weapon against all imperfect institutions—laughter. In the same chapters in which Carol gets this instruction, Will Kennicott comes up greatly in our estimation as a man of intelligence, dignity, and good will. On her return to Gopher Prairie, having been re-won by Will's patient courtship, Carol finds the town somehow easier to accept. She participates in a number of concrete reforms and is herself finally accepted by the town. In short, with both the exterior and interior conflicts resolved, Lewis has written an ending which borders on the happy.

Is *Main's Street's* conclusion, then, a contradiction to Lewis's earlier position? No. It is a modification but not a contradiction. It is the work of neither the satirist nor the romancer, but the realist. At the end of the novel Lewis has denied Carol's way; however, he has also denied Gopher Prairie's way and Will's and even Vida Sherwin's. Carol gives up the battle but not the war, for she asserts that she will continue to exercise her critical intelligence and continue to ask questions—and this action, Lewis tells us, is enough to lead slowly but inevitably to the good society. He is no longer an anarchist, as he had seemed at some stages in *Main Street,* but a social Darwinist. He admits that one girl cannot reform a whole town, but he retains his faith in the need for reform. As the novel closes, Carol points to the head of her sleeping daughter and declares to Will: "Do you see that object on the pillow? Do you know what it is? It's a bomb to blow up smugness. If you Tories were wise, you wouldn't arrest anarchists; you'd arrest all these children while they're asleep in their cribs. Think what that baby will see and meddle with before she dies in the year 2000! She may see an industrial union of the whole world, she may see aeroplanes going to Mars" (p. 450). Thus, while some might call the book's ending a happy one, it is hardly idyllic. Chastened but not maimed, Carol has graduated from the school of disillusionment. She continues to recognize and resist the ugliness of the reality, but she has found a *modus vivendi.* She is still a rebel, though now somewhat tamed, and her attitude lets us continue to like and respect her because she has not sold out, and because she does not praise what she has formerly battled. Her triumph is perhaps the only kind possible, except for martyrdom or dying well, in the realistic novel.

Why, some have asked, did Lewis make Carol as weak as she is, since her weakness complicates the choice between the contrasting ways of life and thought which she and Will represent? Lewis himself later wrote that he had done it deliberately: Carol "should be just bright enough to sniff a little but not bright enough to do anything about it."[12] There are other possible replies, however. First, Carol is not such a pathetic figure as she has been painted, nor is she inferior to her husband. Her main flaws are those of personality and judgment. In her character and values she is admirable. Moreover, while Will represents Gopher Prairie in many of his attitudes, he is more than the total of the town. He is the *best*, not the average, sort of man the small town produces.

Another answer to the problem of Carol's character lies in Lewis's own experience; that is, the relationship between Carol and Gopher Prairie and Carol and Will (which is often more like that of father–child than husband–wife) reflects the relationship between Lewis and Sauk Centre and Lewis and Dr. E. J. Lewis. As much as he resented Sauk Centre and as much as he rebelled against the father who symbolized it, he was neither blind to its merits nor proof against its influence. Lewis admitted to Charles Breasted in 1922 that he had portrayed his father as Will Kennicott and himself as Carol. "Yes . . . Carol is 'Red' Lewis: always groping for something she isn't capable of attaining, always dissatisfied, always restlessly straining to see what lies just over the horizon, intolerant of her surroundings, yet lacking any clearly defined vision of what she really wants to do or be." In 1926, just before his father's death, Lewis told Breasted that his father had never forgiven him for *Main Street*, not realizing "it's the greatest tribute I knew how to pay him."[13]

There are other autobiographical elements in *Main Street*. Some of Carol's reform activities are modeled after those of Lewis's stepmother, Isabel Warner Lewis; the operation in which Carol assists her husband by administering the ether (in the presence of an open flame) occurred in reality in Lewis's own life when he was thirteen.[14] Taken all together, these bits of evidence indicate that Sinclair Lewis could no more reject Sauk Centre utterly and completely than he could un-live his own boyhood. Carol's weaknesses, therefore, are Lewis's weaknesses. His ambivalent attitude toward her reveals his ambivalence toward himself and his home town. When Carl Van Doren wrote, in a review of *Main Street,* that Lewis must despise all dull people, Lewis replied in a letter that he loved many of the town's "dull" characters.[15] His answer no longer seems surprising.

Although Sauk Centre remains today much as Carol saw it, *Main Street* had a tremendous impact upon the American mind, if not upon the architecture of its villages. It was, of course, not the first novel to attack the small town, for E. W. Howe had anticipated *Main Street* forty years before. Twain, Eggleston, Harold Frederic, Garland, Zona Gale, Edgar Lee Masters, Sherwood Anderson, had all written realistically and even caustically about small towns. Moreover, Frank Norris, Robert Herrick, Upton Sinclair, Theodore Dreiser, H. L. Mencken, Randolph Bourne and others had created the critical mood favorable to the novel's fantastic success. A brutal war and an inconclusive peace had also turned the younger generation against their elders and everything they represented. Thus, *Main Street* and the mood of the time made Sinclair Lewis the voice for which the young rebels had been listening. America's intellectuals and a good part of its thinking citizenry had become introspective, self-conscious, and self-critical; Lewis caught the wave at its crest.[16]

The critics added to the novel's momentum by discussing it widely and often with glowing praise. Irvin Cobb explained the book's success in this way: "People in the cities are sure to like it because it makes fun of rural places, and the folks that live in villages and little towns have to read it just to find out what Sinclair Lewis is saying about them." One writer called it "one of the milestones in the discovery of America"; and an English critic wrote, "One is tempted to generalize about American characteristics on the basis of nearly every chapter of this book. It sums up brilliantly and mercilessly everything that the new generation in America detests."[17]

The public took *Main Street* with as much seriousness as the critics, according to contemporary sources. An article in a popular magazine of the day noted the deep influence the book was having:

What seems to me most significant about the whole affair of *Main Street* is the painful conscientiousness of any number of people in regard to it. "This is America," says Mr. Lewis in his own italicized foreword, and far from his being lynched, there is a widespread uneasy fear that his picture may largely be true. . . .

. . . .

For everyone who has revolted against the book one has met a dozen who with a deep discomfort of soul accepted it . . . and asked the Great American Question: What are we going to do about it?[18]

Another of the many testimonials scattered through the books, newspapers, and periodicals, this one written by an English traveler to America, reads as follows: "In common with many other people I read *Main Street* when I was in America. It was hardly possible to avoid buying it and reading it. . . . A lady remarked to me, 'Every American should read *Main Street* as a penance. Gopher Prairie, Minnesota, is the twentieth century substitute for Concord, Massachusetts! Alas!' "[19]

From 1920 to 1930 Sinclair Lewis was, beginning with *Main Street,* a writer who compelled the attention of both his country and the world. The very characteristics which later critics turned against him—his simplicity of theme, the weight of his detail, his didactiveness, the emphasis on environment rather than character, the crude vigor of his style, his faithful transcription of American idiom and sharp portraiture of the surface of American life—made Lewis famous, read, and effective. Other books, before and since, have sold more widely than *Main Street,* but the quality of its success was unique. It was the first book to become popular which attacked a beloved native institution. Dreiser's grimness had repelled the mass audience, Anderson was too fumbling and arty, and Mencken's influence was limited largely to the readers of the *Smart Set*; but Lewis broke through the layers of public indifference and the hostility toward unpleasant novels.[20] He had, after an arduous apprenticeship, arrived.

II *Babbitt*

By late summer, 1920, just several weeks after completing *Main Street,* Lewis was already planning his next novel. It was to be "the story of the Tired Business Man, of the man in the Pullman smoker, of our American ruler." The book's title, Lewis decided, would be the name of its central character. "Babbitt" was the name he chose.

From its inception Lewis intended the book to be a serious

treatment. Both the composition and reception of *Main Street* had wrought a profound, although not a total, change in Lewis and in his attitude toward writing. He saw that he had become a novelist of international importance and that his work would thenceforth be given the most careful attention. Consequently, he found himself unable to return to the potboiling fiction he had earlier found easy and profitable, and he wrote to Alfred Harcourt, "I don't believe I shall ever again be the facile Post trickster I by God was." In the same letter and in a prospectus for the new novel, he declared his intention to depict its protagonist as an individual, for he hoped to correct one of the faults which critics had found in *Main Street,* that of "exterior vision," its superficial and typed characters. But this hero and his environment would also be representative of America, Lewis believed, because only in the United States was life so standardized that a writer could treat one city as if it were like all others of its size, regardless of its location.

The ambitiousness and seriousness of his conception is best revealed, perhaps, in this letter to Harcourt, December 28, 1920:

> I want the novel to be the G.A.N. [Great American Novel] in so far as it crystallizes and makes real the Average Capable American. No one has done it, I think; no one has even *touched* it except Booth Tarkington in *Turmoil* and *Magnificent Amber-sons;* and he romanticizes away all bigness. Babbitt is a little like Will Kennicott but bigger, with a bigger field to work on, more sensations, more perceptions. . . . He is all of us Americans at 46, prosperous but worried, wanting—passionately—to seize something more than motor cars and a house *before it's too late.* Yet, utterly unlike Carol, it never even occurs to him that he might live in Europe, might like poetry, might be a senator; he is content to live and work in the city of Zenith, which is, as everybody knows, the best little ole city in the world. But he would like for once the flare of romantic love, the satisfaction of having left a mark on the city and a let-up in his constant warring on competitors, and when his beloved friend Riesling commits suicide* he suddenly says, "Oh hell, what's the use of the cautious labor to which I've given everything"—only for a little while is he discontented, though. . . . I want to make Babbitt big in his real-ness, in his relation to all of us, not in the least exceptional, yet dramatic, passionate, struggling.[21]

* In the final version of the novel Paul Riesling is sent to prison for attempting to kill his wife.

Much of *Main Street* had been drawn directly from Lewis's experience, for he knew from direct observation the patterns of small town speech and behavior. Although *Babbitt* depended far less upon what Lewis had lived, it also contained something of his personality. A number of Lewis's friends have remarked about the similarity between the character of Babbitt and that of his creator. One has written: "At the bottom, Lewis is solidly bourgeois. He loves real estate and mortgages and bank accounts. Fundamentally, he is a Rotarian." Another has pointed out that in his informality, cordiality, impulsiveness, candor, riotessness, and in his hatred of affected and arty people, as well as in other personal qualities, Lewis resembled Babbitt.[22] An incident related by William Rose Benét concerning what he called the "essential Lewis" further illustrates this matter. Benét and Lewis were dining together when a stranger, a traveling salesman, came to their table and engaged them in conversation. Lewis soon got him talking about himself so that he revealed more than he knew—to the fascination of Lewis but to the boredom of Benét. After the man had gone, Benét asked Lewis if he truly liked that sort of person, and Lewis replied, "That's the trouble with you, Bill. You regard him as *hoi polloi*, he doesn't even represent the cause of labor or anything dramatic—but I understand that man—by God, I love him."[23]

As regards Lewis the artist, *Babbitt* displays his ability to project himself into virtually any environment and capture its essence. His gift for impersonation and mimicry enabled him at any given time to be almost anyone he wanted. He could strike up an acquaintanceship with a stranger on a train or in a hotel or restaurant and, by pretending to be of the same background, completely win the man's confidence. His remarkable memory enabled him to record American speech on a mental soundtrack, to be replayed at will—a talent crucial to the astounding fidelity of detail and idiom both typical of his work and necessary to its satiric effectiveness. In this manner Lewis had been gathering material for *Babbitt* in the years of his travels over the American continent. Moreover, his own experience in the various publishing jobs he had held from 1910 to 1915, including his work as advertising manager for the Doran Company, had given him some insight into the principles of salesmanship. Finally, the student of Lewis's career perceives that in the character of Eddie Schwirtz in *The Job*, and in a number of short stories, Lewis had anticipated some of the characters and situations of *Babbitt*.[24]

Thematically, *Babbitt* is an extension and expansion of *Main Street*. Having described the forces of conformity at work in a typical small town, it was foreseeable that Lewis would now enlarge his canvas. Accordingly, he created an average midwestern state called Winnemac (Wisconsin, Minnesota, Michigan), placed in it the imaginary but familiar city of Zenith, and depicted two years in the life of one of its representative citizens, George F. Babbitt: middle class ($9,000 a year), forty-six years of age, somewhat overweight, resident in a fashionable suburb, father of two children, dealer in real estate, good fellow. Again in *Babbitt*, as he had in *Main Street*, Lewis combined and solidified ideas and attitudes already in existence but awaiting a local habitation and a name. Indeed, we may discern in Lewis's novel certain perceptions about American life which had been advanced by such keen observers of our civilization as Thorstein Veblen, Randolph Bourne, and H. L. Mencken.[25]

While much of Veblen's thought is today in disrepute, especially those concepts based on Sumnerian sociology, Veblen's theories of pecuniary emulation, conspicuous consumption, the pecuniary standard of living and canons of taste (these are developed in *The Theory of the Leisure Class*, 1899), all have great pertinence to the mode of Babbitt's daily life. Furthermore, Veblen's analysis of business enterprise and business principles (*The Theory of Business Enterprise*, 1904) goes far toward explaining the larger structure of Babbitt's society.

As Veblen saw it, wealth symbolizes honor and prestige in modern society; it is necessary for acceptance by our fellows. For status we need money, and without that status there can be no self-respect. Yet once we accumulate a certain sum, it is not enough. We are driven ever to increase what we own, to rise as far above the average as we can. Moreover, money brings power, or the sense of power; and, since man's striving for money also springs from his sense of purposeful activity—what Veblen calls "the instinct of workmanship"—we have come to see success as money and to measure success by money. But the possession of money is not alone sufficient to satisfy man; he must demonstrate his wealth, either by his own freedom from labor and/or by the amount of goods and services he and his family consume. Since money becomes the *summum bonum* and the

surest way in a business society to success and power, the aim
of business is to gain money; all is subordinated to profit, even
if the profit is gained at the community's loss. Nor are profit
and wages necessarily related to true value.

Finally, the members of an industrial and business society,
such as that of the modern Western world, are inevitably affected in their modes of thinking by the machine process upon
which industry depends. Because the machine process inculcates
standardization, exact quantitative knowledge, and a sense of
material causality, it inevitably collides with and weakens tradition, traditional morality, and all conduct based on sentimental
and metaphysical precepts. Only the tradition of ownership
prospers under such conditions; property rights become the
highest rights. However, despite the deterioration and change
ultimately produced by the machine process, the standardization
it enforces tends to prevail in the lives of the industrial popula-
tion and to repress any disturbance which might upset the delicate balance and adjustment between the various parts of the
society. The balance must be maintained.

The ideas of Randolph Bourne apply to *Babbitt* in a different
sense but with no less pertinence. Bourne pointed out that
America's older generation had grown conservative and stodgy.
It had stopped thinking about and trying to answer life's more
difficult questions; in fact, it pretended there were no questions.
While it was no longer so strict in its religion and its belief in
religious dogmas, it persisted in maintaining the forms and
rituals. The elders disengaged themselves from such vital matters as death, which frightened them; sex, which brought them
panic; and psychology, which mystified them. Having fallen
into the comfortable routines of business, church, and family
life, they recognized no change and failed to meet the age's
new needs and demands. The young, Bourne concluded, must
transform all this and must not become victim to their parents'
complacency. Bourne admitted to the friendliness of the American, especially the midwesterner, but warned against its consequences. "An excessive amiability . . . will, in the end, put a
premium on conformity." "Folksiness," he wrote, "evidently has
its dark underlining in a tendency to be stampeded by herd-
emotion." And, "Social conscience may become the duty to
follow what the mob demands, and democracy may come to
mean that the individual feels himself somehow expressed—his

private tastes and intelligence—in whatever the crowd chooses to do."[26]

Likewise, H. L. Mencken in *The American Credo* (written in collaboration with George Jean Nathan) offered an analysis of the American character which is perfectly applicable to *Babbitt*:

> The thing which sets off the American from all other men, and gives a peculiar colour not only to the pattern of his daily life but also to the play of his inner ideas, is what, for want of a more exact term, may be called social aspiration. That is to say, his dominant passion is a passion to lift himself by at least a step or two in the society that he is a part of—a passion to improve his position, to break down some shadowy barrier of caste, to achieve the countenance of what, for all his talk of equality, he recognizes and accepts as his betters.[27]

This desire to rise socially, Mencken asserted, was at the root of American restlessness. However, Americans fear one another. Since the majority determines the individual's status, the individual fears the majority. His only way to success is to assume protective coloration, to lose himself in the crowd, and then to be approved by it as one of its members. Failure consists of being unmasked, of standing out as an individual; consequently, the American fears to question ideas and institutions. Ultimately, he fears simply to question.

Thus, Babbitt lies within a context of economic and social analyses which suggest some of the novel's intellectual affiliations, whether or not they were actually influences upon it. But when we analyze the novel itself, we discover that it has its own entity.

Babbitt begins with the description of a modern city—a city "for giants." The remainder of the novel provides an extended ironic commentary on this statement, as it demonstrates how Babbitt and the others of his kind who live in this city are pygmies, not giants. Our initial glance at Babbitt is likewise focused through Lewis's ironic lens, for the only beauty and magic left in his life are the visitations of an elusive dream girl, reminiscent somewhat of Melville's Yillah, who beckons to Babbitt in his slumbers. As Lewis continues to concentrate on the hero for the narrative's first one hundred pages, the irony deepens.

We are given closely detailed descriptions of Babbitt's house, yard, bathroom; the routine of his morning shave; Mrs. Babbitt's contours; his method of dressing, his eyeglasses, his tie, the contents of his pockets; his minor aches and pains and the state of his digestion; his opinions on dress suits and on his children. We are told of his pride in his automobile, his attitude toward his neighbors, his route to his office. We watch him as he dictates letters, prepares a sales campaign, and composes advertisements for cemetery plots. We follow him to lunch at the Zenith Athletic Club and listen to his badinage and his conversation. We see him, in short, in all the significant activities of his life, at home, at work, with his friends; and in the last five of the one hundred and two pages which have depicted twenty-four hours in the history of George F. Babbitt, Lewis recounts to us the sinful or meaningful or interesting things others are doing and saying in Zenith as Babbitt goes to sleep on his sleeping-porch, gallant and intrepid at last in the pursuit of his dream girl.

The total effect of this first section of the novel is, just as Lewis intended, overwhelming in its emphasis upon the smallness, the pettiness, the triviality, and the lack of joy and freedom in the existence of a typical member of a money society. His house, conspicuous in its material comforts and illustrative of its owner's success, is a shelter but not a home. His stolid wife and his children who insult one another and argue at the breakfast table about who will get the car (less a vehicle than a symbol of status) are, if anything, even more trivial and shallow. Although Babbitt performs no truly useful function in his work as a "realtor," he is successful enough at it financially. His field is real estate but he adds nothing to its value nor is informed about it. He knows nothing about architecture, landscaping, economics. He does not really know such essential facts about his community as how good the police and fire departments are, or the quality of the schools. Although engaged in land development, he is ignorant of the fundamentals of sanitation. Nor does he need to possess any of this information. As Veblen had written, the business system is large enough to absorb those who take profit without rendering service or creating anything of worth.

Furthermore, Babbitt's business ethics are elastic. They can be stretched to condone bribery, lying, bullying, and conspiracy, although Babbitt discharges one of his employees for employing the same methods. The point (Veblen's) is that right and wrong, the traditional morality, are now determined by what is expedient and profitable, by what brings in a financial return yet is not flagrant enough to disturb the system's equilibrium. Where Babbitt might be troubled by moral qualms, the remnants of the old morality and religion, he can justify his practices under the name of good, smart business, which is what everyone is doing. In this way Babbitt also has his efforts rewarded by his peers, for in following them he shares in the recognition which the group provides for the obedient (Mencken and Bourne).

Everywhere Babbitt is surrounded by pals who slap him on the back, call him by affectionate nicknames, joke with him. His entrance at the Athletic Club brings a volley of greetings. He is elected vice-president of the Boosters Club. He is chosen to make a speech before the Zenith Real Estate Board. He attracts attention and praise by his speech-making during an election campaign and by his participation in a drive to raise Sunday School attendance at his church. But Babbitt's conformity and forced geniality have their price because all the while there is only one person, Paul Riesling, to whom he can admit that he is somehow not fully satisfied, not really happy; and his only means of breaking out and still maintaining the appearance of respectability is to take a Maine vacation without his wife and, once there, to sit up late, drink, and play poker.

Only in the hotel barbershop can Babbitt unleash his senses and glory in the sybaritic abandonment of a haircut, a shampoo, and a manicure; the group demands that at least the pretense of propriety prevail. Thus, Babbitt is disturbed by Paul's open hatred of his wife Zilla, shocked at Paul's flagrant violation of the code by carrying on an affair, and horrified when Paul turns on Zilla and physically assaults her. Yet it is acceptable to Babbitt that as "one of the boys" he should get drunk and visit a house of prostitution during the course of an out-of-town convention. He avows dedication to law and order, but with ill-concealed pride at this proof of his status and power, he procures and serves bootleg whiskey at a party.

He declares himself a democrat, yet he is thrilled to meet one of the town's richest men, proud to have another to his home for dinner (a dismal failure), and contemptuous when one of his less successful college classmates in turn invites him to dinner (a dismal failure). When he does get a glimmer of the realities of class and caste structure, it is forgotten in the frenzied activities of the innumerable clubs and organizations which the system provides to keep its citizens from too much thinking. One of the highest moments of his life is his meeting with Sir Gerald Doak, an Englishman, who likes the same pastimes as Babbitt, has the same disdain for the intellectual, the same lust for success symbols, and the same smug sense of the power of his kind. Lewis's point? Babbittry is not only a native disease; it is pandemic.

But somehow Babbitt does grow restless and thoughtful in his constricted existence. Paul Riesling's frustration arouses muted response in Babbitt. At the same party whose success is reassurance of his popularity, he gets another impulse toward revolt; for a moment he realizes how dull it all is, how stupid his friends are, how hollow their congeniality. He comes to see that he neither understands nor approves of his children, nor they of him. When he falls ill for a day or two, he realizes the emptiness of his life, his work. It is "all mechanical." He begins to take the hard look, characteristic of the individualist, the sensitive man, at himself. In a word, he begins to move away from the mass and to search out true value—an act which inevitably threatens the delicate balance of the system and which, consequently, it cannot permit.

Babbitt's rebellion starts harmlessly and predictably enough with some mild and furtive attempts at romance: a weak pass at his secretary, a slightly stronger one at a neighbor's wife, a date with a manicurist, and finally an affair with a pretty widow. The group frowns on such philandering, but it does not absolutely forbid it if in moderation and in secrecy. However, when his affair becomes dissipation and when Babbitt openly declares his independence by publicly defending the cause of labor during a strike—thus challenging both the social and economic bases of his world—it is time for the maverick to be driven back to the herd. Accordingly, representatives of the newly formed "Good Citizen's League," a kind of rotarian Ku Klux Klan, call on Babbitt and ask him to join. He refuses; the pressure builds; he loses business and his friends avoid him. Then his wife falls ill and her illness causes him to realize how much she and the safe, comfortable existence she represents mean to him.

He renounces his liberty, becomes a member of the Good Citizen's League, and with its members pledges himself to uphold the ideal of equality in everything but wealth—and for everyone except the working class. As the novel concludes, only one avenue of hope and freedom is left to Babbitt (and this is, of course, reminiscent of *Main Street*), that his son will not make the same mistakes.

In *Babbitt* we can distinguish the two elements, the two layers of meaning comprising Lewis's method. As a novel it is the story of one man's struggle against the forces besetting him, a man who is closer to the Wellsian than the Sophoclean. On this level *Babbitt* might be read as the story of a man approaching old age—the male menopause—and having a last fling. Typically, he becomes dissatisfied with his daily routine, his work, his friends, his home and family. He almost inevitably seeks an illicit relationship which will restore the sense of life's danger and adventure he had as a youth and reassure him that he is still sexually attractive. He rejects the values he has accepted as an adult, whatever those values, and tries to return to the values and ideals of his youth. In some cases the rebellion goes so far that the man overturns his whole life, takes the firm's money and his secretary, and runs off to Brazil. Babbitt travels a little distance along just such a road.

On the second level, Babbitt is not a realistic character but a parody, a type, a symbol.[28] By means of this Babbitt, Lewis uses the book as a vehicle for satire and social history, the portrayal of a whole way of life in a representative American city. In this context Lewis gives us a superficially authentic but distorted account of the conditions of life in an industrial and commercial society, which is dominated by the profit motive and acquiescent to the pressure toward sameness and standardization.

The success of *Babbitt* as a novel results from the merger of the two elements, for the story of the brief rebellion of one middle-aged man cannot be separated from the account of that man's role in a society which he has made and which has made him. We perceive that the doubts Babbitt suffers are shared by his friends and associates. Paul Riesling revolts even more drastically by trying to destroy his wife, the symbol of his imprisonment in a desolate world. Chum Frink the poet, who is one of the voices of the society, confesses drunkenly, like a character in an E. A. Robinson poem, that he has betrayed his talent; he could indeed have become a poet, not the hack versifier he is. The cameraderie, the noise, the activity of the Athletic Club and the Booster's Club, the Fascistic program of the Good Citizens League—all indicate a basic malaise, an unhappiness with life as it is. As Maxwell Geismar and Ludwig Lewisohn have noted, this sense of fear and dread underlying the novel is a high artistic achievement by Lewis.[29] Like Babbitt, the other inhabitants of this purgatory try to resolve or forget their inner torment by arranging a busy and gimmick-filled outer world, by their frenetic pursuit of money and what it buys, by the chase to acquire class and caste symbols—a chase so exhausting that no energy remains to enjoy what has been achieved. Their symbols become ends in themselves.[30] In such a world individuality and self-knowledge are difficult, perhaps impossible. Thus, individual revolt comes too late for Babbitt; he cannot see himself clearly for the first time at forty-eight and make changes. The children must determine the future, and they must do it by heeding their own desires, by defying the world and doing what they want.

Among the most tragic things which have happened to Babbitt is his loss of capacity for pleasure. He who seeks so ardently for recreation, for entertainment in a culture which has never been more materially conducive to pleasure, cannot really be entertained. Not only is he fearful of what people would say if he followed his dream-girl in actuality, he is so stifled by routine that he has lost most of his capacity to feel. Herein Babbitt demonstrates what Thomas Henry Huxley had said was the penalty of civilization—weariness, ennui. Where there should be standards of taste, value, and beauty adequate to the height of the material existence, where, in other words, there should be a soul, we find a vacuum. Too comfortable, well fed, long-lived, and rational to believe in heaven and hell, not talented or dedicated enough to believe in himself or his work, he can only believe in what his friends and the mass media tell him. Once he learns that they lie, that his gods are brazen idols, he becomes stripped of his capacity for faith.

But Lewis's conclusions about Babbitt's future are not entirely negative. He shares with Lewis's other heroes a yearning for self-realization and fulfillment. If it is too late for him to find fulfillment, at least he may achieve realization. This realization, once established, will never again allow Babbitt contentment or peace of mind, will never again permit him to warm himself against the bodies of the herd, but it is worth more than any of these. Babbitt is not of heroic dimensions—nor could he ever be so in the conditions of his world; but he is an adult or promises to become one at the novel's end. He walks out to face the world and live in it, although it is no longer Eden.

In this portrait of Babbitt there appears once more the question of Lewis's ambivalence toward his heroes. Whereas he had clearly *approved* of his earlier heroes, despite their faults, he obviously does not approve of Babbitt. Babbitt is a coward, a braggart, a hypocrite, a liar, a cheat, a poor husband and father, a worker whose work contributes nothing toward human betterment. Yet we *like* Babbitt and are indulgent to him, just as Lewis is and intends, for Babbitt is also kind, loyal to his friends, basically simple and decent. He is a combination of strength and weakness, vice and virtue. His family and friends sense his decency and lean on him a little for it. He is so perfectly representative that the Good Citizens League feels his membership is important. Why, then, does Lewis portray a way of life so explicitly evil and destructive, and yet convey affection for the man who is its chief type and symbol? Perhaps because Lewis himself, as I have indicated, experienced kinship with Babbitt. Perhaps because at the same time Lewis realized and attacked the power of *things* in American life, he admired the ingenuity of those things, the technology which made them, and the operation and power of the system which markets them. Utterly to damn Babbitt would have meant to damn America.

Although this ambivalence is undeniably present in *Babbitt*, it is much less obvious than in *Main Street* and it is consequently less damaging to the novel and less perplexing to the reader. In fact, Lewis's affection acts as a catalyst in the novel, thickening it and providing a complexity too often missing in his work. Where *Babbitt* falls short of the highest art, it does so from Lewis's inability to leave room for the reader's imagination. Almost nothing is implicit in *Babbitt;* we are told everything. When we share Babbitt's thoughts and fears, we share them all; there are no greater depths to be plumbed. Only two matters are left unclear: how Babbitt came to be the way he is, and what he should do about it. Although he is given a vague family background and a mother and half-brother who appear in the novel briefly, we learn nothing about Babbitt as a child or adolescent. We are told that in college he was a liberal, with lofty ambitions and ideals, but we do not know what changed him. Surely it is hard for us to believe he could ever have been a wild and dangerous dreamer. In this sense Babbitt as a character is weaker than Carol and inferior to Hawk Ericson.

As for the possible methods of change in *Babbitt,* we have already seen that Lewis believes little is possible for Babbitt himself. However, the reader remains confused about what Lewis is *for.* Beyond an obvious sympathy for union labor, a hatred of the kind of Harding–Coolidge policies Babbitt admires, and a contempt for the cultural and aesthetic sterility of middle-class life, we do not know specifically what Lewis wants us to do. If he wants socialism, he does not say so. He simply wants people to be better. The novel's social program here reminds me of the scene in *All My Sons,* when Joe Keller, a more recent Babbitt, turns to his son Chris, and asks him what his son wants from him, and Chris shouts, "You can be better!"

While the book lacks proposals upon which to build the foundations of a new society, its impact upon its own time was very great. Appearing in the same year as Harding's declaration "If I could plant a Rotary Club in every city and hamlet in this country I would then rest assured that our ideals of freedom would be safe and civilization would progress," *Babbitt* reminded Americans that there were higher aspirations than "normalcy." It summarized every criticism advanced against the middle class in the 1920's, and it rendered a superb account of the devastating effects of a material culture. Others have since written of the average American businessman, but only Lewis's name for him survives in our vocabulary—as Lewis predicted it would, as a synonym for both a state of mind and a way of life.[31] It is the outstanding social satire of its generation, if not of American literature, and it continues to engage us by the quantity of its truth and the vigor of its execution. Sinclair Lewis invented Babbitt; his creation endures.

III   *Arrowsmith*

In the summer of 1922 Lewis came to Chicago to visit Eugene Debs, whom he had long admired, and to collect material for the novel he then contemplated dealing with the American labor movement. Chance meetings with Paul de Kruif, a scientist formerly on the staff of the Rockefeller Institute for Medical Research, and with Morris Fishbein, editor of *Hygeia*, started Lewis thinking instead about a book which would have a doctor as its hero. Another meeting with de Kruif in New York in December, 1922, resulted in a formal plan for collaboration between the two men; de Kruif was to help Lewis by providing and authenticating the novel's scientific detail. Less than a month later they sailed for the West Indies to begin the extensive travel and research which was to go into the writing of *The Barbarian*, later *Arrowsmith*.[32]

As for the significance of such a novel to Lewis's own experience, we need not look very far. Lewis has left us this account in his own words:

A small boy whose memory is of being awakened by his father's talking to a patient, down at the door; of catching 3 A. M. phrases: "Where is the pain? Eh? Well, all right, but you ought to have called me earlier, Peritonitis may have set in." A small boy who was permitted to peep at anatomical charts and ponderous medical books in The Office. Then his brother going off to medical school—gossip of classes, of a summer's interneship, of surgery vs. general practice. And behind father and brother, a grandfather and uncle who were also doctors.

With such a background, the work and ideas of doctors have always been more familiar to me than any others, and when I began to write novels . . . I thought of some day having a doctor hero. Part of that ambition was satisfied in Dr. Kennicott of "Main Street," but he was not the chief character, and furthermore I desired to portray a more significant medico than Kennicott—one who could get beneath routine practice into the scientific foundation of medicine—one who should immensely affect all life.[33]

Lewis's idealistic intentions and high purposes for his book are unmistakable here. *Main Street* and *Babbitt* had also been motivated by idealism, but the noise of their satire and the weight of their social criticism had obscured this. Lewis now wanted to do an affirmative book, one in which he could express his idealism openly. He wrote to Harcourt of his desire, even before he had decided definitely on the subject of the book: "I think I shall make my next novel after *Babbitt* not satiric at all; rebellious as ever, perhaps, but the central character *heroic.*"[34]

Indeed, Martin Arrowsmith was to become the symbol of an ideal, the modern reincarnation of the American pioneer spirit, which was to Lewis among the most vital of our native traditions. The novel's opening paragraph, with its portrait of Arrowsmith's pioneer great-grandmother, contains the spirit of intrepidity later to prevail in Arrowsmith's quest for truth. The grandmother's courageous rejection of the immediate and practical, in order to seek the distant and unknown, foreshadows the book's theme: "Nobody ain't going to take us in," she says to her sick father, who wants her to turn the wagon toward relatives living nearby. "We're going on jus' as long as we can. Going West! They's a whole lot of new things I aim to be seeing!"[35] Just as his forebears had in this spirit settled the physical frontier, Arrowsmith explores the frontiers of knowledge.

It is also obvious from the start that this novel will be another of Lewis's tales of self-realization. In each of the novel's basic situations Arrowsmith meets society and is defeated by it, but in each case he surmounts the defeat by growing, by learning from his mistakes. In each of these encounters and defeats he leaves society a little further behind, until, finally, he abandons it completely. The subtitle of the book could well be "All for Truth, or, the World Well-lost."

Arrowsmith could also be read as a highly moralistic allegory, somewhat reminiscent of *Pilgrim's Progress*, with Martin a twentieth-century version of the man of piety in pursuit of the twentieth-century deity, scientific truth; or as a modern Red Cross Knight, the cross, in this case, that we associate with the saving of lives. He is the best sort of character Lewis can make him and still remain within the realm of realism; he is human, at times petty and selfish in his personal relationships, tactless, stubborn (two of Lewis's early titles for the novel, "The Stumbler" and "The Barbarian" suggest this phase of the hero), but he is noble in his ideals, ambitions, career.

In this portrayal of Arrowsmith, biographical parallels exist between Arrowsmith and his creator. In Arrowsmith's case, when marriage becomes a barrier to work, he gives up marriage, and the same situation may have applied to Lewis. Certainly, in writing *Arrowsmith* he was separated from his wife and son for even longer periods than usual and at a time when the marriage was already in jeopardy—partly because of Lewis's already-exercised conviction that he needed complete freedom from familial obligations to write.[36]

We cannot help speculating about yet another possible parallel, the one between Arrowsmith's career and Lewis's. Wherever Arrowsmith goes, he makes enemies and becomes notorious not only for the frankness with which he announces his opinions of what is good and what is bad but also for his well-intentioned but unpolitic attempts to do the right thing, to make people better. They think of Martin as a radical, a crank, while at heart he is sincerely altruistic. The same might be said of Lewis and his books. Ultimately, Arrowsmith stops trying to *like* people and be liked by them because, as in Lewis's case, he *loves* them. He cannot, as Lewis could not, accept, excuse, tolerate, gloss over. He wants to uproot, change, reform—and his motivation is love. Lewis, too, loved America without liking her, just as he loved the small town and Babbitt without approving of them.

Gottlieb, whom some critics have found the novel's most memorable character, is no less essential than Arrowsmith to its theme. In Gottlieb Lewis created for the first time an almost wholly admirable figure, a man the reader can revere as the embodiment of all the chief virtues Lewis respected: integrity, true intellectual attainment, a total inability to compromise by accepting unfinished or imperfect work.[37] Gottlieb, a man at the farthest remove from the affable and well-adjusted good fellow, is the kind of man who carries civilization on his shoulders. He is a pessimist who voices his doubts about the possibility of progress and about man's superiority to animal, yet his own genius advances progress and proves man's superiority. He declares himself an agnostic, but his purposes, his work, and his very name belie this assertion. Joining with Arrowsmith and Gottlieb as truth-seekers, and sharing in their merit, is Terry Wickett, a minor although memorable character.

Set in contrast to this heroic triumvirate are Duer (again notice the characternym), who represents hard, professional competence operating solely on the profit motive; Pickerbaugh, the expert in promotion and self-promotion, a Babbitt of public health; and Holabird, the scientist turned administrator and empire-builder, the intellectual fraud. The novel's female characters also fit into its allegory and strengthen the pattern of contrast which we have come to recognize as basic to Lewis's books. Madeline Fox, Martin's first love, belongs to the type whose ancestress is Istra Nash and whose last descendant is Olivia Lomond (*World So Wide*). Joyce Lanyon, rich, cultured, sophisticated, sexually alluring, is an extension of Madeline and a direct forebear of Fran Dodsworth. In their demands upon Arrowsmith, Madeline and Joyce symbolize the demands of Society and Success. In opposition to them Lewis places Leora, the Western girl, and the prototype of Lewis's good women: quiet, long-suffering, plain, utterly loyal, a little dumb, totally and selflessly dedicated to her husband's fulfillment.[38] She represents personal integrity. The two different kinds of women in *Arrowsmith* summarize more emphatically than in any other of Lewis's books, with the exception of *Dodsworth,* the continuous conflict between what might be called the *hausfrau* and the debutante; and *Arrowsmith* is one of the few novels in which the hero makes the right choice.

To view *Arrowsmith* as purely a morality play, and its characters as mere abstractions, is to view it in distorted perspective, however. Despite Lewis's original intention to make it an affirmative book, sharp satire and social criticism are in evidence. Lewis's heaviest barrage falls upon the commercialism, quackery, pseudo-science, and glory-hunting in medical education, medical practice, and medical research. Beginning with Martin's college and medical school career, which permits Lewis a number of shots at the American university and the professional school, Lewis then moves his hero first to a prairie town, next to a small midwestern city, and at last to Chicago; and all the while he peppers away at targets already riddled in *Main Street* and *Babbitt.*

In these experiences as small-town general practitioner, city public health director, and member of a famous clinic, Arrowsmith is confronted by the same problems facing Carol and Babbitt: if he is to be successful, prosperous and accepted, he must lie, dodge, compromise, do the expected and the profitable. His attempts to reform the health habits of both town and city are nearly as clumsy and ill-advised as Carol's efforts to bring culture to Gopher Prairie and as Babbitt's rebellion; and, like them, he is defeated. Lewis also uses Gottlieb's career as a source of satire and social commentary. Through him we see how genius is feared and thwarted in academic life and how talent is less important than affability, when Gottlieb is driven out of his university position by lesser men. We see the exploitation of the many for the profit of the few in Gottlieb's employment by a large pharmaceutical manufacturer who pressures him to discover a new serum so that the company may monopolize its sale, charging all that the traffic will bear.

Finally, in his depiction of the McGurk Institute Lewis's satire reaches into the top levels of the world of science. It is lamentable, although not unthinkable, that commercialism, venality, and fraud should exist in universities, medical schools, medical practice, public health, and private clinics; but an endowed institute, devoted to pure, non-profit research, ought to be paradise. However, here, too, Arrowsmith finds corruption. Not only are the staff members put on public display by the vain lady whose husband supports the institute, there are also internal politics, intrigues, cliques, jockeyings for position and, worst of all, pressure from the administration to publish for the sake of publication and fame, even though the experiments may not be finished. Only Gottlieb, Wickett, and Arrowsmith are devoted to their work for its own sake. The others coast on reputations earned long before, or they spend their time and energy parading as scientists rather than laboring as scientists. Most are also astonishingly ignorant of anything outside their own specialties. Above all, the McGurk Institute serves to demonstrate the perils of success.

With his discovery of the "X" principle, Martin for the first time experiences Success, which will bring him every possible benefit except the chance to do his work. He finds even a little taste of it heady wine, but he is saved from its influence when a foreign scientist anticipates his discovery in a published paper. The full and deadly power of Success and Position falls instead upon Gottlieb, who is given the directorship of the institute, is immediately caught up in its dissensions, and is ruined as a scientist. There is perhaps a parallel in this situation with Lewis; he, too, had known success and enjoyed its gifts. Perchance he had begun to fear it and its effects upon his work.

The satire and the social criticism in *Arrowsmith* are supported by a solid underlayer of fact. Almost all of Lewis's books, including the poor ones, have this foundation; it gives them a satisfying density and bulk, and nowhere is this truer than in *Arrowsmith*. In it the details of a medical training and internship, of a general practice, of the job of the public health official and the operation of a private clinic, the secrets of the research laboratory, and the hazards of the battle against epidemic are all tremendously appealing to the reader. Americans are worshipers of science but they also distrust certain aspects of it—as they distrust any work which tends to isolate the worker and which depends upon abstract thought. Thus, of all sciences we distrust medicine least because the doctor is a familiar figure. He produces visible, practical, desirable results, and it is possible for the layman to apprehend and admire the doctor's skill in much the same way he would admire the skill of an engineer. Furthermore, the doctor himself justifies the mysteries of research, for we tend to see the medical laboratory and medical research not as Science, distant and unknown, but as manufacture, the production of necessary goods. It is not difficult to understand, then, why medical books and medical novels have been enormously popular in America. *Arrowsmith* both perpetuated and shared the public's enthusiasm for such books. It brought to the reader that especially comforting thought that he was being educated as well as entertained, so that even the most puritanical or pragmatic could not feel that he was fiddling away his time with a storybook.

Beginning with *Main Street* Lewis had given his readers the titillating sense of being on the "inside," a sense which is heightened by *Arrowsmith* because the inside is now that of a hallowed profession, rather than the depressing detail of life as lived in the small town or by the average businessman. Consequently, while Lewis's appraisal of American civilization as manifested in Wheatsylvania, North Dakota, or Nautilus, Iowa, is hardly more complimentary than it was in *Main Street* and *Babbitt, Arrowsmith* did not arouse the public furor that the others did— except for a mild fuss among some members of the medical profession. Both the novel's pervading idealism and its sober factuality overweighed its satire and brought it success, without the success of scandal.

The book's narrative component is also superior to those of *Main Street* and *Babbitt,* for the story moves beyond the conflicts of the hero with his social environment and centers upon the doctor's war against death. More varied in locale and character, more crowded with dramatic incident, swifter in movement, *Arrowsmith* is always interesting. When, in the last quarter of the book, death enters as an antagonist in the Plague, the story becomes gripping. Almost as good is the previous section, which recounts Arrowsmith's discovery of the "X" principle. In this section Lewis captures the intensity and joy of pure research and the conjunction of circumstance and prescription, fate and free will, in the quest for some of the secrets of life itself. While Lewis never attains the profundity and multiplicity of suggestion of a Kafka, a Dostoevsky, a Faulkner (he does not belong in their rank), this grappling with the universal is a rare thing in his work; on this occasion, at least, he climbs above his usual range. In short, *Arrowsmith* demonstrates more of Lewis the philosopher than any other novel.

The crucial issue in the Plague episode is the giving of serum under test conditions—the problem of carrying out a controlled experiment when men's lives are involved—in order to answer the scientific question of the accuracy of Arrowsmith's research and of the serum's worth. But the scientific question includes the human question of whether to let thousands die now so that millions may be saved later. Experimental verification becomes, therefore, more than a matter of scientific curiosity. This is the conflict which Martin must resolve and which he is not strong enough to do. His humane feelings prevail, and by this lapse Martin overturns the course of his whole career, one in which he had in every previous crisis resisted the public's demands at his own expense but for the public's greater good. Ironically, this climactic failure brings Arrowsmith fame and adoration at the same time that his conscience is being eaten away by his knowledge he has failed as a scientist. The Plague stops, whether through the effectiveness of the serum or of its own accord Arrowsmith will never know; another doctor records the experimental data Martin should have set down; and Arrowsmith returns to America a hero. As a final irony, Martin's scientific conscience, Gottlieb, the one man who would have immediately perceived and announced his failure, has suffered a mental collapse and does not even recognize him. The McGurk Institute, as we by now expect it to do, squelches Martin's report that there is insufficient evidence of his serum's value and instead releases an optimistic statement.

The final clash between science and society occurs in Martin's marriage to the rich, beautiful, and suave Joyce Lanyon. Through her Arrowsmith is exposed to and temporarily persuaded by the temptations of wealth and luxury and the responsibilities of fatherhood. Yet we know that sooner or later Arrowsmith, like the Lewis rebel he is and like Lewis himself, will find respectability intolerable. The arguments between Martin and Joyce resolve into a single argument and a single choice: whether to be decent, responsible, and civilized, or to be free to work. Joyce's parting shaft at Martin, after he has rejected her final attempt at reconciliation and a final appeal to his sense of duty as a father, is completely accurate. She calls him a fanatic. He is indeed a fanatic; he has left behind all common sense. But in Lewis's terms and in the novel's terms, that is the better way. While the other men Arrowsmith has known—the righteous, the hypocritical, the conniving—enjoy success and prosperity, he is shut away in Vermont with Terry Wickett, where he plans pre-doomed researches into insoluble problems. However, in his experimenter's utopia in the Vermont woods, removed from humanity save for a few other dedicated *isolatos* and severed from all intercourse with a corrupt society save for the necessity to do just enough commercial work to support pure research, he has at last found independence and maturity as a scientist— so Lewis tells us.

The basic conflict in *Arrowsmith* has become a staple of much recent literature and sociological analysis (for example, *The Lonely Crowd*), and it expresses what is also apparently a basic problem in twentieth-century America: whether to be *liked*— that is, whether to be amiable, to be well rounded, to leave plenty of time for family, recreation, friends—or do one's work. To do one's work, as Lewis structures the situation, means to neglect family and friends, and to be hard, tough, honest, and crude. Furthermore, the man who does his work and is responsible only to its demands, is inevitably and necessarily hard to like. As Lewis portrays Gottlieb, Arrowsmith, and Terry, the only three true scientists in the novel, they are all men who make enemies far more readily than friends, men who can be understood and appreciated only by another of their own rare breed.

This is the definition of the true scientist which Lewis conveys in *Arrowsmith*. He is: (1) utterly dedicated to his discipline; (2) thoroughly educated in all branches of science and not just in his own specialty; (3) an artist in his techniques and methods; that is, he does his work beautifully; (4) unwilling to publish his findings until he is absolutely sure they are completely validated; (5) harshly self-critical; (6) much more concerned with the demands of day-to-day work than with the philosophical or metaphysical meaning or ultimate application of his discoveries, but not unaware of their possible benefits to mankind; (7) fundamentally motivated by a great love for mankind, but it is well disguised, even totally hidden, under a cynical and tough exterior; (8) too concerned with his work to be concerned with the niceties of social behavior or even his duties as father and husband, yet human enough to want and need a wife, children, friends; (9) above all, cautious of success, position, prestige, because nothing can ruin a scientist more quickly, and no one, not even a Gottlieb, is proof against them.

To the problems of marriage and success, Lewis seems to present these solutions: first, the scientist must have a wife, children, and friends who are totally permissive and understanding, who will always be there when he needs them but not there when they might be in the way. Second, the best and perhaps the only possible way to forestall the dangers of the World is to get away from it, to seek isolation. The novel's final conclusion implies, therefore, that the scientist is truest to himself and to mankind when he rejects his own humanity. A provocative implication, it has taken on significance in the years since *Arrowsmith*, for it bears on such topical issues as interspace travel, nuclear explosions, germ warfare, and, in short, on the entire relationship of scientists, scientific principles, and scientific discoveries to the future of the human race. It is too large a question to debate here.

Lewis's definition of the scientist may be approached, however, from another and more limited point of view. In the excitement of the story and in Lewis's contrast of good and bad characters—Leora and Joyce, Arrowsmith and Holabird—we are at least temporarily convinced that easy living, gracious manners, recreation, and high position inevitably lead to mediocrity and failure in real accomplishment. Upon reflection, we wonder whether that is true; whether creative activity is possible only under Thoreau-like conditions, and whether there is so close an association between pure research and asceticism as Lewis declares. We also wonder whether it takes any more time to be pleasant than rude when the scientist does present himself in public. It may be conceded to Lewis that the scientist who is working for the public good must and should on occasion bully and command rather than wheedle and coax, but we wonder if Lewis pays too little credit to the public's intelligence. After all, thousands volunteered to cooperate in tests of the Salk vaccine.

Whatever their answers, the questions *Arrowsmith* raises are not trivial. Many of the points it makes are the same as those in *Main Street* and *Babbitt*, but they are made in a more artistic manner. Heavier weight is carried by the novel's characterizations and action and less by Lewis's tirades, sermons, and monologues. Although the situation is somewhat the same—the individual struggling for self-fulfillment and integrity in a society which wants to keep things as they are and which demands of us above all that we be nice—*Arrowsmith*, unlike *Main Street* and *Babbitt*, has no compromise at the end. The hero wins his fight against himself and against the world; he becomes a scientist, solitary, dedicated, skilled. He makes a separate peace on his terms, not the world's. Actually he is able to do so because, however much it may deride him, the world needs him, and both he and the world know it. The same was not true of Carol and Babbitt. Once isolated from their society, there would be no place for them to go except, perhaps, to Europe.

As in all Lewis's work, *Arrowsmith* blends realism, satire, and romance. The realism is conveyed by the hard core of scientific knowledge in the novel and by the presence of death. The satire appears in the struggle between the society and the individual. The romance enters into the exaggerated, even fabulous portrayals of such characters as Sondelius and Leora (we like Leora far better than Joyce, but Joyce seems more credible); into the black and white conflict between Science and Success; and into the near-melodrama of some of the book's incidents. Withal, *Arrowsmith* is marred by fewer flaws than either *Babbitt* or *Main Street*. It does not have *Main Street's* tedious repetition and occasional hysteria; it avoids *Babbitt's* flatness. The satire is less heavy and obvious. The tone and movement of the novel are swifter, surer, more inspired than in either of his previous triumphs.

Moreover, we are heartened by Lewis's unqualified enthusiasm for science, the true hero of the book. In *Arrowsmith* there is no confusion about Lewis's standards or loyalties.[39] Gottlieb and Arrowsmith are unequivocally gallant and admirable characters whose weaknesses are far less than their strengths. Here we *know* where Lewis stands, for the novel has the consistent frame of reference too often missing in his work. All in all, *Arrowsmith* shows Lewis's growth as an artist; it is the best novel of his great decade and it is among the better American novels written in this century.

IV *Lewis the Public Figure and Elmer Gantry*

With some of the same brilliance and egotism with which he could dominate a private conversation or a large gathering, Sinclair Lewis entered the public life of the 1920's as lecturer, polemicist, and commentator on American civilization. *Main Street, Babbitt,* and *Arrowsmith* had made him pre-eminent as a writer; and he was too vocal, too energetic, too conscious of the limelight, and too passionately involved in the American scene not to take advantage of his position as "Our Own Diogenes."[40]

Upon his return to the United States after eighteen months abroad, where he had written *Arrowsmith,* he first embroiled himself in the 1924 Coolidge–Davis–La Follette presidential campaign by publishing a series of strongly pro-La Follette articles in *The Nation.* In these articles Lewis returned to the locales of *Main Street* and *Babbitt* and interviewed some of his own character creations, posing the liberals and intellectuals—such as Guy Pollock and Paul Riesling—on the side of La Follette, and the conservatives and philistines—such as Will Kennicott and Babbitt—on the side of Coolidge. As Lewis saw it, the contest between the two candidates (Davis was virtually ignored in the series) was the same one he had described in his novels, that between progress and immobility, freedom and conformity, cosmopolitanism and provincialism.

In many ways Lewis was a product of the Progressive Movement and mood of the period from 1900 to 1914. His deeply felt but irregular socialism, his distrust of big business and banking interests, his sense of outrage at the predicament of the farmers, the ambivalence of his attitude toward the American social structure—part optimistic acceptance, part suspicious denial—are all typical of the Progressive era. But Progressivism had lost force as a political movement and as a temper, and when La Follette campaigned in 1924 on an independent ticket and on a platform which featured public ownership of water power and railroads, recognition of the right of collective bargaining, greater government aid to farmers, stronger legislation of child labor and the procedures of popular democracy, Lewis and his fellow liberals saw in him a resurgence of the mood and hope missing from the country since before the war. Lewis's attitude may be summarized by this comment, taken from one of his campaign articles: "It seems to me La Follette is almost the first presidential candidate since Lincoln (the first with a chance to win—that's why I leave out Debs) who has had *greatness*, who has combined a desire to let human life be free and happy with a hard, solid, practical, food-raising competence."[41]

In other essays written in the mid-twenties Lewis turned from politics to other matters, asserting in one piece that much anti-German sentiment still existed in the United States. Another article surveyed the condition of the artist in America and concluded that this, the most self-conscious country in the world, had imposed the same intolerable burden of self-consciousness upon its artists, which did not permit them full development of their creative powers. We may discern in this essay some of the strain Lewis himself was experiencing, for he lashed out not only at the arbitrariness of our literary criticism (he was always terribly sensitive to criticism and was pleased with nothing less than the highest praise) but also at the insistence that the artist fulfill the public's image of him (which Lewis, with his unpredictability, could not consistently do); and he concluded that the artist could save himself from the public's dictatorship only by working at what he enjoyed. A third essay, which extended Lewis's comments on the artist and which had special reference to the expatriate movement then in full force, declared that a writer could work just as well in America as elsewhere.[42]

Mantrap, a novel based on a vacation trip which Lewis had taken with his brother Claude into northern Saskatchewan and Manitoba, seemed to fill Lewis's own prescription for the novelist to please himself. Written primarily for publication as a magazine serial, it is slick fiction of the *Saturday Evening Post* level and variety, although it also contains some spoofing and debunking of such traditions as the beauty of the great outdoors, the joys of camping out, and the silent, strong, and noble Indian. In *Mantrap* the great outdoors is filled with mosquitoes, camp-

ing out is drudgery, and the Indians are scrawny, dirty, treach-
erous, lazy, and loquacious. The book's humor is labored, its
situations contrived, its tone so facetious it sometimes borders
on self-parody.

To put it bluntly, *Mantrap* is a bad book, a return to the
romantic melodrama and comedy of Lewis's grubstreet days;
it is worse than anything he had done except *The Innocents*.
Despite one contemporary reviewer's strong defense of *Mantrap* (and this is one measure of the height of Lewis's reputation)
as a superior adventure yarn, and while we may grant Lewis
the prerogative to do a change-of-pace novel, it is difficult to
excuse *Mantrap*, especially in the light of its obviously slapdash
composition and commercial intent. Furthermore, Lewis seems
not to have balked at the book's demands upon his integrity.
He wrote Harcourt: "Looking back at it I recall nothing shoddy
in it, and as far as the critics who insist that I have no right to
do anything but social documents, they may all go to hell." Yet
he also admitted to George Jean Nathan "that he was, to use
his own locution, turning out a swell piece of cheese to grab
off some easy gravy."[43]

But with the same contradictoriness so puzzling to the student
of Lewis, in the very year of the publication of *Mantrap*, 1926,
he performed an act of considerable courage when he refused
the Pulitzer Prize awarded to him for *Arrowsmith*. We would be
naive not to recognize that Lewis was also motivated by some
desire for personal revenge and a thirst for publicity. A selection
committee had chosen *Main Street* for the Pulitzer Prize in 1920,
but the trustees of the award had not accepted the committee's
choice; instead, they had honored Mrs. Wharton's *Age of Innocence*, which was far less openly critical of America. *Babbitt*
had likewise been ignored, and Lewis was stung by these af-
fronts. Therefore, when *Arrowsmith* was chosen, Lewis saw the
chance both to return past favors and to attack the conservative
elements in American intellectual life that he believed the Pulitzer Prize represented. In a letter addressed to its administrators
and also released to the press, a letter that is convincingly honest
and serious whatever Lewis's private motives or the wisdom of
his actions, he denounced the terms of the award, attacked the
prize itself as a false symbol of excellence, and declared that
it was one of the forces working to make American writers "safe,
polite, obedient, and sterile."[44]

Meanwhile, Lewis's preparations for his next book were also keeping him in the center of the stage. Having for several years planned a novel about religion, he had now begun work on it. In collecting the material Lewis tried, as always, to immerse himself in the environment he would treat. Accordingly, he went to Kansas City, engaged L. M. Birkhead, a liberal clergyman of the community, as a consultant and assistant, and spent the spring of 1926 in such activities as preaching, attending religious services of all sorts, conducting a "Sunday School Class" for ministers, posing as a Bible salesman in order to interview rural clergymen, and reading voluminously. Many of Lewis's activities were well publicized, especially his "Sunday School Class" and a sermon in which he had reputedly defied God to strike him dead.[45] Looking back, we wonder how much of this was truly necessary for Lewis as preparation and background, and how much of it was evidence of instability and uncontrolled nervous energy.

Lewis's investigations into religion and the writing of *Elmer Gantry* could well be interpreted as but another phase of that private insurrection which had begun during his Minnesota boyhood, and it seems inevitable that Lewis's rebellion against Sauk Centre's norms should eventually include the denial of its articles of faith. Undoubtedly Lewis spoke for himself when he wrote of Carol Kennicott: "Always she perceived that the churches . . . all of them . . . were still, in Gopher Prairie, the strongest of the forces compelling respectability." And: "When she ventured to Sunday School and heard the teachers droning that the genealogy of Shamsherai was a valuable ethical problem for children . . . when she experimented with Wednesday prayer-meeting and listened to store-keeping elders giving their unvarying weekly testimony in primitive erotic symbols and such gory Chaldean phrases as 'washed in the blood of the lamb' and 'a vengeful God' . . . then Carol was dismayed to find the Christian religion, in America, in the twentieth century, as abnormal as Zoroastrianism—without the splendor" (p. 328).

Apart from a brief conversion, while Lewis prepped for Yale at Oberlin, his hostility to religion and its ministry was constant. A number of his Yale writings present unflattering portraits of clergymen, and other pieces of his work from 1908 to 1917 contain guarded but unmistakably hostile references to religion and the clergy. When Lewis declared in *Main Street* his independence from the restrictions of popular fiction, his attack on religious practices and religious hypocrisy moved into the open. In *Babbitt* he continued the assault with even greater ferocity by introducing the minor character "Mike Monday," who is both an obvious takeoff on Billy Sunday and a preliminary sketch for the caricatures Lewis developed in detail in *Elmer Gantry*. Lewis's heaviest fire in *Babbitt* was directed, however, at Babbitt's modern, "liberal" church, clergyman, and worship, which, together with the other strongholds of conformity and respectability of the middle-class world, serve to keep him captive. Aside from one or two minor characters and episodes, Lewis ignored religion in *Arrowsmith;* in it he was concerned with the only sort of truth he consistently recognized, scientific truth. Gottlieb and Arrowsmith serve only the gods of the laboratory, nature's impersonal and immutable laws, and in one of the novel's more significant speeches Gottlieb places the scientist in mortal conflict with the preacher.

Through Gottlieb and Arrowsmith Lewis expresses what for him came closest to replacing God: a humanistic faith in science and a concern with the possibilities of man's perfectibility through his own efforts. In his belief that deity arises from within the individual, in his anger at religion's pomp and show, in his scorn at the pretensions of the clergy, Lewis reminds us of what another nonconformist, Emerson, had said in the Divinity School address. The difference between the two men is more than that between a profound mind and a merely clever one; it is also the difference between their centuries, for Emerson had the oversoul to occupy the vacancy left by the departure of the Trinity.

In short, neither the ideas nor the inspiration for *Elmer Gantry* came upon Lewis suddenly. Moreover, the time was right for a book of this sort. The Scopes evolution trial at Dayton, Tennessee, and the fantastic careers of Billy Sunday and Aimee Semple McPherson are evidence that some aspects of popular religion in the 1920's had come to seem more appropriate to the circus tent than the church. Their careers may even have suggested to Lewis the outlines for the two chief characters in *Elmer Gantry*, the hero himself and the sexually appealing lady evangelist Sharon Falconer. At least two episodes in *Elmer Gantry* exactly parallel real incidents. The boisterous activities of Sharon's evangelist troupe are based on 1915 court proceedings in which a Philadelphia landlord sued Sunday for the damage caused to his house by Sunday's party of assistants. Elmer Gantry steals one of his most effective sermons from Ingersoll, as did Billy Sunday in a speech given in 1912. In addition to these exhibits Lewis had for years collected news items about religious fanaticism and errant clergymen, a collection he utilized extensively in *Elmer Gantry*. Finally, the activities of two other prominent men of the cloth—Dr. William L. Stidger of Kansas City, a Methodist, and Dr. John Roach Straton of New York, a Baptist—provided Lewis with material which he employed and adapted in the characterization of his hero.[46] From these facts we may conclude that Lewis's imagination did not travel in uncharted territory.

But Lewis seemed never to have learned the lesson, as is observable in *Elmer Gantry* and some of his later books, that an artist must not hope to justify his characters solely on the basis of their resemblance to real people. That resemblance may give the character topicality, momentary life, and perhaps added force and gusto; but ultimately the character itself stands alone. If it is to last, it does so on the basis of art, not photography or caricature. Washington Irving's William the Testy is an amusing satirical sketch of Thomas Jefferson, but that knowledge does not confer immortality upon the character; it merely adds a dimension to the reader's appreciation of the character. Consequently, we must examine Lewis's Elmer Gantry, whose words and deeds are admittedly no more exaggerated or bizarre than those of Billy Sunday or Father Divine, as an artistic creation and not as a snapshot from life; and, when we do, we must agree with the majority of Lewis's critics that Gantry is a grotesque, a hobgoblin.

Lewis's intention was simple enough. He merely tried to hit off in Gantry, as he had in Babbitt, a symbolic prototype, a perfect average. His technique had been for centuries a favorite of polemicists, although traditionally it was used by the devout against the heretical. Thus, Lewis's main syllogism in the novel is a familiar if invalid kind of logic: Elmer Gantry is a clergyman; Elmer Gantry is a monster; clergymen are monsters. Furthermore, in order to thoroughly defame his clergyman hero-villain, Lewis focused on the sensational to the extent that the novel's sexuality, which was so lurid as to completely dominate the early drafts, remains a weakness in its published form.[47] The portrayal of sex is not among Lewis's specialties, and he handles it well only when it is part of a deeply-felt love relationship.

In fact, *Elmer Gantry*, more than any other of Lewis's books, approaches naturalism, and its central character the naturalistic hero. Elmer is a man driven—driven by the lust for money, power, fame. He is also a strongly physical being whose sexual desires demand constant gratification; and, since he is in an exposed position as a clergyman, his urges keep him in constant trouble. Although he has moments of self-recognition, of humility, of shame, he is—like the naturalistic hero and unlike Lewis's previous heroes—completely incapable of deep self-examination. Furthermore, although he is a clergyman, he has no sense of the spiritual, resembling in this both the naturalistic hero and Lewis himself. He even evokes from the reader the same reactions elicited by the naturalistic hero: pity for his weaknesses where they do not affect us, fear of them where we are threatened by them.

However, one vital aspect of Elmer's portrayal distinguishes him from the naturalistic hero—his success. Life for Elmer is neither a Dreiserian trap nor Fitzgeraldian disintegration; his is not even a case of the mildest variety of American-style naturalism in which Success becomes a Force and ruins Character. To Elmer, as to his creator Sinclair Lewis, success is real and tangible; Elmer wants it and he gets it, but he is neither corrupted nor changed by it. If he is weak or vicious or evil, he was that way before success reached him. Yet for all his naturalistic traits, there is something saving about Elmer, something amusing, vital, a Rabelaisian or Dickensian quality. He is, despite everything, not dull. He has American bounce and brashness as only Lewis could capture it. Even if he were to become moral dictator of America, which seems likely at the novel's end, we cannot shrink from the prospect with total horror; we sense that Gantry's rule would be a benevolent despotism and that, after America's Wednesday Night National Prayer Meeting (Compulsory), a man could always find a girl, a drink, a game.

But the question remains. Granted that Lewis has created an amusing hero, rogue-hero, or antihero, how successful is he as a symbol of the death of religion in America? As I have already suggested, not very. In *Elmer Gantry* Lewis proves only that the ministry is large enough to harbor a scoundrel, as it is large enough to harbor fools and hypocrites. Nor can we believe that of all the clergymen in the novel—and Lewis has populated it thickly—the barest few are decent and intelligent men who are well trained and sincere in their ministry. We could believe Lewis when he told us that small towns were dull and culturally barren, that our businessmen were loud of mouth and shallow of soul, and that our doctors were venal; but at least in those cases he gave us exceptions. However, of the characters who appear in *Elmer Gantry* only two deserve the least respect, Frank Shallard and Reverend Pengilly, and then the first is destroyed and the second so vaguely portrayed he eludes comprehension. The best that we can concede to Lewis in *Elmer Gantry* is that religion in America has become partially infected by Babbittry; at the same time we must, however, assert that Lewis's representation of religion is biased. Nowhere in the novel does Lewis deal with any concept of God other than the fundamentalist; this he handles with sarcasm and in passing. His references to Christianity as a whole are likewise fleeting, and here he makes but two familiar points: (1) that some Christian rituals and symbols have their origins in primitive religions (he does not further specify); (2) that the phenomena of conversion spring from hysteria rather than the holy spirit. The passage toward the novel's end in which Frank Shallard, serving as Lewis's spokesman, attacks the personality and teachings of Jesus is the sole portion of the book concerned in any detail with theology, but Lewis's approach is less sophisticated than that of either Ingersoll or Mencken, *Elmer Gantry's* godfathers.

As for the sources of Lewis's theology in *Elmer Gantry*, about a dozen of the more important ones are stated in the novel itself. Lewis read the books Frank Shallard reads, including: James's *The Varieties of Religious Experience*, Renan's *Jesus*, Davenport's *Primitive Traits in Religious Revivals*, White's *History of the Warfare of Science with Theology*, and scores of others apparently not important enough to list in *Elmer Gantry*.[48] But these books served to lead Frank Shallard, not Lewis, away from orthodoxy. He had long since departed it. In fact, except for a few passages in Renan's *Jesus* which may have suggested a part of Shallard's long diatribe against Jesus and Christianity (*Elmer Gantry*, pp. 369-78), and an occasional echo of Mencken, Lewis's reading seems merely to have supplied a few details for the expression of an old grudge. Curiously, a close scrutiny of the sources mentioned in *Elmer Gantry* shows that they could have worked just the other way; for, while most are "modernist" approaches to religion and regard the Bible as allegory, and religion as a way of life rather than a set of rituals and an established church, and while they supply plenty of ammunition for an assault on fundamentalism, all are also basically theistic, even pietistic, books. We conclude, therefore, that Lewis's religious opinions did not stem from his reading—at least from his adult reading.

Whatever Lewis's shortcomings as a theologian in *Elmer Gantry*, we must grant him recognition in other ways. In dealing with some of the social usages of modern Protestantism and in portraying the words and deeds of some of its clergy, Lewis is both sharp and convincing. He was doing in this instance what he did best, documenting manners and mores. Thus, he is successful in poking fun at denominational colleges and at the quality of training in provincial seminaries. He succeeds in capturing the spirit and exposing the methods of a touring evangelist troupe. He successfully records what ministers think and say (so a friend of mine, a clergyman, assures me) at the annual conference when new pastorates are to be assigned. He is effective in his portrayal of the big-city clergyman's need to use huckstering techniques to build attendance and get publicity. He is so successful in these matters we almost forget how little he says about the minister's visits to the sick, the counseling, the funerals. These are barely mentioned.

Elmer Gantry is, in a sense, as Mark Schorer has noted, "pure" Lewis.[49] It strongly demonstrates his abilities and his limitations. It has snap, flavor, a strong narrative line, a good deal of authenticity, and that peculiar Lewisian tone of simultaneous love and hatred for the hero, although much more hatred than love. But it is distorted, even too much for satire; it lacks conflict and contrast. Although its very subject is the transcendental, it conveys no sense or grasp of the transcendental. We see religion only as Lewis saw it: a kind of carnival, a show, a hoax, a monstrous but profitable fraud in the big city churches; and in the seminaries and small towns, a creeping, snuffling, dingy, paralyzing affair. While the novel aspires to record the death of religion in America, it conveys no feeling of catastrophe because Lewis himself obviously lacked it. Even Shallard's fate, effective and moving as it is in context, is pathos rather than tragedy. If the novel attacks religion at all, it attacks only the extreme fundamentalism and evangelical Protestantism of the 1920's and earlier, the literal and orthodox and rigid religion of Sauk Centre, and the hysterical Billy Sunday kind of religion, modes of worship which Lewis apparently confused with all religion. Consequently, while he was certainly able to recognize *intellectually* the differences and subtleties of religious thought, Lewis makes it clear in *Elmer Gantry* that he could not apprehend them emotionally. To Lewis, religion continued to be a vicious mixture of nonsense and repression.

We must also remember, in judging *Elmer Gantry*, that Lewis was writing in the most hotly charged religious atmosphere in America since the Salem witch burnings. Even as Lewis wrote the novel, the Scopes case was still being deliberated by the Tennessee Supreme Court. The Monkey Trial had served to climax the entire conflict between fundamentalism and modernism; and, while the trial itself had left the front pages, the arguments it aroused raged on. Accordingly, Lewis saw in *Elmer Gantry* a chance not only to deliver himself of a personal demon but also to champion the modernist cause before a reading public which he knew would number in the hundreds of thousands. Perhaps, then, the heat of his anger and the subsequent loss of his perspective and control were a result of his concern over what he saw as a grim threat to native freedom. The events of the trial are clearly reflected in one passage in the novel in which Lewis mocked the biblical story of the sun standing still (one of the very points on which Darrow examined Bryan in that unprecedented scene wherein Darrow had called Bryan as a witness for the defense; *Inherit the Wind* makes great use of this episode), ridiculed the attempt of illiterate preachers to prescribe proper subjects for the schools, and concluded by characterizing all fundamentalists as "men superbly trained to ignore contradictions" (p. 389). When Frank Shallard is maimed and blinded by a gang of fundamentalist vigilantes, at the same time that Gantry climbs to ever-greater popularity and power, Lewis intended to suggest a bitter parallel to what he feared might happen in the United States. Frank Shallard is the only Lewis rebel to be completely defeated.

Whatever Lewis accomplished in *Elmer Gantry*, he succeeded in doing what Mencken called "stirring up the animals."[50] The novel sold over two hundred thousand copies in the first ten weeks after publication, and it provoked dozens of incidents as well. Two Kansas City clergymen reviled Lewis from their pulpits and announced that they were the originals of the book's hero. When each realized he had a rival, he stopped the attack on Lewis long enough to denounce the other as an impostor and a liar. A prominent midwestern evangelist regaled his audiences with the story of how he had shamed Lewis by refusing to shake his hand when they were introduced, but in reality Lewis had never met him. A well-known Los Angeles minister invited Lewis to visit the city, promising he would personally lead a lynching party in the novelist's honor; at the same time another clergyman started proceedings in New Hampshire to jail Lewis for writing *Elmer Gantry*. The stage version of the book was delayed when its adapter withdrew from the project, announcing that he feared the play would seriously hurt the American theater.[51] For a time it seemed that Lewis's prediction that he would be thrown out of the country for *Elmer Gantry* might be coming true. But at least he had calculated correctly on one point. He had wanted the book to make the nation take notice, and he was not disappointed. With all its faults, *Elmer Gantry* continues to remind us of the bitterness of the struggle in Lewis's generation between religious liberalism and literalism, modernism and fundamentalism; and it remains to this day one of the two or three best American novels centered upon religion, challenged only by Frederic's *The Damnation of Theron Ware* and by Wilder's *Heaven Is My Destination*.

Elmer Gantry both leaves no doubt as to Lewis's own religious beliefs and foreshadows other things he was to write. Although he once mused, after a prolonged attack on the conventional concept of heaven, "Supposing after they throw the last spadeful of dirt on us, we find out it's all true!", he continued to be an archfoe of religion and the ministry.[52] For example, Lewis's fear of the thought-control power of the clergy was expressed in his characterization of Bishop Prang, who is a thinly veiled portrait of Father Coughlin, in *It Can't Happen Here*, Lewis's only novel of the 1930's depending mainly on satire for its substance. His anticlericism was again evident a few years later in a 1937 speech attacking church censorship of books and movies.[53] In his 1943 novel *Gideon Planish* Lewis depicts crooked fund-raisers who use their church affiliations to stuff their own pockets (Elmer Gantry makes a brief appearance in the same novel). An episode in the best-selling *Kingsblood Royal* (1947), in which the hero goes to his pastor for help in making a crucial moral decision but finds in him a deplorable bigotry and hypocrisy, reminds us of a similar scene in *Babbitt*. However, it was not until Lewis's penultimate novel, *The God-Seeker* (1949), that he returned to the fray with anything like the zeal of *Elmer Gantry*.

The God-Seeker is one of Lewis's worst and a strange potpourri. It contains some of the material which Lewis had collected for the labor novel he had never finished; it is in part a historical romance; it is a tribute to the courage of Minnesota's early Protestant missionaries and simultaneously a biting satire on their lives and failures; it is a defense of the Indians against the whites; and, finally, it is an assault on Christianity, both nineteenth-century New England and frontier-missionary varieties. Into its satire of evangelical Protestantism Lewis weaves caustic commentary on the entire civilization which Christianity has produced, and his spokesman is Black Wolf, a college-educated Indian chief. Black Wolf has written a "book" which views the white man and his culture with the same contempt the whites felt for the Indians. The technique, of course, is standard in Lewis's work; for example, Carol Kennicott looks at Gopher Prairie and judges it as she herself has been judged.

To suggest the contents of Black Wolf's book, it is sufficient to cite some of its chapter headings. Among them are: "Religion and Superstition," "Improvidence and Dirtiness," "Senseless Love of War," "Greed and Commercialism," "Gambling and Lying," "Lack of Common Sense," "Lewdness, Incontinence, and Position of Women." In other words, Black Wolf's mordant tract is very nearly a review of Lewis's entire body of social criticism; and its religious opinions—that Christianity is idolatrous, barbarously ritualistic, hypocritical, cruelly fanatical, intolerant, and stolen from the Hebrews—are either already familiar charges or extensions of earlier indictments. In the near-hysterical tone and the repetitiousness of these and other elements in the novel, *The God-Seeker* is convincing evidence that the once firmly knotted strands of Lewis's power had unravelled.

V *The Man Who Knew Coolidge*

Granville Hicks has remarked that *Elmer Gantry* completed a cycle in Lewis's work. Carol Kennicott had been a naive rebel; Babbitt, a likable conformist; Arrowsmith, the rebel for positive good; Gantry, the conformist for evil ends. To that cycle we might add the protagonist of Lewis's next book *The Man Who Knew Coolidge* (1928), Lowell Schmaltz, who is a sort of combination of Babbitt and Gantry, a pathetic and despicable conformist. Schmaltz is Babbitt without soul or brain; a summation of everything Lewis found hateful in the American character; and as Alfred Kazin has called him, a "monstrous, incarnate, average."[54] He is Lewis's version of Mencken's "Boobus Americanus"; indeed, the novel was an expansion of a piece originally written for Mencken's *American Mercury*.

The Man Who Knew Coolidge consists entirely of four monologues. As we read them, we realize with mounting horror that in this fantastic parody Lewis has also caught certain truths about us: the blindness to our own faults; the braggadocio; the Fascism and class consciousness hidden beneath the spoutings about democracy; the utter faith in appliances and cars and objects as the standard of civilization; the lack of taste in literature, music, and art; the search for personal privilege and exemption which is covered by an announced belief in the equality of all men before the law. Yet Lewis has perceived as well the love of home, wife, and children; the spontaneous geniality and cameraderie; the touching naiveté and idealism; and, above all, the yearning to be liked.

All of these characteristics Lewis renders through one character and in a perfect impersonation of American popular speech. Lewis's detractors are loathe to call it art (although the same kind of mimicry is admired in Mark Twain), but it is something that no one in Lewis's generation or since—including Ring Lardner, Lewis's closest competitor in this genre—has done better:[55]

> Yes sir, Cal is the President for real honest-to-God Americans like us.
> There's a lot of folks that pan him, but what are they? You can bet your sweet life he isn't popular with the bums or yeggs or anarchists or highbrows or cynics——
> I remember our pastor saying one time, 'A cynic is a man who

sneers, and a man who sneers is setting himself up to tell God that he doesn't approve of God's handiwork!' No sir! You can bet Coolidge ain't popular with the Bolsheviks or the lazy boob of a workman that wants fifteen bucks a day for doing nothing! No sir, nor with the cocaine fiends or the drunkards or the fellows that don't want the prohibition law enforced——

Not that I never take a drink. What I say about prohibition is:

Once a law has been passed by the duly elected and qualified representatives of the people of these United States, in fact once it's on the statute books, it's *there*, and it's there to be enforced. . . . But at the same time, that don't mean you got to be a fanatic.

If a fellow feels like making some good home-brewed beer or wine, or if you go to a fellow's house and he brings out some hootch or gin that *you* don't know where he got it and it isn't any of your business, or if you have a business acquaintance coming to your house and you figure he won't loosen up and talk turkey without a little spot and you know a good dependable bootlegger that you can *depend* on, why, then that's a different matter, and there ain't any reason on God's green earth that *I* can see why you shouldn't take advantage of it, always providing you aren't setting somebody a bad example or making it look like you sympathized with lawbreaking."[56]

But the very intensity of such a performance demands that it be brief, and brief it is not. The first of Schmaltz's monologues, occupying ninety-two pages, would have been enough; when Lewis adds nearly two hundred pages more of the same, it becomes tedious and nearly insufferable. *The Man Who Knew Coolidge* is Babbitt's speech before the Real Estate Board multiplied thirty times. No book demonstrates better than this one how necessary the *balance* of satirist and storyteller was to Lewis's success, for *The Man Who Knew Coolidge* shows us Lewis's satiric impulse run amok.

VI *Dodsworth*

Fortunately, this novel did not close Lewis's great decade. It was an interlude—and here the term is appropriate—preceding Lewis's seventh and last book of the period, *Dodsworth*, which rivals *Arrowsmith* as the best novel of his career. While it lacks the fast pace and excitement of *Arrowsmith,* it also avoids the slickness which creeps into some passages of the earlier work.

Dodsworth is an honest, sober, serious book which improves with re-reading. It is written from the heart; and, although it does not deal with America's destiny as do *Main Street* and *Babbitt,* nor with the causes of disease as does *Arrowsmith, Dodsworth* is ultimately as consequential because it deals candidly with a love situation, a marriage, and the co-existence of love and pain. In fact, the novel could accurately be called a love story, or a story about the death of love. It suggests that as we start to know ourselves, when we leave the protective coloration of our native habitat, we also begin to see ourselves and our mates clearly for the first time; and, once this occurs, we can no longer go on with them. That, at least, is an outline of what happens to the novel's hero, Sam Dodsworth, whose search for self-knowledge and for the good life lead him to Europe and then to the loss of his wife, Fran. Tangentially, *Dodsworth* is also a comparison of two civilizations, American and European, as well as a repetition of much of Lewis's social criticism of the 1920's.

Sam Dodsworth, the American millionaire and self-made aristocrat, appears to be a new character type in Lewis; actually he is a composite. He has Will Kennicott's physique, looks, and temperament and Arrowsmith's skill and pride in his work. There is also a little of Babbitt in him, some of the inner loneliness and a very small part of the delight in possessions and material surroundings. Lewis makes it very clear, however, that in tastes, values, intellect, and achievement Dodsworth is far superior to Babbitt. He is one of the Zenith aristocrats whom Babbitt admires from a distance. He is, in brief, the highest type of representative man Lewis believed our culture could produce.

Although the trip to Europe, upon which the plot of *Dodsworth* hinges, is originally Fran Dodsworth's idea, Sam makes it his own. The European tour becomes his rebellion, the shattering of the mold, and the search for fulfillment we have come to see as central to Lewis's fiction. However, this search inevitably means a break with Fran, for it is she who has enslaved him, kept him from fulfillment as a man and as a husband. *Dodsworth* thus combines Lewis's basic themes of rebellion, freedom, travel, and the quest for identity with the poignant narrative of a disintegrating marriage.

Yet in this novel we find Lewis the realist, not the romancer.

Part of the novel's realism is its restrained but accurate suggestion of sexual incompatibility and of Fran's frigidity; from the first, she is described as "an angel of ice." She makes her husband feel clumsy, unsure, confused, ashamed of his natural urges toward her. Skillfully, Lewis demonstrates how Fran's physical coldness expresses itself in her personality: her insatiable wants and desires, her need to know the right people, her social consciousness, her flirtatiousness. She can respond only to men she knows will be transient in her life, not to anyone who threatens to possess her emotionally. What keeps Sam with Fran so long after he has realized not only the shallowness of her nature but her unfaithfulness to him is his conviction that she needs him. Fran's very weakness is her strength; her dependence is her freedom. To a good man like Sam, nothing can be more enslaving than the sense that someone needs him, even when he knows that they may not deserve his caring.

Once the reader has marked Fran's frigidity, infidelity, and the mode of her castration of her husband, he can appreciate the sharpness of Lewis's irony in giving her the role of spokesman for the doctrine of liberty, of finding the true self through the abandonment of routine and through travel. She says it with great feeling and sincerity, but Lewis's point is that she has confused freedom and personal fulfillment with the recapturing of a lost youth and fading allure. Lewis permits her a convincing argument to cover her own petty needs for flirtation and adoration by men, and he continues throughout the novel to let Fran voice persuasive speeches about what's wrong with American husbands and the unhappy role of American women. Indeed, so passionate are Fran's statements that at first reading we are inclined to accept them at face value and to take, correspondingly, the marriage of Sam and Fran Dodsworth as typical. Upon reflection we realize, however, that Fran generalizes largely to salve her own conscience.

While *Dodsworth* may be read in part as Lewis's version of "the battle of the sexes" so well advertised in the 1920's, and while there is surely some credence in Fran's complaints that American men are too preoccupied with business to be good husbands and lovers, or that our industrial and commercial society is responsible for the lack of communication between mates and for woman's having freedom because her husband is too busy to care what she is doing, these are not Lewis's final conclusions. The novel offers substantial evidence to refute Fran. Although Fran praises European marriages and European men as better lovers and as more sympathetic and understanding of women, a minor character in the novel (a European wife) complains bitterly that Continental men are just as courtly to their mistresses as to their wives, and that if the wife's role is more clearly defined, it is also more clearly inferior. Furthermore, when Fran herself leaves Sam to plan marriage with a European nobleman, she finds herself grossly abused by her prospective mother-in-law and overridden in all important decisions.

Lewis also indicates that Fran is not representative of all American women. In plain contrast to her we have Matey Pearson and Fran's own daughter, Emily, both friendly, open, straightforward, loyal women who do not castrate their men. Finally, we must remember that although Lewis had drawn more than one unflattering female likeness, he had before been generally a strong feminist and a liker of women for their own sake. He kept on being so in *Ann Vickers* (1933), *Bethel Merriday* (1940), and elsewhere, with only one or two important exceptions in his last few books. If Fran Dodsworth is considered as typical of a class or kind of American woman, it would be of only a limited segment. We must, therefore, not trust her assertions; they are more glib than profound.

For the reader who is used to identifying the author's opinion by which character voices it and by the wisdom or seeming wisdom of the words, it is confusing to have the villain (Fran has this role in *Dodsworth*) argue so well and be portrayed with such insight. Thus, to many in the audience Lucifer still carries off the show in *Paradise Lost*. But that is Lewis's way. He had always done it in his marital situations. Will Kennicott sometimes makes more sense than Carol, and Joyce more than Arrowsmith. It is a symptom of Lewis's own ambivalence, the "schizophrenia" present in the man and the artist, a duality which allowed him to love Babbitt while he ridiculed him, feel nostalgia for small towns while he flayed them, follow a book like *Arrowsmith* with trash like *Mantrap*.

This same ambivalence persists in *Dodsworth,* and it not only generates artistically desirable tension and conflict but also makes it difficult for the reader to come to any conclusions. Europe is praised and debunked. Travel is urged and denied as a way to salvation. America is attacked and defended. Fran is simultaneously right and wrong; Sam is at the same time wise and foolish. What are we to believe? Lewis himself did not really know. He believed in no solutions, in no way to improve people, marriages, civilizations; but he also spent much of his life and the best part of his energy trying to do it.

Is Lewis's ambivalence, then, an aesthetic flaw here? No. In its very ambiguity and lack of resolution *Dodsworth* displays Lewis as a realist who scans the human condition with somber eye and concludes that man is doomed to perpetual striving, searching, finding, and then not liking what's found. In this sense *Dodsworth* shows us what happened to Hawk Ericson and Ruth twenty-five years later. They have gotten exactly what they wanted, travel, freedom, success, yet they have found no happiness . . . The Zenith that the Dodsworths live in and the Europe they tour are the culmination of Carol's dream, yet it is insufficient. For readers still so naive as to look to novels for solutions to life's problems, *Dodsworth* is not very satisfying. For those who look to novels for a sharper representation of life than they have themselves perceived, *Dodsworth* offers considerable pleasure.

Of all Lewis's books *Dodsworth* is the most directly and deeply autobiographical. Its love story is essentially Lewis's version of his marriage which ended in divorce in 1927, and Fran is his depiction of Grace Hegger Lewis. We believe that the poignancy which distinguishes *Dodsworth* springs from this.[57] To explore the matter in much detail is, however, a task for Lewis's biographers; suffice it to say here that Mrs. Lewis presented her account of the marriage in her novel *Half a Loaf,* which she intended as a reply to *Dodsworth;* and she has more recently told the story of her life with Lewis in *With Love from Gracie.* If we read *Dodsworth* as autobiography, then, we must read it in conjunction with these books because they contain a number of important differences with Lewis's version: they assert that Mrs. Lewis was her husband's loyal companion and helpmate in his work and not his denigrator and foe; and that he, not she, was guilty of infidelity. Knowing what we do of Lewis's complex personality, erratic behavior, and general inability to maintain enduring human relationships, we must be very cautious in reading *Dodsworth* as a *roman à clef.*

Whatever the biographical accuracy of *Dodsworth,* its personal element undoubtedly helped Lewis to create in Sam and Fran his best-realized and most credible characters. Fran is already recognizable to us as a development of what Martin Light, who has studied Lewis's characters, calls "nervous, neurotic women," while Sam is one of his "mature, capable, creative, men." Imagination enters into both portraits, of course, but especially so in Sam. He is not Sinclair Lewis; he is a projection of the sort of man Lewis may have wished to be. They are very unlike in both appearance and temperament, for where Sam is quiet, somewhat stolid, predictable, occasionally imperceptive, Lewis was noisy, meteoric, razor-keen. In any case, it is necessary for Sam to be reticent and long-suffering to permit contrast with Fran and to allow Lewis to register more effectively his complaints against her. Without Lewis's obvious admiration for Sam, enabling the reader to use him as a standard of judgment, Lewis's tendency to present all sides of the novel's debate with equal fairness would indeed become a grievous flaw.

Although the focus remains on the Dodsworth marriage throughout, we see Sam's growing consciousness of his wife's snobbishness, superficiality, and sexual frigidity against a variegated background of European locales. In this way Lewis adds to the book's impact by making it also an international novel of considerable interest and pertinence. As an international novel *Dodsworth* has three interrelated functions.

First, it presents Lewis's own impressions of Europe gathered in his trips and residence abroad (most of *Babbitt* and *Arrowsmith* were written in Europe). These cover such matters as food, terrain, cities, architecture, and the movement and atmosphere of European life. On the whole, Lewis is favorably, even enthusiastically, inclined toward this life style. At the end of *Dodsworth* Sam is on the way back to Europe, perhaps to stay there permanently; and it was to Europe that Lewis turned, exhausted, at the end of his life.

Secondly, *Dodsworth* evaluates the experience of living in Europe through the eyes of an American who is much like Henry James's Christopher Newman, ·a man of affairs, successful, rich, but culturally deficient—or so he feels. But there are two main differences between Newman and Dodsworth. Newman has come to Europe searching for a wife, which makes him more vulnerable than Dodsworth and which also distracts him from the civilization itself. Newman is also apparently less able than Dodsworth to tell the true from the false, the sham from the genuine. However, they are alike in being Americans of the highest type—strong but humane men who are trying to learn relaxation, the art of enjoying oneself, and the appreciation of beauty.

Finally, through Dodsworth's European experience we are given a new context in which to assess America. Carol is aware of Gopher Prairie's faults, but her vision and her standards of judgment are shallow and secondhand. Babbitt has only a dim sense that a better life is possible; he does not know of what it would consist. But once Sam Dodsworth, already a man of some culture and intellectual attainment, leaves the United States and tastes an older civilization, he becomes the best-equipped commentator Lewis provides us. In other words, we may presume that Dodsworth's opinions of America epitomize all that Lewis had to say on the subject up to that point in his career.

Most of this social criticism we recognize; a new element, however, does appear in *Dodsworth*. In *Main Street*, *Babbitt*, and *Arrowsmith* we were led to infer that the lives of the American aristocracy—the bank presidents, corporation executives, professional men—were rich and full because of their education, money, and increased opportunity for leisure and travel. Now, by means of Dodsworth's experiences, we see that this is not so. Dodsworth's best friend, Tub Pearson, banker and prominent resident of Zenith, may lead a somewhat better life than Ezra Stowbody, banker, of Gopher Prairie; but he is still dull, provincial, unimaginative, and even cruder and noisier in Paris than he is in Zenith. Sam observes that American aristocrats drink too much, are incapable of good talk, are not *interested*, and have no real understanding of politics, women, the arts. They are surpassed in intellectual vitality by such expatriate frauds and bohemians as Endicott Everett Atkins and Mme. de Penable, whom Dodsworth and Lewis despise. Consequently, Dodsworth resolves to become more like the Europeans and expatriates in their curiosity and engagement—to learn what James called "awareness."

The contrasting values of Europe and America are crystallized in the debate between Professor Braut and Sam Dodsworth (Chapter 23), with Braut serving merely as another voice for Lewis. Although they supposedly represent different worlds, there is really essential agreement between the two. Dodsworth admits to the validity of Braut's test of the excellence of a culture—the number of truly great men it produces—rather than the American aim of average achievement for the many. However, Dodsworth protests convincingly that Europeans have consistently misjudged and undersold Americans and that they persist in holding a comfortably false picture of the United States as a land of moneygrubbers, gunmen, and rustics. Europeans are no less materialistic than Americans, Dodsworth declares; and he ends his part of the debate by asserting that more Americans are thinking deeply and that their desire to grow culturally is proved by the number of them who visit Europe.

Lewis's conclusions on the issue, to wed the best of America to the best of Europe, are actually quite near those of Henry James. Lewis admires European manners, grace, leisure, cosmopolitanism; he dislikes very little. He also likes American creativeness, zest, vitality, curiosity; he abhors America's vulgarity and blind preference for everything American. Both *Dodsworth* and *The American* convey their authors' great sense of the importance of class and family background to the European. The chief difference here, of course, is that the period separating Lewis and James had witnessed the collapse of a social system which James saw as still potent although deteriorating. Both James and Lewis share the feeling of European immorality and decadence, although James, as befits the better artist, is able to convey a more profound and pervasive atmosphere of depravity. The distance between Lewis and James is in their points of view. Lewis is always natively American; he may speak as Professor Braut but that is an obvious impersonation. James is far closer to Europe; he looks at an American as Lewis would look at a European, or else with cool detachment. Even when we have American heroes in James, Newman or Lambert Strether, there is nothing of Lewis's passionate, patriotic involvement and self-projection.[58]

Our admiration for *Dodsworth* grows as we analyze it, and we must endorse Maxwell Geismar's statement that it displays Lewis as a mature and reflective writer. The book's quiet tone extends to its social criticism; where Lewis is most often shrill elsewhere, he is here modulated. Although *Dodsworth* contains a goodly portion of satire, the novel could not be called satire. Rather, it is exposition and inquiry. Lewis still tends to orate where the more resourceful writer would demonstrate, but even this tendency is controlled. As Clifton Fadiman has noted, the foreign journey of Sam and Fran Dodsworth is also a journey inward in search of a way of life absent in Zenith. Sam Dodsworth reveals the split in the American businessman who can be neither wholly business nor man. Furthermore, Lewis has achieved in *Dodsworth* one of his two best criticisms of American life (the other is *Babbitt*); while Lewis devotes proportionately much less space and emphasis to denunciation and satire, we can believe in the Dodsworths as characters and through them grasp some of our own successes and failures.[59]

The critics who have complained that Lewis was incapable of anything but mockery, those who have asserted that Lewis's characters are flat or grotesque, those who deny Lewis any stature beyond that of historian of part of the mood of the 1920's could not have read *Dodsworth*. We wonder with amazement how Leslie Fiedler, one of our most gifted critics, could write a large and brilliant book whose thesis is "the failure of the American fictionist to deal with adult heterosexual love" and himself fail to deal with the American fictionist who treats the matter so memorably in *Dodsworth*.[60] Love, marriage, and the death of love are too often, it is true, the specialties of soap opera; their treatment by the mass media has made them so hackneyed and banal they defy serious depiction. Thus, when we return to *Dodsworth* after three decades and find it still fresh, honest, direct, and moving, we ought to pay it and its creator at least a moment's homage.

VII *The Significance of the Nobel Prize*

On November 5, 1930, Sinclair Lewis received word that he had been awarded the Nobel Prize in Literature, an honor never before bestowed upon an American writer. The award was a fitting conclusion to Lewis's great decade in which he had published five important books, *Main Street, Babbitt, Arrowsmith, Elmer Gantry,* and *Dodsworth;* it was impressive evidence that Lewis was, at least in 1930 and in European estimation, the most eminent American writer of the time; and it was also proof that, through Sinclair Lewis, Europe was finally compelled officially to recognize the existence of an American culture.[61]

To Lewis, the Nobel Prize was the culmination of his ambitions. As early as 1921 he was suggesting that his publisher send copies of his books to influential literary men in Sweden so that he might be considered for the Nobel award. While he had refused the Pulitzer Prize both out of pique and an honest contempt for its terms, he was proud to accept the Nobel Prize because it stood as a tribute to the quality of a writer's entire body of work. His deep patriotism strengthened his personal satisfaction in being chosen—a patriotism manifest in his acceptance speech—for Lewis realized that he had become the symbol of a cultural achievement which Europe had previously slighted. In *Dodsworth* Lewis had portrayed Europe as the repository of the beauty and grace missing in America; now Europe had honored him as a pioneer representative of a healthy new American literature and as a "new builder."[62] Whatever the effectiveness of his attempts to make America better, the Nobel Prize proved to Lewis that his efforts had been neither misguided nor overlooked.

Certainly no other of our writers was so widely read in Europe in the 1920's as Sinclair Lewis. By 1930 eleven of his thirteen books had been translated into either Russian, German, Swedish, or Polish; seven into Hungarian, Danish, Norwegian, or Czech; six into French; four into Dutch; two into Spanish; and one, *Babbitt*, into Italian and Hebrew.[63] Of the writers more or less contemporaneous with Lewis, Jack London, Upton Sinclair, and H. L. Mencken were also widely known to European readers, but none of these had the general respect of serious readers necessary to qualify an American as a Nobel candidate.[64] Therefore, it was Theodore Dreiser, although less familiar to the European than Lewis, who became his chief opponent for the prize. In the opinion of the Award Committee of the Swedish Academy, Lewis had reached the acme of his achievement in *Babbitt* and Dreiser had done so in *An American Tragedy;* however, in finally choosing Lewis, the Academy selected the writer it felt to be more significantly and typically American in his vision, humor, and creation of typical characters.[65] The presentation speech delivered by Erik Axel Karlfeldt, secretary of the Swedish Academy, glowingly summarized Lewis's accomplishments and fully set forth the reasons for his selection.

Karlfeldt called *Main Street* one of the best descriptions of small town life ever written, stated that Babbitt probably approached the "ideal of an American popular hero of the middle class," and remarked what many Americans had missed: that behind Lewis's depiction of Babbitt there was love and that in his books Lewis attacked values, not people. Karlfeldt praised *Arrowsmith* as a learned and accurate book, recognizing the intensive preparation and research supporting Lewis's work when he said, "Lewis is least of all superficial when it comes to the foundations of his art." He also lauded *Elmer Gantry* as "a feat of strength, genuine and powerful." Perhaps the most remarkable aspect of Karlfeldt's speech was its emphasis on the positive elements of Lewis's work—his achievements as a literary artist rather than his effect as a social critic and satirist.

Unfortunately, many observers in the United States did not see the matter through such rosy spectacles, nor did Lewis's acceptance speech soothe their inflamed vision, for in his address he assailed a number of venerated American literary men, institutions, and beliefs. Lewis, his opponents declared, had been given the Nobel Prize because his books satisfied the European desire to humiliate America and reinforced European prejudices against it. One of Lewis's own colleagues, Sherwood Anderson, whom Lewis had praised before the world at Stockholm, summarized this hostility when he said that Lewis had received the prize "because his sharp criticism of American life catered to the dislike, distrust, and envy which most Europeans feel toward the United States."[66]

There is, of course, some truth in these charges, but they make of the Nobel Prize a tool of literary politics, which, despite some peculiar selections, it never has been; they overlook the fact that Lewis's criticisms of American life were widely accepted by our intelligentsia as valid; that many European critics had taken Lewis's indictments of provincialism, philistinism, commercialism, and hypocrisy as fully pertinent to their own countries; that Lewis was almost universally considered among the two or three best writers of his generation; and that he was by far the mostly widely read. Finally, Lewis's detractors failed to perceive that the superstructure of satire in Lewis's work was erected upon a foundation of affection.

Lewis's acceptance speech, delivered at Stockholm on December 12, 1930, made plain both his profound love for America and his impatience with her flaws. The address, still one of the most memorable public utterances by an American writer, combined high praise and sharp denunciation. The abuse was directed at such targets as Henry Van Dyke, whose voice had been among the loudest in the outcry against the choice of Lewis for the prize, and whom Lewis characterized as a living example of "the American fear of literature" (the title of Lewis's speech); at the American Academy of Arts and Letters, which Lewis asserted "does not represent literary America of today—it represents only Henry Wadsworth Longfellow"; at the New Humanism, which Lewis termed "a doctrine of the blackest reaction introduced into a stirringly revolutionary world"; and at William Dean Howells, whom Lewis blamed for taming both Mark Twain and Hamlin Garland.[67]

These were the agencies, Lewis charged, which had suppressed honest writing in the United States. "Most of us," he said, "are still afraid of any literature which is not a glorification of everything American." Moreover, American higher education had perpetuated this lamentable condition, Lewis said. "In the arts our universities are as cloistered, as far from reality and living creation, as socially and athletically and scientifically they are close to us. To a true-blue professor of literature in an American university, literature is not something that a plain human being, living today, painfully sits down to produce. No; it is something dead."

Because of these hostile forces, the artist finds himself in a perilous predicament, Lewis concluded. "'The American novelist or poet or dramatist or sculptor or painter must work alone, in confusion, unassisted save by his own integrity." He is paid well, too well for his own good, but not seriously regarded by his countrymen. Above all, the artist is hindered by the lack of a unified and coherent code of critical standards against which he could test his work.

In spite of these handicaps the American writer is creating work of quality and significance, and here we have the affirmative element in Lewis's speech. Among those he singled out for praise or as fit candidates for the very award he had won were Theodore Dreiser, Willa Cather, Sherwood Anderson, James Branch Cabell, and Eugene O'Neill. To Dreiser Lewis paid special homage:

> Dreiser more than any other man, marching alone, usually unappreciated, often hated, has cleared the trail from Victorian and Howellsian timidity and gentility in American fiction to

honesty and boldness and passion of life. Without his pioneer-
ing, I doubt if any of us could, unless we liked to be sent to
jail, seek to express life and beauty and terror. . . . Dreiser's
great first novel, *Sister Carrie* . . . came to housebound and
airless America like a great free Western wind, and to our
stuffy domesticity gave us the first fresh air since Mark Twain
and Whitman.

As in *Main Street* and *Babbitt* Lewis ended his address with
a strong assertion of his optimism. He said:

I have, for the future of American literature, every hope and
every eager belief. We are coming out, I believe, of the stuffiness of safe, sane, and incredibly dull provincialism. There are
young Americans today who are doing such passionate and
authentic work that it makes me sick to see that I am a little
too old to be one of them.

There is Ernest Hemingway . . . Thomas Wolfe . . . Thornton
Wilder . . . John Dos Passos . . . Stephen Benét . . . William
Faulkner . . . and there are a dozen other young poets and
fictioneers, most of them living now in Paris, most of them a
little insane in the tradition of James Joyce, who, however
insane they may be, have refused to be genteel and traditional
and dull.

I salute them, with a joy in being not yet too far removed
from their determination to give to the America that has moun-
tains and endless prairies, enormous cities and lost farm cabins,
billions of money and tons of faith, to an America that is as
strange as Russia and as complex as China, a literature worthy
of her vastness.

With this ringing declaration closed Lewis's great decade.
The boy from Sauk Centre, Minnesota, had become the first
American privileged to speak to the world from a platform at
Stockholm, and he had made the occasion a memorable one.
It was the summit of his career.

CHAPTER 4

Reaction and Confusion: The Thirties

IF LITERARY CRITICS were more openly given to superstition than they are, we might have had by this time a
number of articles or a book which advanced the thesis that
the Nobel Prize casts an evil spell upon its American winners.
Such a thesis could be quite firmly buttressed. Without de-
bating the cases in which the Nobel selection was an obvious
error (Pearl Buck), it could be argued that the deserving
winners—Lewis, O'Neill, Hemingway, Faulkner, and Eliot—
thereafter failed to surpass or even equal the work for which
they had been rewarded. Certainly in the case of Sinclair Lewis
the Nobel Prize marked the apogee of his literary career. While
there was little slackening of his output—he continued to average
a novel every two years until the end of his life—and while some
of his later novels contained fine work, exceeded the sale, and
aroused some of the stir of his books of the 1920's, nothing he
wrote after 1930 would have distinguished him to the Swedish
Academy.

I   *The Labor Novel*

This decline in the quality of Lewis's work, which is sharply
evident in the 1930's, had been predicted by certain signs visible
at virtually the same time as his greatest success. Lewis's activities as celebrity and orator, the energy wasted in writing *Mantrap* and *The Man Who Knew Coolidge,* the pain of his divorce,
the courtship and marriage of Dorothy Thompson, and the
establishment of a new home in Vermont—all these tended to
pull Lewis away from his serious work, although he was able
to turn some of these experiences into literary capital in *Dodsworth.* Winning the Nobel Prize also had an unhappy effect on
Lewis; it made him more self-conscious and egotistical than he

already was. Lewis's letters show that the honor was partly responsible for his abrupt break with the publishing firm of Harcourt, Brace, which had shared in and contributed to his success. We can also see in the letters of the late 1920's that Lewis, always involved with the advertising and promotion of his books, became almost feverishly concerned with these matters, for nearly every communication advances a new circulation or money-making proposal. There is more than a little truth in James Branch Cabell's observation that the falling-off in Lewis's work came from what Lewis himself called "whoring," although Lewis persisted in the belief a professional writer could turn out commercial fiction and then return to his serious work without ill effects.[1]

But by far the most crucial factor bearing upon Lewis's career after 1929, perhaps the turning point in it, was his failure to complete a novel dealing with the American labor movement. As early as December, 1921, Lewis had contemplated a book on labor. He first visualized it with a hero who would be based on Eugene Debs, but in collecting material for the project he had encountered the people and conceived the ideas which instead resulted in *Arrowsmith*. Although he put aside the plans for the labor novel to write first *Elmer Gantry* and then *Dodsworth*, it continued to fascinate him. Again in the late 1920's and on several occasions during the 1930's he made attempts to write the book, each time finding himself unable to make headway with it. Yet he continued to work at it sporadically for the rest of his life. In 1945 and in 1947 he mentioned it to a young writer who was his guest, and in 1948 he told an interviewer that the book was to be the portrait of a "plain, hard-boiled labor leader."[2] We infer from the deterioration of Lewis's writing after 1929, from his repeated efforts to complete the labor novel, and from the frequency with which he spoke of it, that it was perhaps the most important of all his unfulfilled schemes and ambitions.

A number of those who knew Lewis intimately have set forth their analyses of his failure to finish this pivotal book. Grace Hegger Lewis has written that Lewis's middle-class attitude, his inability to understand and sympathize with the working man, and his distaste for the bickerings within the labor movement itself were the causes of his failure. Dorothy Thompson concluded that he gave it up because he became convinced that labor leaders were mere power-grabbers and moneygrubbers. Louis Adamic, one of Lewis's collaborators on the project, has suggested a number of personal factors, among them his fear of doing an unpopular book and his competition with his wife Dorothy. Benjamin Stolberg wrote that Lewis was intellectually unsuited to the task. Ramon Guthrie, another of Lewis's collaborators, saw his failure as the product of his relationship with his father and his own complex personality. We must also remember, in considering the whole matter, that if Lewis did not complete a novel on American labor, neither has any other American writer managed to handle more than a small part of this massive and mercurial subject.

In any case, Lewis wanted to write the book, did his best to carry it through, and could not.[3] Had he succeeded, especially in his efforts during the 1930's, he might have drawn from the success the momentum he needed to get his career through the doldrums. But with the coming of the Depression, the stable middle-class world based on peace, prosperity, and business as usual, the world to which Lewis was inextricably attached, fell under assault by political, social, and economic forces which Lewis was either not fully equipped to comprehend or unable to depict convincingly. As we will see in the discussion to follow, he tried in his own way to deal with the turmoil of the 1930's, but too often his methods made his work—so fresh and original in the previous decade—appear self-contradictory, tired, confused, contrived, and even anachronistic.

The causes for which he had fought valiantly in the 1920's— personal integrity, nonconformity, the liberation from village standards—were now overshadowed by lengthening bread lines at home and the totalitarian menace overseas. As Bertolt Brecht put it succinctly, in the lyrics of one of the songs in *The Three-penny Opera* (1928): "So learn the simple truth from this, our song/ Whatever you may do; whatever you aspire/ First feed the face, and then quote right and wrong/ For even saintly folk may act like sinners/ Unless they've had their customary dinners." The very affluence of American life, which Lewis had turned to artistic advantage in the 1920's by attacking it, had vanished. After the events of October 24, 1929, Babbitt could sustain no further onslaught nor furnish the substance for additional satire. Lewis's best work had depended on the premise that material prosperity without deeper values would engender spiritual poverty; suddenly he was confronted by a rich society which had grown poor overnight. He never quite got over the shock.

Not only Lewis, but Dreiser, Cabell, O'Neill, E. A. Robinson, and Mencken had already done—with the possible exception of O'Neill—their best work, and Mencken and Cabell plummeted into almost total obscurity as literary figures. Lewis himself seems to have known that his great days were over, for in his Nobel speech he had referred to himself as already too old to share in the work being done by Wolfe, Dos Passos, Hemingway, and Faulkner, the younger writers Lewis correctly named as his successors.[4] It was a tragically accurate assertion.

II *Ann Vickers*

Lewis had intended the first book of the new decade to be the labor novel, which would have anchored him in the main channel of the period's literary current. Instead, he wrote *Ann Vickers* (1933), an imperfect fusion of realistic–satirical novel and romance which traces the private and professional life of a modern woman. Ann Vickers is another of Lewis's nonconformists and his first female protagonist since Carol Kennicott. She grows up in a small midwestern town, graduates from an eastern college, becomes first an agitator for women's suffrage, then a social worker, and finally a penologist. Along the way she has an affair with an army officer, which necessitates an abortion; marries and later separates from another man; and finally falls in love with Barney Dolphin, a judge of questionable moral character, whose child she bears out of wedlock.

Despite the book's rather racy plot, the reader coming to it after Lewis's slashing books of the 1920's would immediately have detected a new and unsettling note in the novel's first paragraph, in which Lewis depicts children at play "blissfully unaware that compromise and weariness will come at forty-five" (Lewis was, at the time of its publication, forty-eight). There are other disturbing hints. Although the novel's heroine is described from the start as a free and proud girl, highly idealistic, Lewis's treatment of her village background is an interesting departure. For one thing, it is not stultifying. For another, we are told that it leaves a deep and favorable impression upon her, teaching her a basic and permanent sense of decency and values and also introducing her to a wide variety of human types. Furthermore, Ann shares with rural America the awakening awareness of national destiny and pride. In short, Lewis presents a portrait of the small-town environment which is not only autobiographical but also complimentary.

A number of other passages contribute additional detail to this sketch of a new, or at least an unfamiliar, Lewis. He characterizes the pre-World War I era as a time of windy optimism, of faith, of certainty that Utopia was at hand, and of "Christian socialism."[5] He asserts that this era made those who grew up in it (Sinclair Lewis, Dorothy Thompson, and Ann Vickers) seem somewhat ridiculous to their children in 1930, for the older folks had "buoyant, Shavian, liberal, faintly clownish notions" (p. 59). Throughout the novel Lewis offers similar statements, at one point ridiculing radicalism (pp. 216-18) and at another affirming that the human race ought to be left alone by reformers (pp. 256-57).

The tone has changed. It is neither that of the raging satirist, filled with snap and snarl—"America's Angry Man" a reviewer once called him—nor is it the cheery and whimsical voice of the romancer. Now it is nostalgic; an older soldier *hors de combat* is questioning the need of the battles he once fought. It was to be the tone and attitude dominant in Lewis's work of the 1930's. He has become the historian, not the reformer; he is the scribe of what has been, rather than the maker of what should be. Further, he addresses an audience he assumes are friends he had met long ago, who are growing old with him and sharing his bemusement at the times. This self-admitted displacement, this bewilderment, this weariness are not what we had come to expect of Sinclair Lewis, even the Lewis of *Mantrap* and the early romances.

Another unusual element in *Ann Vickers* is its sexuality. While it rarely becomes indecorous and while it completely avoids the erotic, sexuality is important to both the novel's story and message. Until *Elmer Gantry* Lewis had been proper, even puritanical about sex. Ann's affairs are the first in Lewis's books in which a hero or heroine engages in illicit relations without some feeling of shame. Will Kennicott and Babbitt had indulged in such relations, but in their cases Lewis had portrayed the situations as sordid. The same disapproving tone is evident in *Dodsworth;* and Lewis, who permits Sam Dodsworth only one weekend of unsanctioned sex, justifies it as therapy. In *Ann Vickers* he suspends judgment altogether. Moreover, he demonstrates quite emphatically that love and satisfying sexual experience may be had outside of marriage, that women have as much right to sexual pleasure as men, and that, once awakened, they have need of it. He also justifies abortions under extenuating although not desperate circumstances. None of these concepts and suggestions were radical in the fiction or discussion of the 1930's, but for Lewis they were.

The novel's sexuality cannot be discussed as an isolated factor, however. It is woven into the heroine's destiny and it is part of the novel's larger moral statement. The biography of the heroine follows the pattern of Lewis's search-for-identity or growth tales: small-town environment, instruction by the village atheist, stimulating college years, career, travel, disillusionment, and deeper experience in love, all resulting in maturity and fulfillment. Although Ann Vickers, unlike Una Golden, achieves prominence, like the earlier heroine, she finds that a career is not enough for a woman. She suffers loneliness; she even regrets her own talents and accomplishments because they frighten men away. Upon this base Lewis erects a Nietzschean theory of romance: that great women need great men to love them. Since both are rare, the superior will marry an inferior. Then, the inferior will strive to drag the other down, humble him, and thus remove the difference between them.[6]

The Nietzschean influence may best be observed in the heroine's liaison with Barney Dolphin, which combines some of the romantic notions and complications of a *Saturday Evening Post* story (love at first sight, idyllic trysts) and the *übermensch* theory that great men and great women can have love affairs above the law. The fact that both Ann and Barney are already married causes no hesitation or qualms in either. Indeed, as the novel ends, the two lovers are living together while each awaits a divorce from his spouse, and Ann is now depicted as a complete woman, with her career, her man, her child, and a legal union planned in the near future. Thus Lewis conjoins the miracle ending of popular melodrama with a naturalistic amorality in which everything viable is permissible.

The moral confusion apparent in Lewis's treatment of Ann's sexual and marital experience carries over into his portrayal of Ann's lover, Barney Dolphin, who is a wonderfully clever, able,

kind, sincere judge, and only incidentally a criminal. Although
Lewis has him confess his guilt in using his public position for
personal profit, the immorality of his conduct is presented in
such mild terms that we can not condemn him. He is also much
too likable to condemn. In view of all this, why does Lewis stir
up moral issues? Why should morality be important in *Ann
Vickers,* or if not morality, the law, since one of the novel's
theses is that morality and the law are not the same? Morality
consists of treating people decently; the law consists of treating
them harshly, or so Lewis interprets it. The novel asks: since
the law demands and justifies prisons, how can we respect it?
Further, Lewis implies that if we were all brought before the
law, we would all be guilty of some infraction or crime. Ergo,
we cannot hold to the law.

Lewis is forced, perhaps unwittingly, into this dilemma by
the best thing in the book: its exposé of the intolerable conditions
in American prisons and its assault on the widespread belief
that imprisonment is the best way to punish wrongdoers and
deter wrongdoing. In this social criticism, at least, we perceive
no confusion, no uncertainty in *Ann Vickers.* This is the good
Lewis, sticking sharp pins into our follies. In its monologue-
parodies of a sadistic deputy warden and a lady do-gooder, and
in passages describing the filth and degradation of prison life
and the brutality of a hanging, the novel moves swiftly and
surely. At times Lewis approaches naturalism as he amasses
grim details in the prison episodes; he is kept from it only by
the fierce indignation which did not permit him clinical detachment.

However, even as social commentary—Lewis's specialty—*Ann
Vickers* is shaky. There are jibes at social work, communism, the
too-clever talk at New York liberal–intellectual cocktail parties,
but none are keen enough to cut. It advances a number of
worthy causes, true, and it takes a firm stand on penology, but
these episodes do not dominate the entire novel. On the whole,
it conspicuously lacks the vision which had transfigured *Main
Street, Babbitt,* and *Arrowsmith;* it is without *Elmer Gantry's*
sheer malice, nor does it possess *Dodsworth's* deep seriousness.
Lewis seems to have surveyed the panorama of American society
in the first years of the thirties and found nothing worthy of his
full and concentrated attention. Even the thrust at penology is
somewhat blunted when the heroine actually sets up and oper-

ates a model house of correction and rehabilitation. In other words, Lewis allows his heroine what he had denied his other nonconformists: a measure of success gained through integrity and a solution to the problem. Since the heroine's private life has also been neatly arranged, the novel concludes with everything settled and resolved and with real happiness just ahead. As a consequence, the reader is left entertained and solaced rather than disturbed, but it had been disturbance that Lewis had earlier used to his best artistic advantage.

At times, in fact, in his assertions that people are probably better than those trying to improve them, Lewis nearly refutes his major position of the 1920's. He is even capable of such reactionary remarks in *Ann Vickers* as the statement that the Depression is beneficial to the American people because it has again reminded them of the joys of honest poverty and because it may restore the iron to their souls. Only the sparks of rebellion remaining in Lewis's unconventional attitudes toward love, marriage, the law, and prisons, keep him out of the camp of his former enemies, propriety and respectability. Although in *Ann Vickers* we continue to be warmed by the heat of Lewis's inquisitional fires, they no longer burn with the same consistency and incandescence.

The conservatism, reaction, and retreat hinted at in *Ann Vickers* were even more obvious in Lewis's next novel, *Work of Art* (1934); a volume of short stories, *Selected Short Stories* (1935); a play, *Jayhawker* (1935); and in two later books of the decade, *The Prodigal Parents* (1938) and *Bethel Merriday* (1940). *Work of Art* deals with hotel-keeping. *Jayhawker* is a Civil-War melodrama. *The Prodigal Parents* offers as its hero a Babbitt-like automobile dealer. *Bethel Merriday* has to do with the theater. All are primarily affirmative of American life and all are the work of Lewis the romancer; taken together or separately, they constitute a lamentable retrogression in the career of an important novelist who also seemed willing to depend all too frequently on elements of plot and theme he had used in his earlier work.

III *Work of Art*

In its narrative *Work of Art* is concerned with two brothers, Myron and Ora Weagle. Ora is the poet: as a youth, charming, graceful, imaginative, and unbearably superior, while Myron is the stolid, hard-working, older brother who does most of the chores for the village hotel which is the family's livelihood. Myron forms the resolution to learn the hotel business from top to bottom, and in one job after another he perseveres in his ambition, eventually winning a directorship in a large hotel corporation and momentarily fulfilling his lifelong desire to build and operate his own "dream hotel." Meanwhile, Ora has become a hack writer, a drunkard, a chiseler, and a squanderer of his own talent, who has written only one honest book in a literary career of fifteen years. But Myron's dream hotel becomes a disaster and he is ruined, by wordly standards, although remaining true to his private ideals. Ora, on the other hand, becomes rich and famous at the same time his brother's career disintegrates.

Therefore, *Work of Art* is essentially a book about success, its types, varieties, and meaning. The novel's thesis and conclusion are plain and simple: to do a job well, any job, is better than to do a job badly, no matter how much the world may praise and reward the meretricious. More specifically, Lewis labors the point from beginning to end that hotel-keeping is as important to society as writing, and that good hotel-keeping is more important, more worthy of respect, and more honest, however much the bad writing pays in money and fame. At first glance this appears to be a new philosophy for Sinclair Lewis, but on closer inspection it may be seen that it is a mere adjustment in already established conclusions. For example, we can find pronounced similarities between *Work of Art* and *Arrowsmith*, with virtually the same ending in both novels: the hero has isolated himself (in *Work of Art* he is not in the woods but running a tiny hotel in a Kansas village) while the villain enjoys "success" and luxury in the large world outside. Moreover, Lewis's interest in hotels was both a personal fetish and the source for material in *The Job* and *Dodsworth,* to name two instances. We may also see reflected throughout his work, early and late, the admiration for practical competence which he apotheosizes in *Work of Art.* Finally, the contemptuous portrayal of the writer, Ora Weagle, and the deliberate depiction of hotel management as a kind of art and music and poetry are but manifestations of Lewis's old philistinism and abiding hatred for anything that smacked of the bohemian.

But are comfortable and well-run hotels a matter of such importance as the novel declares? Furthermore, in Lewis's contrast of the writer who has sold out with the honest drudge of a hotelkeeper he suggests there are none other but corrupt writers. We meet many sorts of hotel men in the novel, some admirable, some not; but only one representative of the arts appears and he is intolerable.[7] Consequently, there is an insidious implication that the one is the all, the prototype. And, to carry Lewis's suggestion to its logical end, *Work of Art* rejects the very craft of its author in favor of life in the business world. It is a deplorable conclusion to draw about the author of *Babbitt,* but there is some evidence for it. Whatever Lewis intended in this novel, the character of Ora Weagle does convey his belief that Americans are such fools they cannot tell the difference between the true and the false and the original and the imitation; all a writer need do to succeed, therefore, is combine the right ingredients. As we reflect further, we realize that *Work of Art* also contains a caustic commentary on the level of American taste in hotels, for a large proportion of the public seems to prefer glittering but shoddy places to those honestly and carefully operated—just as it prefers the vulgar in literature.

While the book makes passing reference to what is happening in the world, parallels larger events with developments in innkeeping (how the automobile will revolutionize the hotel field), and briefly alludes to the Depression, it has an even lesser quantity of realism than *Ann Vickers.* When we read *Work of Art* today, it has a curiously antique quality, as if it were written in 1894 or 1904 instead of 1934. Nor is there anything in the novel's style to distinguish it. It shows great knowledge of the details of the hotel business and it is passably written, but it is only slightly superior to Lewis's pre-1920 romances in its avoidance of their cuteness and sentimentality.

Unfortunately, at the same time that Lewis was falling from critical grace because of *Ann Vickers* and *Work of Art,* he chose to publish a collection of stories and a play which further evidenced his decline. Of the thirteen stories in his *Selected Short Stories* (1935), all but a few range from the canned, slick, or unforgivably sentimental to the merely contrived. Such a collection forces conclusions hostile to Lewis. If we presume that these stories are Lewis's best or representative of his best short fiction, then his best was inferior. It is also impossible to trace any consistent values or standards in the stories; rather, they contain some direct contradictions. For example, "Things" (1919) attacks the materialism and values of a business society; "Go East, Young Man" defends those very values. The shift might be explained by saying that one is an early story and the other late; however, in another late story, "Land" (1931), Lewis reverses his field again and denies profit, respectability, and urban life. Obviously, Lewis paid no attention to consistency or harmony of theme in issuing this volume. Although the better stories, "Things," "Young Man Axelbrod," and "Land," affirm individuality and integrity, the collection on the whole manifests the romantic, affirmative, and commercial Lewis. Perhaps most disturbing of all, these tales show no development or progress of any kind. The best of them, "Young Man Axelbrod" (1917), is the earliest; one of the worst, "Let's Play King" (1931), is the latest and a piece of pure claptrap.

Jayhawker, which had its New York premiere on November 5, 1934, and which appeared in published form in 1935, is less objectionable than the story collection, although it, too, stemmed from Lewis's commercial rather than artistic instincts. Written in collaboration with Lloyd Lewis, dramatic critic of the *Chicago Daily News*, the play abundantly reveals Lewis's hand in its characters and plot. The plot revolves around a plan (based on a proposal actually advanced by one of Lincoln's advisers) to end the Civil War by uniting North and South and marching against Mexico. With its combination of romance, war, heroism, and political intrigue and with its Gantry-like central character, Ace Burdette, *Jayhawker* may have been diverting entertainment but, again, it was not a tribute to America's winner of the Nobel Prize.

IV The Prodigal Parents

There is a scene in *Our Mr. Wrenn*, Lewis's first novel, in which the hero returns from Europe to find one of his old friends gone to seed and to drink, takes him in tow, and sets him back on the straight and narrow. Exactly the same scene occurs in *The Prodigal Parents*, Lewis's sixteenth novel, but with a significant change in its personnel. The central character is now Fred Cornplow, whom Lewis depicts with all seriousness and respect as the "eternal bourgeois," and the sot is his son, Howard Cornplow. Before Lewis permits the protagonist to enjoy this final triumph, however, he has allowed him victories over a business rival, a sinister young Communist, a psychiatrist, leeching relatives, and even what was forbidden to Babbitt—the conquest of the mundane and routine via a spectacular dash to Europe. But of all the antagonists Fred Cornplow must face, the most noxious are his own two children.

The Prodigal Parents was published in 1938, nearly twenty years after *Main Street*. The children whose sleeping heads Carol said were bombs to shake the foundations of respectability have now grown up. However, they are not bombs, they are duds. They are not what's right with the world but what's wrong with it. They are the villains, not the heroes. The heroes are the former villains, the Will Kennicotts and the George Babbitts, who are now portrayed as decent hard-working folks who are the backbone of civilization and who have the backbone their children lack. In short, Lewis has traveled full-circle in *The Prodigal Parents*. He has reversed his identifications and values. The herald of the new in 1920 has become in 1938 the guardian of the old.

Sara and Howard Cornplow, the children, are so devastatingly rendered in their selfishness, incompetence, and self-indulgence and are so greedy in the sucking of their parents' sustenance that, although Lewis provides moral rejuvenation and reform for them by the end of the novel, we fail to be convinced by it. Lewis has made us hate them too thoroughly. And in contrast, so warm and friendly and approving is his treatment of Fred and Hazel Cornplow, the parents, that we can neither believe nor accept any fault on their part in what the children have become; and it is necessary to the credibility of the novel that such fault be established. Although Lewis says on several occasions that the parents are paying for pampering their offspring, he says it without much conviction and completely falls short of proving it. Furthermore, the children have none of their parents' traits—emotional, mental, or physical. Fred and Hazel are stable; their son and daughter are flighty and unreliable. Fred and Hazel have common sense; the children are completely lacking in any sort of insight. Fred and Hazel are hard workers; the children are lazy and feckless. Fred and Hazel are self-reliant; the children are almost totally irresponsible and dependent. Fred and Hazel are short; the children are tall. Perhaps Lewis intended these antitheses to make his point, but if he did, it was a sad misreckoning.

Another defect of *The Prodigal Parents* is its inconstant tonality. Like many other of Lewis's affirmative books, this one is only half-serious. The tone fluctuates between the serio-comic of slick fiction and the sincere, or even the hortatory, in the long passages in which Lewis defends Fred Cornplow as the eternal bourgeois and in which he has him question the meaning of life. In its view of the Cornplows' marriage, the novel is thoroughly sentimental and sticky, for the parents' still-active romantic feelings for each other are woven of spun sugar. Lewis gives his hero all sorts of desire to cast aside routine, to stop being so dutiful, to travel the road to Samarkand; yet he fails to give him an iota of real passion.

Still, we cannot classify the novel purely as escape fiction because it includes realistic episodes and problems: communism, the relationship of parents and children, references to the chaotic state of world affairs, etc. *The Prodigal Parents* could best be described, perhaps, as another romance of the commonplace. In any case it is the result of a struggle between Lewis the realist and Lewis the romancer, with the romancer winning a dominance which did further mischief to Lewis's reputation.

V *Bethel Merriday*

There is no such struggle in Lewis's last novel of the decade, *Bethel Merriday* (1940). It is unadulterated syrup. In *Work of Art* and *The Prodigal Parents* Lewis had at least admitted to the existence of a real world; *Bethel Merriday* repeatedly denies such a world in Lewis's preference for the theater and his concern with the professional and romantic struggles of the young actress named in the novel's title. Bethel is another of Lewis's sympathetically portrayed heroines (although by far the dullest) with a quest. Hers is to be an actress, and, after experience in summer stock, part-hunting in New York, and a role with a touring company, she fulfills her ambitions. In fact, she overfills them because, as the novel closes, she can look forward not only to a career on the stage but also to a compatible marriage.

The plot of *Bethel Merriday* is harmless enough, but its theme —if such an insubstantial piece can have a theme—is downright irritating. Actually, we derive our conclusions about them less from what happens to the characters than from Lewis's running commentary, which avows that *the theater contains the only*

reality left in life. Witness these remarks: on page two we find
the assertion that Barrymore in *Hamlet* and the productions of
Anna Christie and *Back to Methuselah* were "so much less stagy"
than the Italian Fascists and Hitler. A character in the novel
declares that "the rest of the world outside the theater . . . seems
pretty shabby" (p. 30). The novel's heroine concludes that she
would much rather act than worry about what was happening
to the Jews in Europe or the sharecroppers in Oklahoma (p. 47).
Thirty pages later, there is the statement that the illusion created by the theater is "more real than reality" (p. 87). What does
one say about such a novel? The writer has the right to deal
with what he knows and loves, and there is logic in Lewis's
doing a book on the theater after several years' involvement with
it as playwright, performer, and director.[8] Furthermore, if *Bethel
Merriday* is considered merely as light fiction, it might be allowed that it is amusing and divertingly told, although too many
of its four hundred pages are given over to an account of a road
performance of *Romeo and Juliet.*

But from Sinclair Lewis, the winner of the Nobel Prize, it is
another one of those romantic and/or commercial transactions
which makes us unhappy, which makes us suspect the worth
of his best books, and which makes us disbelieve that the same
writer was responsible for *Bethel Merriday* and for *Arrowsmith*
and *Babbitt.* True, *Bethel Merriday* is a better book than *Mantrap* and perhaps better than all but one or two of Lewis's first
five, but it is not the sort of novel a writer of his achievement
should have published. Ideologically, it shows Lewis still retreating, in fact, reaching the furthermost boundaries of with-
drawal from the troubled events of the time, for in the repeated
assertions in *Bethel Merriday* that the world of the theater is
valuable precisely because it avoids the real world, precisely
because it lives in fantasy, and in his own theatrical activities
during the years when Steinbeck was traveling with the Okies
and Hemingway was on the scene of the Spanish Civil War,
we have Lewis's apparent decision—both personal and artistic—
to cope with the real world by ignoring it and by playing at
make-believe.

Moreover, Lewis's insistence on the triumph of the theater
through fantasy is weakened by one of the conflicts in the book
itself: the question of how *Romeo and Juliet* is to be played.
Lewis speaks through the character of Zed Wintergeist, who

feels that the production is a flop because it is not being acted naturalistically, that it only pretends to be modern by using modern dress, but that in its performance it is still being treated as a romantic costume drama. Zed objects to the leading man's reading of Romeo because he elocutes and recites, stressing the verbal poetry of the lines but not the psychological poetry of the character, the interplay of emotion and conflict which gave the play greatness. It is this which leads to the tour's demise. Modern audiences are no longer interested, the novel discloses, in stage romance, and thus they stop attending. Produced and performed Zed's way, as he acts his own part of Mercutio, the play would again be true to life. This Lewis approves and conveys to the reader. Yet he also stops to tell us repeatedly that the theater is wonderful because it is "illusion," "children's play," "magic." In this contradiction, another of those Lewis neither saw nor intended, there is represented the elemental conflict in Lewis's work, that between fantasy and verisimilitude, with, as always, failure when the fantasy prevails. When Lewis offers no message, or when the message is thin, as in *Work of Art,* or trivial, as in *Bethel Merriday,* Lewis is bad—not bad by *Saturday Evening Post* standards, but bad when judged seriously as an artist of continuing importance. He wrote his own doom as a popular writer once he had published *Main Street.* After that novel it was impossible for his critics to think of him again as another hack. Inevitably, we measure all his work, whatever Lewis's intention in a particular book, against his best and most serious work; by that yardstick, *Bethel Meriday* is minute.

But there must be some justification for this phase of Lewis's career, this return to the romance of the commonplace in *Work of Art* and *The Prodigal Parents;* to entertainment in *Bethel Merriday* and *Jayhawker* and in that collection of short stories which should have remained buried in the magazines first publishing them.[9] Had Lewis lost *all* conscience and reason as well as all taste? No. The quality of his writing slumped badly, almost beyond recovery it seemed, and he was mistaken and confused in his purposes; but he did have purposes, especially in *Work of Art* and *The Prodigal Parents.* Despite the critical disfavor— with the exception of *It Can't Happen Here*—which Lewis's work of the 1930's deservedly brought him, he kept his audience. *Ann Vickers* and *Work of Art* sold more than 90,000 copies each. The volume of stories sold 266,000. Even *Bethel Merriday* reached a sale of 63,000. As Lloyd Morris has pointed out, the common readers recognized Lewis as one of them. His mass audience heard the increasingly affirmative tone of his books and knew that Lewis was now singing them lullabies where earlier he had shouted battle cries. Lewis's vision, like that of many of his readers, had grown misty. He reminded them of the American Dream, of Horatio Alger, and of their faith in an individualistic, republican, middle-class utopia.[10]

Accordingly, *Work of Art*, which appeared during the depths of the Depression, may be taken as a prop for the sagging ideals of a mercantile society. By writing an old-fashioned success story of the hero who rises from mean origins, fails, and then rises again, Lewis was perhaps trying to reaffirm what most needed reaffirmation.[11] Perhaps, in a system whose values were deteriorating, Lewis wanted to remind his audience of the value of hard work, thrift, loving one's job and knowing it well, the virtue of work and the goodness of work for its own sake. In an age without integrity, he proclaims the importance of integrity, for whatever else the novel's hero, he is honest. And in choosing hotel-keeping for the hero's metier, Lewis settled upon just the kind of work which appeals to Americans: white collar but not cerebral; demanding but soiling neither hands nor clothes; requiring know-how but drawing it from experience, not books; work which is also varied, lively, potentially profitable, yet comforting in its sense of service to others.

Likewise, *The Prodigal Parents* shores up the class most threatened by the rumors of war from abroad and by economic instability at home. Again Lewis reiterates the worth of what the times were challenging: salesmanship, productivity, self-reliance, the profit system. If Lewis had seemed to condemn these in *Babbitt*, he now champions them. He remains loyal, however, to the belief that Americans need to upset their routines, do the unexpected, seek travel, search within, and so he differentiates Fred Cornplow from Babbitt by making his revolt more successful, his hunger for beauty and excitement more fully satisfied (although far less intense). Cornplow yearns for Europe and sails there, while Babbitt had scoffed at it. In other words, *The Prodigal Parents* is a comforting book in a discomforting age, a book in which Lewis stages a revolt of the parents against the revolt of the children, assailing all who would harm the parents: Communists, leeching relatives, undeserving children, psychiatrists—everything representative of destructive change.[12] Nor would a careful reader of Lewis have been taken utterly by surprise at these developments. As early as 1928 Lewis had written that his version of utopia would not differ substantially from that of George Horace Lorimer, editor of the *Saturday Evening Post*, and in 1935 he expressed his conservatism, his rejection of the reformer's or diagnostician's role, by saying: "There are two equal sins for a thinker or a doer in this year of 1935: to despair of the noble future of mankind; and to believe that this savage race, mankind—so much more savage than the tigers because we kill not just for meat, but for our highest ideals— can be made all sweet and holy just by a few fine phrases."[13]

Lewis's novels of the 1930's were also the expression of his own revolt. He was always neurotically sensitive about his freedom as a man and as a writer, and in publishing the kind of books he did Lewis deliberately swam against the literary currents of the period. In 1938 he accepted membership in the American Academy of Arts and Letters—which he had characterized in his Nobel address as being representative only of Henry Wadsworth Longfellow—an act symptomatic both of his conservatism in this period and of the baffling contradictions in Lewis, the man and the writer. Ramon Guthrie has speculated that even Lewis's labor novel was unfinished as a result of this compulsion to do the opposite of what was expected of him, because, we might further speculate, in writing such a novel Lewis would have affiliated himself with the social-conscious, proletarian, and Marxist writers who held the center of the stage. Above all, he refused to be a member of any "school." So, in a decade generally poor in its literary product and in which many of the best books—Dos Passos' *U.S.A.* and Steinbeck's *The Grapes of Wrath*—evidenced grave social concern and were sharply critical of America, Lewis wrote romance and affirmation. One of his favorite poses was that of storyteller, and he had never given it up, even in his great decade. In the 1930's he seems to have preferred that role to all others, as may be observed in this autobiographical statement appearing in 1936:

> I read in the public prints that the man Lewis . . . is a raging reformer, an embittered satirist, a realist dreary as cold gravy, and a bustling journalist. I don't know. Maybe. The critics ought to know—it's their job. True, these categories are mutually contradictory, but the same critics can undoubtedly explain a

little matter like that. Only, I should have thought Brother Lewis was essentially a story-teller—just as naive, excited, unself-conscious as the Arab story-tellers beside the caravan fires seven hundred years ago, or as O. Henry in a hotel room on 23rd Street furiously turning out tales for dinner and red-ink money. In his stories Lewis does not happen to be amused only by the sea or by midnight encounters on the Avenue, but often by the adventure of the soul in religion and patriotism and social climbing. But they are essentially stories just the same. And as for the man Lewis himself and his private personality, I rather doubt his having any, outside those stories.[14]

However, in one novel of the 1930's, *It Can't Happen Here*, Lewis abandoned the unflattering guises of romantic storyteller and weary retired veteran, and confronted the issues of his time squarely. Looking back on the novel after a quarter century, we see that it is a faulty and poorly constructed work, but in its own day it had great impact and timeliness.

VI *It Can't Happen Here*

Written in four months and published late in 1935 so that Lewis could exploit public interest in the forthcoming presidential election, *It Can't Happen Here* is Lewis's version of how America could become a Fascist dictatorship. The novel's hero is Doremus Jessup, an elderly newspaper editor of Fort Beulah, Vermont. Its villain is Senator Berzelius "Buzz" Windrip, who becomes President and then dictator of the United States when, after taking office, he suspends the democratic processes and declares martial law, replaces the system of separate and sovereign states with a form of corporate government, and begins to milk the country of its riches. Concentration camps are established for enemies of the "Corpo" regime, as it is called; persecution of racial and religious minorities begins; and the conditions of life become steadily more intolerable for any decent and intelligent citizen. By the end of the novel, however, Lewis has chronicled the start of a rebellion against the Corpos, with Doremus Jessup taking an active part in the resistance movement.

From this brief summary it is obvious that the rise of Mussolini and Hitler and the seizure of power by their parties in Italy and Germany provided Lewis with a general pattern for the novel, while the career of Huey Long in the United States specifically suggested a native parallel and a model for the character of Buzz Windrip.[15] Other parallels might be drawn between the fictional characters of Lee Sarason and Bishop Prang and the real figures of Goebbels and Father Coughlin. In the rantings of Eugene Talmadge and Gerald L. K. Smith, in Huey Long's "Share Our Wealth" plan, Father Coughlin's National Union for Social Justice, the Townsend Plan, Upton Sinclair's EPIC (End Poverty in California), and Technocracy, Lewis had true-to-life precedents for Buzz Windrip's "Fifteen Points of Victory," a weird conglomeration of most of the dangerous forces and crackpot schemes unsettling American life and a grouping which Lewis used as a summation of the social and economic disturbances of the 1930's. Finally, Lewis had in his wife Dorothy Thompson an expert analyst both of the political scene and of European Fascism, for she had interviewed Hitler at the time of his accession to power and had, in fact, been expelled from Germany as the result of her derogatory remarks about *der Führer*. This passage from her book *I Saw Hitler* (1933) may contain the germ for *It Can't Happen Here*:

> Imagine that in America, an orator with the tongue of the late Mr. Bryan and the histrionic powers of Aimee Semple McPherson combined with the publicity gifts of Edward Bernays and Ivy Lee should manage to unite all the farmers, with all the white-collar unemployed, all the people with salaries under three thousand dollars a year who have lost their savings in bank collapses and the stock market and are being pressed for payments on the icebox and the radio, the louder evangelical preachers, the American Legion, the D.A.R., the K.K.K., Mathew Woll, Senator Borah, Henry Ford—imagine that and you will have some idea of what the Hitler movement in Germany means.[16]

In each generation there had been a character whom Lewis obviously admired and who acted as Lewis's spokesman—in 1915, Hawk Ericson; in the 1920's, Arrowsmith and Dodsworth—and in the 1930's that character is the protagonist of *It Can't Happen Here*, Doremus Jessup. His politics, his favorite reading, his work, his personality, all are matters in which Lewis either shares or approves. When we survey America, we do so through the eyes of Doremus. What do we see?

The main threats to America and those most directly producing Fascist dictatorship are Lewis's favorite demons: big business united with folksiness; mass cult taste and values united with the desire, especially sharp in the 1930's, to get something for nothing; and the forces of conformity which the Corpo regime now masquerades as patriotic necessity. "Buzz" Windrip is a super-Babbitt, but a Babbitt nevertheless. He is to politics what Gantry was to religion; and, like Gantry, Lewis depicts him as not really an evil man, just an ambitious and unreflective one. To put it simply, the rise of the Corpos in the United States in *It Can't Happen Here* is merely an extension of what Gopher Prairie felt about someone not joining in its boosting, or an enlargement of the Good Citizen's League in *Babbitt*, or an expansion of what the fundamentalist vigilantes did to Frank Shallard. Thus, the novel employs the same conflicts preponderant in Lewis's other books. *It Can't Happen Here* culminates and diagrams in detail the sort of native Fascism he had warned against since 1920. Now, in the 1930's, with one of three citizens unemployed, with totalitarianism abroad, with the truths of democracy and the precepts of capitalism under duress, Lewis cautioned that we were never more ready for dictatorship. The argument early in the novel between Doremus Jessup and some of his important fellow citizens contains Lewis's resumé of conditions, with Doremus, of course, as Lewis's spokesman.

In a peroration that runs for two pages, Lewis amasses the evidence for Doremus's declaration: "God knows there's been enough indication we *can* have tyranny in America." He cites the exploitation of the southern sharecroppers, the miners, and the garment-makers, and the unjust imprisonment of such labor leaders as Mooney. To the remark that America is "a country of freemen" who would not tolerate tyranny, Doremus replies that America is capable of greater hysteria and obsequiousness than any other nation in the world, and in support he offers an impressive group of exhibits: Huey Long's complete rule over Louisiana; Father Coughlin's influence upon millions of his radio listeners; America's tolerance for Tammany graft, Chicago racketeering, and the corruption in Harding's administration; the activities of the Ku Klux Klan; American war hysteria and the hatred of all things German to the extent of renaming sauerkraut "Liberty cabbage"; the wartime censorship of the press; the popularity and influence of such religious frauds as Billy Sunday and Aimee McPherson; the unwarranted fear of Catholics and Communists; the influence of William Jennings Bryan upon state legislatures in their passing of laws to forbid the teaching of evolution; the government's overzealous attempts to enforce Prohibition by firing indiscriminately upon anyone even suspected of transporting whiskey; and the delight of many Americans in lynchings. Lewis summarizes all this with the emphatic question to which he has already supplied the answer: "Why, where in all history has there ever been a people so ripe for dictatorship as ours!"[17] And the answers of Doremus' listeners confirm the argument. They say that a strong leadership, like that of Hitler and Mussolini, would be good for the country, save it from the Reds and the lazy workmen on relief. This is the background for the novel; this is Lewis's rendition of the climate of opinion. From this point, it will be merely a matter of technique, of *how* it happens here.

Despite the bleakness of all this, which, like Lewis's denunciations in *Main Street* and *Babbitt,* leads the reader to believe that Lewis hates America, *It Can't Happen Here* does offer some hope. The very existence of Americans like Doremus Jessup, who has in the past (like Lewis) asserted Tom Mooney's innocence, questioned the Sacco–Vanzetti verdict, condemned the interference of the United States in Haiti and Nicaragua, and supported labor's right to organize, is in itself one source of optimism for the nation's future. Another is visible in Lewis's declaration that a new America must be built on the proposition that government is not a contest to be won by the best political athletes "but a universal partnership, in which the State must own all resources so large that they affect all members of the State," and in which the worst crime shall not be a murder but a crime against the people's welfare (pp. 441-42). A third is Lewis's recognition of the many Americans who do not tolerate tyranny and who lead a revolution against it, a rebellion starting in Lewis's homeland, the West: "the land of the Populists, the Non-Partisan League, the Farmer-Labor Party, and the La Follettes" (p. 447).

Finally, *It Can't Happen Here* contains one of Lewis's most affirmative and idealistic social statements. Although it, too, advances the notion that the revolutionaries and idealists have hindered human progress more than they have helped it, the novel also declares Lewis's deep-rooted faith in the "Liberal" as the only hope of civilization. Unlike many of his literary colleagues of the 1930's, Lewis was never deluded into thinking that communism had the only remedy for the ills of capitalism or the spreading infection of Fascism, and in *It Can't Happen Here* he emphatically rejects communism. These statements are the crux of Lewis's convictions, and the speaker is Doremus:

> He saw now that he must remain alone, a "Liberal," scorned by all the noisier prophets for refusing to be a willing cat for the busy monkeys of either side. But at worst, the Liberals, the Tolerant, might in the long run preserve some of the Arts of Civilization, no matter what brand of tyranny should finally dominate the world (p. 432).

And:

> "More and more, as I think about history," he pondered, "I am convinced that everything that is worth while in the world has been accomplished by the free, inquiring, critical spirit, and that the preservation of this spirit is more important than any social system whatsoever. But the men of ritual and the men of barbarism are capable of shutting up the men of science and of silencing them forever" (p. 433).

The public responded to the timeliness of *It Can't Happen Here* by purchasing more than a quarter of a million copies, while shortly after the novel appeared the Federal Theater Project produced a dramatic version staged simultaneously in thirteen cities. The critics, too, once more hailed Lewis as the man of the hour. "Probably the wisest and most human, the most searching and suggestive piece of realistic political thinking that has been done in America for a dozen years," one declared.[18] A reviewer pointed out that at the same time he was composing his review, the morning papers carried remarks by Governor Eugene Talmadge and speeches at a convention of the Daughters of the American Revolution which would have been called incredible and exaggerated burlesque had Lewis written them.[19] Such prominent leftist critics as Granville Hicks and V. F. Calverton, generally hostile to Lewis in the 1930's, found words of praise for the novel. In 1939 Charles and Mary Beard wrote, "In all the years of depression and turmoil, no novel written in the United States portrayed more dynamically the ideals of democracy pitted against the tyranny of the demagogic dictator." In 1943 Merle Curti noted, "When Sinclair Lewis published his own personal alarm call to the nation, *It Can't Happen Here,* there was widespread discussion of the book and few leaders of American thought stood up to call it foolish."[20] Even now, read either as history or narrative, the novel offers excitement, insight, and information; and although the events have passed which made it so vital to its own decade, the career of Senator Joseph McCarthy indicates that *It Can't Happen Here* retains some pertinence to American life.

But held up against Lewis's best and against other notable political novels of its generation—*Man's Fate, Darkness at Noon, Bread and Wine, 1984,* to give only a partial list—we can see why *It Can't Happen Here* falls short as a work of art, or even as a permanently significant political document, where the others succeed.[21] They are engendered not only by a set of conditions or a type of society but also by deeply held convictions about the nature of man. The events they describe are based not only upon a Depression, a period of political unrest, or even the characteristics of a single nation, but upon the writer's conclusions regarding the destiny of the human race. They are ultimately not about politics but about people. This is exactly where Lewis miscarried in his novel and where we may perceive one of his great failings.

Lewis tries, via Doremus' musings about war and about how idealists have hurt mankind more than they have helped it, to establish some connection between Fascism in America and the eternal bloodshed and tyranny in man's history. But he does not convince us. The only conclusion of which Lewis persuades the reader is that the ends of idealism and reform—the establishment of a utopian and edenic state—do not justify the means. However, because the aims of the Corpo regime were clearly ignoble from the start, *It Can't Happen Here* provides scant opportunity either to the hero or the reader for progress, change, or learning. The sole development which takes place in the novel is that in Doremus Jessup's concentration camp experiences he has beaten into his body the lessons about political tyranny that his head knew all along. The theme of the novel affirms that it *can* happen here if the decent folk, whom Doremus represents, merely stand by as well-behaved spectators of the legions of evil. We must all resist, Lewis says. But is this not a contradiction to the doctrine voiced by Doremus and so persistently by Lewis throughout the 1930's—that we would be better off without reformers and rebels and idealists? Furthermore, at the end of the novel Doremus has become precisely such a rebel and idealist—an active revolutionary engaging in espionage activities just as much a part of violence and bloodshed as the pulling of triggers. Also, Doremus had never been merely a bystander; he had gained a reputation in his town as a radical because he had continually spoken out in his influential position as newspaper owner and editor. In short, we must conclude that there is no evolution in the novel. The hero knows what he knows from the beginning. We have seen this fault elsewhere in Lewis, but there had before been greater compensations.

What *It Can't Happen Here* most lacks, considering it thematically, is a code of political or economic or philosophical convictions which would serve as a frame of reference. The critics had always complained that Lewis diagnosed sicknesses without prescribing medication for them, and the same criticism might be applied even more appropriately to this novel, for in it Lewis is dealing with specific political and economic conditions as well as a particular state of mind. Yet the only remedy Lewis proposes is some sort of welfare state—a kind of benevolent democratic socialism—in which civic responsibility is rigidly enforced, and this proposal is given but a paragraph. The only solution Lewis advances for human betterment is the preservation of the free, inquiring, liberal mind. Well and good, but that's like being for Virtue. We are all in favor of it; how do we get it? I again admit that judged as a satirist and as a writer of fiction Lewis is not obligated to provide remedies. This is the work of statesmen, professors, and philosophers. But evaluating Lewis as a political scientist, and he leaves himself open to such an evaluation in *It Can't Happen Here,* we can call him to account here where we could not in his books of the great decade.

Lewis's own politics were never fully or consistently developed; his views ranged from an early Fabian socialism, to a support of the New Deal and other Roosevelt programs in the 1930's and in the early 1940's, to a belief that Senator Vandenberg would make a good presidential candidate. While he was capable of brilliant political analysis (his wife used many of his opinions in a series of articles called "Conversations with a Grouse"; Lewis was the grouse), and while he was always keenly sensitive to any kind of injustice, he tended, like Mencken, to see all political activity as farce and all politicians as rogues. "He was basically apolitical," Dorothy Thompson has written, "but insofar as his social ideas were articulate and consistent, he was an old-fashioned populist radical."[22] We recall his ardent support of La Follette in 1924 and his admiration for Eugene Debs. In 1948 he told a visitor that his socialism most closely resembled that of the German Social Democrats, that he believed socialism would eventually come to America as the government gradually took over more and more functions, as it had the Post Office; but in the next breath Lewis said he would vote for a Republican if he felt like it.[23]

Quite apart from Lewis's hold on politics, the looseness of his grip as a novelist is apparent in *It Can't Happen Here* in the handling of characters, plot, and narrative structure. "Buzz" Windrip, for example, is the most incredible of all Lewis's creations. In Windrip and in such other characters as Adelaide Tarr Gimmitch, Hector Macgoblin, and General Emmanuel Coon —whose names in themselves testify to the state of Lewis's artistic sensibility—the distance between the concrete world and fantasy world of Lewis's imagination becomes too obvious. He conveys quite well the mood of the 1930's and a sense of the chaos in the decade's events, but the fantasy spills over into the reality and dilutes it, sometimes making a witch's brew of the whole thing. The book departs too often from a firm grounding in emotional and psychological truth for us consistently to project ourselves into it and shudder, as we do Orwell's *1984;* nor is *It Can't Happen Here* dignified by the total seriousness of Orwell's masterpiece. Because Lewis's material is itself so volatile, it should have been handled with more care and restraint.

Instead, Lewis piles one weird character and speech and proposal upon the other, his propulsive imagination working unchecked. Perhaps his haste in writing the book, his urge to make it completely topical, was responsible for its excesses; and he probably did not take the year or more to write and revise, as he usually did, because he feared he would delay the publication of the book too long. However, he might have gained in durability what he would have lost in timeliness and verve. In any case, more than any other of Lewis's novels, *It Can't Happen Here* has the furniture of realism without the reality. More than any other it approaches that realm of nightmare which some of Lewis's most perceptive critics, T. K. Whipple, James Branch Cabell, Mark Schorer and others, have found to be the true setting of Lewis's books.

The form, loose and episodic in Lewis's best work, is less controlled than usual in *It Can't Happen Here.* While the focus remains more or less upon Doremus Jessup, there are also long expository passages, done in a newsreel-like fashion, about what's happening in the rest of the United States. This robs Doremus, the only really interesting and credible character in the novel, of some of his stature. Since, as I have already pointed out, Doremus undergoes no change—not even the traditional education or counter-education of the Lewis hero—the novel must depend upon exterior action, and so it does. By far the largest amount of space is devoted to the details of the rise of the Fascist regime, its wickedness, its atrocities, its abuse of the public welfare, and herein Lewis comes very close to the techniques of popular fiction. Although Lewis generally avoids the sensational—it occurs earlier only in some episodes of *Elmer Gantry* and *Ann Vickers*—he makes plentiful use of it in *It Can't Happen Here,* including accounts of physical torture and brutality and continual hints at sexual promiscuity and/or deviation. Lewis's intention in describing the violence is to remind the reader of the realities then taking place in Germany, Italy, and Russia, while his purpose in employing the sexual material is to suggest that Fascism promotes perversion and lechery. This material results in the sort of novel which the mass audience finds readable and lively, but in *It Can't Happen Here* Lewis is neither a skillful enough craftsman nor possessed of the profundity of vision necessary to transform such material into art.

To give the novel its due, it was intended as a tract for the times and it carried out its function. In it Lewis showed that he was still aware, still in possession of some of the qualities which had brought him eminence. But when we consider that it was his best book of the decade, and when we test it against *Babbitt,* or even *Elmer Gantry* which it faintly resembles, we can descry a marked, perhaps a tragic, weakening of Lewis's artistry.

CHAPTER 5

The Final Phase

F RAZIER HUNT, one of Lewis's close friends in the 1920's, has reported an incident which illustrates the essential Sinclair Lewis. Hunt wrote of Lewis's reaction to seeing the Glasgow slums one night, just after the pubs had closed for the weekend and when drunken men and women were brawling or lying unconscious in the streets: "Finally Red stopped and raised his clenched fists to high heaven. Tears were streaming down his cheeks. 'I can't stand it any more,' he cried. 'I can't stand it.' All the way back to the hotel he cursed and raved. 'God damn the society that will permit such poverty! God damn the religions that stand for such a putrid system! God damn them all!' "[1]

This passion and high seriousness had been missing in the 1930's, except momentarily in *Ann Vickers* and *It Can't Happen Here;* and, without these qualities, Lewis fell into mediocrity and confusion. While there is also too little passion and seriousness in the books of Lewis's final years, we may remark a brief resurgence of power in two of his last five works, *Cass Timberlane* and *Kingsblood Royal.* These novels likewise demonstrated that Lewis still knew the way to the readers' hearts; the combined sales of the two totaled nearly 2,500,000 hardbound copies. Sales figures are, of course, no proof of a book's merit or lack of it, only of its possession of some ingredient for which its audience hungers. The ingredients which Lewis offered were, in *Cass Timberlane,* an honest portrayal of American marriage, and in *Kingsblood Royal,* a scathing indictment of racial prejudice. If they are not Lewis at his best, they are at least good Lewis; in quality they are just below the masterpieces of the great decade.

I *Cass Timberlane*

Cass Timberlane invites comparison with both *Main Street* and *Dodsworth,* for it utilizes some of their situations and conflicts. Like *Main Street* it deals with the marriage of a young, rebellious, high-spirited girl to an older, more stable, professional man. Like *Main Street* it is set in Minnesota, reflecting Lewis's re-identification with his native state and his residence in it during the early and mid-1940's. As in *Main Street* the young wife of Cass Timberlane must cope with the town's scrutiny (although the locale is a city, not a village) and with the attitude of her husband's upper-crust friends who feel that she does not belong. As in *Dodsworth* the story is told from the male's point of view, and the male is obviously the bearer of the author's identification and approval. As in *Dodsworth* the husband must suffer first his wife's flirtations, then her infidelity. Finally, as in *Dodsworth,* Lewis has chosen an American of the highest type—the hero is a judge and has served in Congress— to convey his thesis that even when one of the marital partners is a person of intelligence, maturity, and good will, matrimony is a strenuous experience.[2]

Despite these similarities, *Cass Timberlane* avoids Lewis's lamentable tendency to repeat himself, for a vital difference between *Cass Timberlane* and *Main Street* resides in the writer's intention and focus. *Main Street* was about small-town life; *Cass Timberlane* is about marriage. Another important difference, illustrative of the difference between Lewis in the 1920's and the 1940's, is the assertion throughout *Cass Timberlane* that life in Grand Republic, Minnesota, is the same as life in New York and Chicago (and, we might presume, Rome and Paris); that people look and act the same, that conversation is no less sparkling (because all talk is dull everywhere, Lewis says); and so on. The issue of whether to live in Grand Republic, Minnesota, or New York City is a minor one, growing out of the marital situation. Moreover, *Cass Timberlane* subordinates all extraneous elements and avoids the familiar Lewis conflicts— integrity versus success, individualism versus conformity, America versus Europe—to fasten more firmly than any other novel on the basic relationship between men and women.

In *Cass Timberlane,* the central characters are Cass, a lonely man approaching middle age, and his loved one, Jinny, a gay and attractive although emotionally unreliable young woman; and Lewis intends their problems to be those common to all: coping with personality differences, sexual and domestic adjustments, the maintenance of mutual affection and regard. Here, too, Lewis has attempted to purify the situation by omitting some of the usual causes of friction: money, in-laws, religion. He has in *Cass Timberlane* reduced the world, even with a great war raging in it, to one man and one woman. This statement in the novel contains its theme and indicates why Lewis should have published a tale about marriage in a year of global conflict: "If the world of the twentieth century . . . cannot succeed in this one thing, married love, then it has committed suicide, all but the last moan, and whether Germany and France can live as neighbors is insignificant compared with whether Johann and Maria or Jean and Marie can live as lovers."[3]

The great danger in any novel which depends on such a situation—and it is a danger to which Lewis was especially vulnerable because of his vices as a writer—is that it can degenerate into soap opera. Nor is Cass Timberlane entirely free from such corruption. There are some unforgivably cute passages about cats, a last-minute rescue of Jinny (who is in a diabetic coma) by the hero, and an upbeat ending that threaten the whole novel. It is saved, however, by the fundamental sincerity of Lewis's approach, by his candid yet restrained handling of sexuality, and by the conviction behind his disturbing assertion that marriages are usually ruined by two people—even when one of them is loving, decent, and forgiving. This undercurrent of deep and honest feeling exalts *Cass Timberlane* far above the level of Lewis's romances.

What message, then, does the novel deliver? It says that marriage is hard; that men and women cannot live together without colliding, simply because they are men and women; that people in love hurt each other—sometimes intentionally; and that they continue to find others sexually attractive and occasionally irresistible, even when their own marriage is a good one. Although these are hardly unfamiliar lessons, there is a more sinister proposal in *Cass Timberlane,* one which works against the grain of a cherished American tradition, and that is the novel's suggestion that men are better than women, that they love more tenderly, do not hurt their mates so deeply or so frequently, and that they are the strength and redemption of most marriages. Herein Lewis invokes not only the example of Cass and Jinny but much else in the novel as well. In a series of interchapters, to which Lewis gives the title "An Assemblage of Husbands and Wives," he unrolls a panorama of American marriage. Incidentally, these passages contain some of the best writing Lewis ever did, tight, sharp, uncluttered by specious or ambiguous emotion, and sexually frank but not erotic or embarrassed. They provide counterpoint to the story of Cass and Jinny and add depth to the entire novel.

There are fifteen "assemblages," covering perhaps twenty different marriages, alternating between bad and good, or bad and "average" marriages. Of the twenty, perhaps five are truly successful and happy. Of the bad marriages, cruel or selfish husbands are at fault in three cases; husbands inadequate as men and as lovers are to blame in a few other instances. The worst man of the lot is far less evil and cruel than the worst of the women. Furthermore, the majority of the women consistently nag, demean, or sexually humiliate their men, and a half dozen of them range from the totally callous to the fiendishly cruel. It would seem that Lewis has turned antifeminist after all these years, but this is not completely true. He continues to display considerable sympathy for women and an understanding of their problems; however, intentionally or not, he has also left the reader with the conclusion that women are inferior to men as human beings. Accordingly, while we are never allowed to despise Jinny for very long as we did Fran Dodsworth (Jinny is impulsive but Fran was malicious), we remain angry at her for a good part of the novel and are not nearly so ready to forgive her at its end as Cass seems to be.[4]

To take another fix on *Cass Timberlane,* the novel could be seen as another instance of Lewis's satiric investigation of American life and as an exposé or a revelation of confidential information about marriage. The book does have something of that quality, and the "assemblages" could serve that function. But I read it differently. The main impulse in *Cass Timberlane* is not satire; it is realism. The novel is not a distortion but a representation. It seems to have no purpose beyond that of describing a segment of human experience and saying some sincere things about human relationships. In this sense the book is rather refreshing, especially to the student of Lewis's career. If *Cass Timberlane* lacks the sweep and excitement of his best work, it does show Lewis as a highly competent novelist of manners and morals, as a convincing storyteller, and as a writer interested in matters other than the spectacular, the fraudulent, and the corrupt. At the same time that it avoids the excesses of Lewis's romances, it manages to be one of the most idealistic and patient of Lewis's books. It urges men and women to love one another, understand one another, forgive one another. It urges them to solve their own problems so that civilization can begin to solve its. And it proffers hope, although not assurance, that those problems are soluble.

II *Kingsblood Royal*

The emotionality in *Cass Timberlane* is poignant, intense, bittersweet, but understated and controlled. It is radically different in *Kingsblood Royal* (1947), for in it we find Lewis the blazing satirist at white heat. Not since *It Can't Happen Here* had the tempo of attack been so rapid and the amount of indignation, scorn, and ironic detail heaped so high. Before the book passes a hundred pages, Lewis has poked and prodded and slashed at every imaginable racist attitude by reciting horror stories from the South and humiliation stories from the North.[5] He pronounces sermon after sermon, poses indictment after indictment; and, while the reader finds it difficult to challenge the veracity of any single piece of evidence of the injustice and inhumanity inflicted upon the American Negro, Lewis makes the weight of our guilt so oppressive that we tend to escape from it rather than to shoulder it. As in *Elmer Gantry*, the sheer fury of Lewis's onslaught nearly carries it past its objective.

The novel's hero, Neil Kingsblood, is one of the few in Lewis's later work to undergo the educational or counter-educational experience characteristic of Lewis's story line. As the novel opens, Kingsblood holds many of the standard notions about the Negro's inferiority—notions which contribute to the pleasing assurance of his own white, Protestant, middle-class, Aryan superiority. But when he learns that one of his ancestors was Negro, his smugness vanishes. At first he is crushed and humiliated; then he begins to identify himself with the Negro and to learn more about him. Next, when some of his "white" friends begin anti-Negro activities, he publicly declares himself a Negro and thus exposes himself to the Negro's indignities. He loses his position, his erstwhile friends shun him, his social life is abruptly curtailed, etc. In short, Kingsblood's reaction against the racism of Grand Republic, Minnesota, and the penalties he suffers for it are reminiscent of Babbitt's rebellion and the retaliatory tactics of the Good Citizen's League.

Although the novel's basic plot device is questionable—that a man who has lived all his life as white would suddenly announce himself a Negro on the basis of a one-thirty-second blood inheritance—Lewis is entitled to the reader's willing suspension of disbelief. After all, by the laws of some of our sovereign states that is enough to make a man Negro; and, by Lewis's own canon, Neil had to make the announcement because he was an honest man.[6] We may reserve judgment, however, on whether an individual's psyche could collapse so suddenly, whether he could indeed begin to think and feel instantaneously as a member of a minority group. This borders on popular melodrama, on the immediate character change to which Lewis too often resorted. The reader is also faced with the dilemma in which he almost *wants* to read much of *Kingsblood Royal* as escape fiction; for, if he does not, he is then forced to accept as true the incredible humiliation imposed upon the Negro, all the more painful to the novel's hero because he was formerly white. In this way Lewis also ingeniously fulfills a common fantasy by allowing a person with whom the reader can identify, born and bred white, to see life from the underside. As one who is both white and Negro and can thus know both worlds, Neil Kingsblood is empowered to know what no white man can know.

The theme of *Kingsblood Royal* also involves a curious reversal, again nearly overreaching itself. As the book progresses, we realize that there are few decent white people in the community although decent Negroes are present in abundance. Consequently, the novel's implicit thesis, one typical of Lewis in the heat of argument or when attacking a dragon: Not only are Negroes as good as whites, they are better. When Negroes are stupid, vicious, or depraved, their actions may be excused by the bitterness and deprivation of their status and environment. When whites are sadistic or moronic, they have no excuse.

Kingsblood Royal reminds us how superbly Lewis was equipped as a propagandist. He could conjure scenes running the gamut from subtle social insult to stark physical violence. He had not only the gift of stereotyping his opponents for easy recognition and classification, but also the ability to give them such hateful things to say and do that one forgets they are straw men. He could portray his own cause and heroes as partaking of just enough foolishness and weakness so that the conflict did not seem to be between saint and devil but between folks like us and the unmentionables on the other side. Further-more, *they* are the troublemakers, the aggressors; and he makes them unjust, unreasonable, and undemocratic. While these spe-cial gifts are on display in much of Lewis's work and while they were integral to his fame, only a few of his novels depend almost wholly on them: *Elmer Gantry, The Man Who Knew Coolidge, It Can't Happen Here,* and *Kingsblood Royal.* I have elsewhere referred to these novels as satires, but they might also more accurately be called *tracts.*

All possess the same common elements. All are heavily epi-sodic, virtually plotless: they describe no struggle or conflict but present instead a basic situation and a series of episodes which show that the good are succumbing to the bad. Characters and events are totally manipulated to support a thesis, and the events are usually arranged in a scale of gradually ascending horror. It would be unfair to say that these novels are wholly without suspense; however, the suspense is not that springing from the dynamic interplay of character and situation but that created by the experienced and resourceful *jongleur* who has a large bag of tricks and who keeps one waiting for the next trick. In none of these books is there true character development or much possibility for interpretation. Beyond Lewis's specialties, the parody and monologue, the style is not experimental or unpre-dictable, nor is there much symbolism or allegory other than the simplest verbal allegory, as in the last few lines of *Kings-blood Royal.* The policeman taking the Kingsbloods to the lock-up tells them, "Keep moving," and Vestal Kingsblood, now a spokesman for the struggle for racial equality, says, "We're moving."

Those who deride Lewis's accomplishments as an artist gen-erally charge that his characters are flat, that he lacks restraint and discrimination, that his thought is shallow, and that he is not original. We have commented at length on these matters elsewhere and we confess to their partial truth. But the critics also customarily fail to distinguish which Lewis they are re-proving: the satirist, the realist, or the romancer. Since Lewis was all of these and yet wholly none of them, the charges must be applied carefully to individual books before they make much sense. Judged as a realist—by the criteria of fidelity to experience, credibility of motive, complexity of character—Lewis achieved much in *Dodsworth,* and moderate success in *Cass*

Timberlane. Considered as a satirist—by characters who are recognizable types illustrating particular modes of behavior, by a grasp of that detail conveying a sharp sense of milieu, and by incidents emphasizing the distance between ideals and deeds or between the society's self-image and its actual appearance— Lewis reached the heights in *Main Street* and *Babbitt*. Viewed as a moralist—one concerned with eternal verities and fundamental passions—Lewis's attainment in *Arrowsmith* is not to be forgotten.

While Lewis could be called *immature* as both man and writer, immaturity launches satire. The immature reaction is immediate, intense, rebellious; the mature man is deliberate, resigned, accepting. The loudness and directness of Lewis's method came from the fervor of his convictions, his personality, his training as a journalist and popular writer, and his preclusion that the American audience would hearken more quickly to a shout than to a whisper. Consequently, he employed those devices closest to his gifts, his nature, and his intentions: caricature, mimicry, denunciation.[7]

In short, to judge *Kingsblood Royal* as a realistic novel or perhaps even as a "satire," in the traditional literary vein, is to judge it wrongly. This is Lewis the fanatic, the crusader, the inquisitor; and the extremities in his novel are precisely those which attend crusades and inquisitions. If *Kingsblood Royal* falls short as a work of art—and we do not defend it as a work of art—it succeeds as a public service. It is a tract, a broadside, made all the more effective because Lewis has glossed it with an entertaining and quickly paced narrative which will not withstand acute analysis but is just credible enough to keep the mass audience involved and uncomfortable—aching in conscience yet inextricably committed to find out what happens next. The series of episodes which replaces plot in Lewis's tracts all center in the novel upon the Negro's debasement by his countrymen, and it builds to two crises in the novel's final fifty pages: (1) the attempt to force the Kingsbloods out of their home in a "white" neighborhood; (2) the fight against an organized racist movement which purposes to drive all Negroes out of the North. At last, the accumulated tension is released in a melodramatic but satisfactorily purgative scene of violence at the novel's conclusion, when a mob assaults the Kingsblood house and is repulsed by gunfire. There have been so many insults levied upon the hero and so much iniquitous racist talk that the reader has felt a building urge to break someone's jaw. Now he has found a means of release. Furthermore, the ending implies what Lewis thinks is the solution: to meet direct action with direct action. It may not win, but the novel suggests that it feels mighty good just to be hitting back.

Any tract, however compelling, must lose force as soon as the conditions which engendered it are past—or passing. Already *Kingsblood Royal* seems a little dated, but not because racism is a closed issue; it was never more alive. However, Lewis did not predict in *Kingsblood Royal* that the Negro would soon make himself heard or that the rise of the African nations and the pressures of international politics would coincide to add such great volume to the protest of the American Negro. He no longer waits and scrapes; he now leads the offensive and it is the white who retreats. All this has happened in less than a generation after the publication of Lewis's novel.

But if Lewis could not foresee current events, he must be allowed some credit for helping them to happen. Appearing in 1947, immediately after the war's end and with the country's conscience still sensitive to injustice and still committed to democracy for all, Lewis's book was shrewdly timed. Again and again it capitalizes on the climate of opinion, sermonizing and demonstrating that the Negro good enough to fight for freedom in war is not good enough to share it in peace. Moreover, in directing his attention at the Northern Negro, Lewis gained the advantage of surprise and the opportunity to strike once more at his oldest enemy, complacency. In *Main Street* Lewis had written a passage in which he equated the rebellious heroine with the suppressed black and yellow races, prophesying that their time was coming. *Kingsblood Royal* is the consummation of that prophecy. The rebellion *has* come to Main Street.

Unfortunately, *Cass Timberlane* and *Kingsblood Royal* contained the last of Lewis's vitality; they are the only substantial books of his final decade. The three others which Lewis published have their moments of quality, but they are only moments. On the whole, these novels manifest· Lewis's exhaustion as an artist. We will heed the wisdom of Maxwell Geismar's advice that we must not pay so much attention to Lewis's bad books that we forget the good ones, although for the sake of thoroughness, mention must be made of them.[8]

III *Gideon Planish*

Gideon Planish (1943), Lewis's first novel of the period, declares his decision to return to satire after the disasters of *The Prodigal Parents* and *Bethel Merriday;* the attempt is only half successful. In its story Lewis records the career of the weak but likable Gideon Planish, who begins as a college teacher; marries a pretty, charming, and heartlessly ambitious girl, Peony; gradually drifts into the field of professional philanthropy and organized charity; and then is finally forced by his wife to remain as a public relations executive for the millionaire advertising magnate and publisher Colonel Marduc, although Gideon yearns to return to the serenity and dignity of academic life.

Throughout *Gideon Planish* Lewis makes satirical forays against a variety of antagonists and gives plentiful exercise to his stock satiric techniques, but at the same time the novel exhibits the affirmative Lewis in its solid defense of the little man and the middle class, and in its emphatic assertion that the best citizenship and worthiest philanthropic activity consists of quietly cultivating one's own garden. The hero is a composite of familiar Lewis types, borrowing most heavily from Babbitt and Gantry, although without the memorability of either. The narrative line is also standard: it traces the hero's life from childhood ambition to middle-age weariness; it shows him getting older but, unlike Lewis's admirable heroes, no wiser. Plot consists largely of the hero's various experiences in moving from job to job, ever upward materially, ever downward spiritually.

The novel's central conflict is the classic conflict of Lewis's work, a man's inner wishes pitted against society's demands, with society winning. There is also present the sentimentality which invariably accompanies and is symptomatic of Lewis's failures. However, the pathos of the book's ending is something relatively new to Lewis. Some of his best novels do conclude with the hero's defeat or with evil triumphant, but they always involve contrast, defiance, juxtaposition. No other has the wavering pathos of *Gideon Planish*. Herein we discern what is wrong with this novel, as well as the last two of Lewis's career: it is tired. Above all, it lacks conviction; and if there is one sensation which the satirist must communicate to the reader, it is conviction. Consequently, while *Gideon Planish* is not Lewis at his worst, it is the worst of the genre in which he worked best.

The part of Lewis which remained a youthful iconoclast, although in 1943 there seemed to be little need for iconoclasm, is revealed in *Gideon Planish*. The novel aims at deflating idealism, charity, and fund-raising at the very time when the war both spurred and justified the proliferation of philanthropic organizations. At first glance it appears that Lewis had chosen his target at random; yet he had a strategy. Such organizations, public speaking and speakers, committees, titles, impressive-sounding names, causes, lobbies, all symbolized to Lewis one of America's cardinal faults—its proclivity for "bunk."[9] As a public figure himself and through his marriage to Dorothy Thompson, an even more public figure in those years, Lewis had gotten to know this phase of American life well. Indeed, some reviewers recognized Miss Thompson herself in Lewis's acidulous portrait of Winifred Homeward, "The Talking Woman." As his stature had declined in the 1930's, hers had risen; it was predictable that Lewis's ego would suffer damage and later seek reprisal, although to be fair, the portrait is far from the ugliest in Lewis's gallery. *Gideon Planish* also decrees Lewis's scorn for the kind of life which must be led by the oracle and celebrity, who is forever surrounded by intellectuals and experts and who is forever involved in causes and movements. His feelings are summarized in the closing pages of the novel when he writes, in a nakedly expository passage, "God save poor America . . . from all the zealous and the professionally idealistic, from eloquent women and generous sponsors and administrative ex-preachers and natural-born Leaders and Napoleonic newspaper executives and all the people who like to make long telephone calls and write inspirational memoranda."[10]

Two other phases of *Gideon Planish* demand comment; in each Lewis has achieved something of value. First, Lewis demonstrates in the characters of Peony and Winifred that the female—and this is a prelude to *Cass Timberlane*—is deadlier than the male; she is smarter, tougher, and more efficient at getting her way. Especially terrifying is her ability to use the male's strength for her own ends and, if necessary, against him. Second, *Gideon Planish* once more employs the predicament of the man who tries to make a living but finds his energies constantly being directed toward the acquisition of *things*, not toward living. His activity becomes less and less willed, more and more compelled; yet at the same time he despises what his money buys. In this Lewis has accurately delineated a facet of modern America: its installment-plan economy and the average man's sensing that he will never break out; that he will always be the slave of his own or his family's lust for gadgets disguised as necessities. Here Lewis nearly repeats his great triumph, the ability to chronicle the quiet desperation of middle-class life in the twentieth century.

IV *The God-Seeker; World So Wide*

Although *Gideon Planish* is not without its merits, Lewis's last two novels, *The God-Seeker* (1949) and *World So Wide* (1951), have much too little to redeem them. In Lewis's penultimate novel he moves his hero, Aaron Gadd, from New England to Minnesota. Called by the desire to Christianize the Indians, a series of disillusioning experiences in his missionary work lead Aaron to return happily to his original trade, building houses. Although the narrative is not without interest and although Lewis's description of frontier Minnesota of the 1840's is written with verve and consistent tonality—indicating Lewis's thorough research and deep affection for his native state—the novel, tested by any respectable standard of quality, is an ill-contrived piece of work.[11]

The God-Seeker is ruined by melodramatic incidents (Huldah's sudden appearance to save Aaron and Selene from the blizzard; this is as incredible as anything in Cooper); by extraneous characters (Davy Queenslace and Aaron's brother) who are brought in momentarily to give the story variety and then quickly dispatched; by dependence on spurious conflicts (Aaron's religious zeal, which from the beginning is patently self-deception); and by mawkish romance. Furthermore, the novel's satire plays repeatedly upon the same old topics: the mockery of evangelism, the ridicule of reformers, the vitriolic comments on hypocrisy, the assault on prejudice. While *The God-Seeker* is the only book in which Lewis used historical material extensively, this innovation does not save it. Instead, the novel shows Lewis retreating more and more rapidly from a society he had ceased to understand except in its more overt problems, such as the race issue in *Kingsblood Royal;* consequently, he turns back to the incontrovertible past.[12] One could almost have predicted that in his next novel, *World So Wide,* Lewis would leave America entirely.

Mark Schorer has demonstrated several ways in which *World So Wide,* Lewis's last book (published posthumously), resembles his first, *Our Mr. Wrenn.* Both are tales of Innocence abroad; both heroes find themselves suddenly freed from routine and go to Europe; both are lonely; both encounter and fall in love with a sophisticated American girl whom they finally reject for a homespun type; both possess a yearning for deeper experience and are kept from it by their loneliness and naiveté.[13] However, what was suitable for popular fiction in 1914 might no longer have been adequate in 1951; in *World So Wide* Lewis seems to have grasped that lesson imperfectly.

To pursue the matter a bit further, about half of the book is a quiet, rather engaging story, with some good scenes and good talk about Americans abroad, conveying much of Lewis's fondness for Italy, Florence, and the leisurely movement of European life. Then, as if Lewis didn't know what to do with it, the novel swiftly degenerates into a soap-opera love tale and shoddy satire about Babbitt-types and hobohemians who have come overseas to exploit and commercialize European culture. Although there is some value in Lewis's message, much of it is delivered in dated idiom and by itinerant characters who appear in the novel only to relieve themselves of a few by-now hackneyed opinions on what's wrong with America and Americans.

World So Wide aspires to represent itself as an international novel, but it does not succeed. Aside from brief glimpses at an innkeeper or doctor, we meet no Europeans. We meet only *expatriate* Americans (yes, including Sam Dodsworth), and these are given less space than the new, loud Americans who have come overseas to exploit Europe, not learn from it. What seems to be the subject in the first third of the book, the travel to Europe of an admirable American, a younger Dodsworth, in order to find himself, becomes submerged by tired romance and tedious denunciation. The only Europe which Lewis presents with any emphasis or clarity is that inhabited by American frauds, so that when the hero must choose between two girls, he has no real choice between those typifying different ways of life but only between two kinds of American girls, the true and the false, the earthy and the pretentious.

At the novel's end, with the hero, Hayden, and his new wife, Roxanna, en route to the Orient via the Near East (a lifelong Lewis ambition) and ultimately home to America, Lewis has come full circle; he is back to *Our Mr. Wrenn* and also to an affirmation of the elements of American life he had earlier rejected and some of which he has attacked in this very novel. Both Hayden and Roxanna know and confess that Europe has something precious to offer them, something better than American life can give, yet both are willing to return home with a sort of concession that perhaps they have come to Europe too late in their lives to really partake of it and be transformed by it. It is an interesting but unsatisfying position, one which reveals the unsettled state of Lewis's mind but also leaves the reader midway between poles—pulled by each and able to attach himself to neither. So ended Lewis's career, in ambivalence, as it began. We would have wished for a better and more resolute novel to conclude it.

V *The Significance of Sinclair Lewis*

This account—written by Professor Perry Miller, who came to know Lewis well in the last year of the writer's life—is of great pertinence both to his last novel and to the entire body of his work: "Over and over again, after he had mailed the manuscript of this last book, when he would try to enjoy Italian scenery or the Swiss Alps, he would come back, with the reiteration of obsession, to asserting that he had written twenty-three novels about America, that nobody could ask more of him, that he had done his duty by his country. 'I love America,' he would shout into the unoffending European atmosphere; 'I love it, but I don't like it.' "[14] Lewis was, indeed, a man divided in his loyalties, both to his homeland and to himself as a writer. His was not a transcendent talent; and, when we consider how the conditions of American life tend to stifle or corrupt artistic talent, Lewis perhaps did well to travel as far as he did.

The passage of time and a vital change in literary taste have also conspired to make Lewis seem worse than he is. He was never a very sophisticated novelist; yet we judge him, as we must judge the artist, by prevailing standards of criticism. As it happens, that criticism is itself highly sophisticated, more so than the work of Sinclair Lewis and more so than the work of many of the very novelists, poets, and playwrights to which it applies. Lewis's aims were simple: he told a story, he recorded a fact, he exposed an evil; or, most frequently, he did all three at once. He was too rarely a *novelist,* in the fullest sense. The novelist seeks to exhibit men and women and to search for a common emotion or basis of understanding. The satirist, on the other hand, pursues and scourges a common failing in men and women. His characters are most effective when they are "types of their failures."[15] When the writer tries to be novelist and satirist simultaneously, or, in Lewis's case, novelist and romancer, he risks failure in either or both attempts. Sympathy is almost always the result of the novelist's search to understand, to find the source of character; the satirist's purpose is to deride; and the romancer's intent is to evade or compensate. Since derision and sympathy are thought to be incompatible, we have one measure of Lewis's achievement in the frequency with which he succeeded in combining them, from *Main Street* to *Dodsworth* and occasionally thereafter.

Several years ago one astute critic took the position that Lewis would survive because he had re-created in the twentieth century an earlier literary form with a long tradition of its own, the Theophrastian Character.[16] The "Character" writer differs from the novelist in two special ways: (1) he deliberately ignores all qualities which would distinguish *an individual;* (2) he selects, invents, and borrows from a large number of individuals only those qualities or mannerisms or attitudes which express a particular type or trait (The Flatterer, The Braggart, The Pretender to Learning); he then makes these into a composite character who becomes the perfect and typical representative of the desired trait. This is what Lewis did, the critic concludes, although in his very accomplishment as a "Character" writer Lewis removes himself from serious consideration as a novelist. The novel is an imitation of life, eliciting a direct response from the reader and permitting the reader's projection into it, while the creator of "Character" deliberately kept the reader and the work apart in order to evoke an intellectual response, an evaluation.

This is in part a satisfying approach, although conceptually its author merely plays a variation on a cliché of Lewis criticism (the view of Lewis's characters as composites). What he and the others tend to overlook is crucial to Lewis's books. The characters who are types and not individuals are such because their society—as Lewis sees it—does not allow them development as individuals. America, the land of personal liberty and individual freedom, produces types: this is Lewis's recurrent thesis. His characters yearn to be individuals and some of them make progress toward it, but their environment and fellows enslave them. In Lewis's books the reader gets a far stronger impression of the milieu in which things happen than he does, with a few exceptions, of the people to whom they happen. To put it plainly, the "Character" writer disregards environment, while Lewis, in his best books, is concerned precisely with environment; if not in *how* the character became the way he is, at least—as in *Babbitt*—in *what* keeps him that way.

Lewis was always conscious of environment and believed that in capturing it a writer would also capture life. We see this clearly in a foreword which Lewis wrote in 1940 to David Cohn's *The Good Old Days*, subtitled "A History of American Morals and Manners as seen through the Sears, Roebuck Catalogs 1905 to the Present." These are Lewis's words:

> The superior survival value of novelists to historians may not be altogether in the eloquence with which fictioneers communicate Mildred's agonies over the virile high diving of Peter, or the glories of Kansas City by moonlight. It may be that the permanence of such institutions as Dickens is due to their recording not the dreary magnificences of coronations and battles, but instead the dear diminutive excitements in commonplace characters which make us identify ourselves with them: what they eat, with what weapons, exactly, they kill one another, and the precise wording of the acid pomposity with which a duke or a dustman complains of his breakfast porridge. Mankind is always more interested in living than in Lives.
>
> .   .   .   .
>
> By your eyebrow pencils, your encyclopedias, and your alarm clocks shall ye be known. The most scrupulous statistics on the increasing acreage of alfalfa and soy beans, the most elevated dissertations on our tendency to chronic philanthropy, could not make us understand that cranky, hysterical, brave, mass-timorous, hard-minded, imaginative Chosen Race, the Americans, half so competently as Mr. Cohn's parade of the wares that we have been buying and paying for and actually lugging into our homes and barns and offices, these past fifty years.[17]

This passage describes Lewis's angle of vision, his way of sighting his material as satirist and realist. It implies his strengths and his weaknesses. And it can lead us to understand why Lewis is no longer in critical favor. He wrote the novel as *history;* we prefer the novel as *poetry,* although there are indications that this, too, is changing.

Yet in the limitations of Lewis's view, with its focus on surface and its belief that the exterior communicates the interior, we can see the distance between Lewis and Tolstoy, or Lewis and Flaubert. He has grasped a portion of the truth and has taken it for the whole truth. They knew what he did not, and they had the artistic resources to say what he could not. We also cannot but perceive how much cleaner and straighter the line of his career would have been drawn without such smudges and waverings as *The Innocents* and *Free Air;* without *Mantrap, The Prodigal Parents, Bethel Merriday;* without *The God-Seeker* and *World So Wide.* These romances were, unfortunately, as much an expression of Lewis as *Main Street, Babbitt, Arrowsmith,* and *Dodsworth;* we can only recognize them for what they are and forgive them.

The forgiveness is especially difficult, if not impossible, because they are not glorious failures deriving from too daring leaps of the imagination or too grand an ambition; they are failures caused by a hunger for profit; an inability to wait, observe, and reflect; and by a crucial weakness in Lewis's sensibility. His childhood reading and dreaming, his inner conflicts and contradictions, his apprenticeship as a writer of potboiling fiction, his lifelong blindness to the consequences of his own personal and literary conduct, his possession of the satirist's hard eye and the romancer's soft heart—all these made him what he was and kept him from becoming more than what he was. Despite his errors and omissions, we will remember him nevertheless. An acquaintance of Lewis once observed that Lewis's fearlessness and honesty in exposing humbug and hypocrisy led others not brave enough to speak the truth to call Lewis's work satire.[18] It is a provocative point.

Indeed, at his best he fulfilled a basic American need for a bold and passionate writer who would assist us toward self-recognition. The portrait of *Babbitt* still hangs in our national consciousness, as a family will hang a painting of "Father" in the drawing room. It may be "unrealistic," but it is the only picture of "Father" ever imaginable. In 1909 Herbert Croly had called for new critics of American society. He wrote this prophetic passage, which appears close to the end of *The Promise of American Life*:

> The function of the critic hereafter will consist in part of carrying on incessant and relentless warfare on the prevailing American intellectual insincerity. . . . He must stab away at the gelatinous mass of popular indifference, sentimentality, and complacency, even though he seems quite unable to penetrate to the quick and draw blood. . . . In all serious warfare, people have to be really wounded for some good purpose; and in this particular fight there may be a chance that not only a good cause, but the very victim of the blow, may possibly be benefited by its delivery. The stabbing of a mass of public opinion into some consciousness of its own torpor, particularly when many particles of the mass are actively torpid because of admirable patriotic intentions,—that is a job which needs sharp weapons, intense personal devotion, and a positive indifference to consequences.[19]

We have seen no better statement of the significance and achievement of Sinclair Lewis; he fulfilled the need of a "new critic" for he indeed stabbed away at the "gelatinous mass of popular indifference." His powers to agitate the reader have not been equalled in America except by Paine, Twain, and Mencken.

If Lewis's foes permit him nothing else, they must at least concede his historical importance, an importance fixed by the Nobel Prize. *Main Street, Babbitt,* and Lewis's other serious books of the 1920's surpassed in circulation the *American Mercury,* published by H. L. Mencken, Lewis's closest rival as the country's most popular and influential iconoclast.[20] In Lewis's books the readers got a sense of *discovery;* and later they were to see verified in their own experience and in scholarly researches what Lewis had told them. Whitman had called for a "literatus" out of the West, a poet-prophet who would provide the nation a literature worthy of its democratic spirit. Instead, we were given Sinclair Lewis, a realistic idealist and romantic satirist, most appropriately described by Horace's phrase as a *genus irritabile*, a fighter. With Anderson, Lewis opened the way for the kind of realism which has prevailed in much American fiction of the twentieth century: the concentration on the domestic scene, on common life, on familiar types, on what might be called middle tragedy. In his art he hit a perfect average; had he been more profound he would have been less successful; had he been less skillful, he would not have been so influential.

Although his treatment of American life was less powerful than Dreiser's and less subtle and sensitive than Fitzgerald's, Lewis felt no less than they the basic urge of his generation to locate and transmit the truth about the national experience, and he was listened to by his generation more than they. He gave us his own version of the fundamental polarity in American life, that between idealism, the future good life, and materialism, the practical and the now.[21] Beginning with *Main Street* he showed us that when these become combined, as they inevitably do in the American dream, they become mutually destructive. Materialism destroys beauty; money becomes the maker not the made. Nor have Lewis's successes gone unsung. Bernard de Voto, who in 1944 attacked Lewis for betraying America by his fierce criticism of it, confessed at the same time that Lewis was the best novelist of his decade. Harlan Hatcher has called Lewis's work in the 1920's the most stimulating in American literature, stating, "By the sheer energy of his mind he helped the modern American novel into maturity and recognition," while the *Literary History of the United States* says of Lewis, "He was the most powerful novelist of the decade when American fiction in general matured in scope and in art."[22]

My position is a reasonable one and easily summarized. It is simply that when we ignore Sinclair Lewis, as the new generation of critics has done and is doing, we forget Lewis's accomplishment in his great decade. This is an omission which does grave injustice both to him and to ourselves.

Notes and References

Chapter One

1. I have written in greater detail about Sinclair Lewis's youth in "Sinclair Lewis's Minnesota Boyhood," *Minnesota History*, XXXIV (Autumn, 1954), 85-89. For many years the major source for biographical information on Lewis was Carl Van Doren, *Sinclair Lewis: A Biographical Sketch* (New York, 1933), which also contains a bibliography by Harvey Taylor. However, Mark Schorer's comprehensive biography, *Sinclair Lewis: An American Life*, the result of several years of research, will undoubtedly become the standard work on Lewis's life. Although Schorer's book will have appeared (it was scheduled for release by McGraw-Hill in October, 1961) before the present study, *Sinclair Lewis* was completed before Schorer's work was announced for publication.

2. The source for the grass-eating anecdote is *Time* (April 11, 1960), 48. The same anecdote is repeated by Dorothy Thompson in "The Boy and Man from Sauk Centre," *Atlantic*, CCVI (Nov., 1960), 39-48, which is an indispensable general reference. The sources for the other quoted statements are, in order of their appearance, Betty Stevens, "A Village Radical Goes Home," *Venture*, II (Summer, 1956), 19; and Cyril Clemens, "Impressions of Sinclair Lewis, with Some Letters," *Hobbies*, LVI (April, 1951), 138.

3. Clifton Fadiman, "Party of One," *Holiday*, XIII (March, 1953), 6; and Christian Gauss, "Sinclair Lewis vs. His Education," *Saturday Evening Post*, CCIV (Dec. 26, 1931), 20-21, 54-56. Another important source which discusses the duality in Lewis's work is Leo and Miriam Gurko, "The Two Main Streets of Sinclair Lewis," *College English*, IV (Feb., 1943), 288-92.

4. I have a letter from Dr. Claude Lewis, dated Sept. 30, 1954, which points out two errors in my *Minnesota History* article and which states emphatically that Dr. Lewis made no attempt to influence his sons to study medicine. As regards the first matter, I had, unforgivably, written Lewis's father's name as Emmet rather than Edwin, and that Lewis was named after a touring actor, rather than, in reality, after a friend of his father. Both errors came from my uncritical reliance upon an article by Bennet Cerf, "Tradewinds," *Saturday Review of Literature*, XXVIII (Nov. 3, 1945), 20. In regard to the second matter, whatever Dr. Lewis did or did not do, his youngest son always felt that he had grievously disappointed his

father, and he confessed this feeling on dozens of occasions throughout his lifetime.

5. Thompson, 42; Allen Austin, "An Interview with Sinclair Lewis," *University of Kansas City Review*, XXIV (1958), 204.

6. Ramon Guthrie, "The Labor Novel Sinclair Lewis Never Wrote," *New York Herald Tribune Book Review*, XXVIII (Feb. 10, 1952), 1, 6.

7. Grace Hegger Lewis, *With Love from Gracie* (New York, 1956), pp. 89-90. Also see the same author's *Half a Loaf* (New York, 1931), an autobiographical novel written in reply to *Dodsworth*. *With Love from Gracie* repeats much of the material in the earlier book.

8. I have treated Lewis's college years in "The Education of a Rebel: Sinclair Lewis at Yale," *New England Quarterly*, XXVIII (Sept., 1955), 372-82.

9. Leonard Bacon, "Yale, '09," *Saturday Review of Literature*, XIX (Feb. 4, 1939), 13; Chauncy Brewster Tinker, "Sinclair Lewis, a Few Reminiscences," *Yale Alumni Magazine* (June, 1952), 10. Cf. also Harrison Smith, "Sinclair Lewis: Remembrance of the Past," *Saturday Review of Literature*, XXXIV (Jan. 27, 1951), 7-9, 36-38.

10. Quoted in Gauss, 54.

11. William Rose Benét, "The Earlier Lewis," *Saturday Review of Literature*, X (Jan. 20, 1934), 421.

12. This editorial from the Waterloo, Iowa, *Daily Courier* (Aug. 3, 1908), is preserved in the Yale Collection, which also contains Lewis's essays for his literature class.

13. Benét, 421. Cf. also Franklin Walker, "Jack London's Use of Sinclair Lewis Plots," *Huntingdon Library Quarterly*, XVII (1953), 59-74.

14. The Socialist Party membership card, showing that Lewis paid dues from Jan. 16, 1911, to April, 1912, is preserved in the Yale Collection. "The Passing of Capitalism" has been reprinted in Harry E. Maule and Melville H. Cane, eds., *The Man from Main Street: A Sinclair Lewis Reader* (New York, 1953), pp. 327-39. The quotation is from page 336.

15. Tinker, 10; Benét, 421.

16. For accounts of Lewis's personality see Thompson and *With Love from Gracie, passim*. The statement by Michael Lewis is quoted in Thompson, 40. Two other valuable sources are Dale Warren, "Notes on a Genius: Sinclair Lewis at His Best," *Harper's*, CCVIII (Jan., 1954), 61-69; and chapters 33-37 of Thomas Wolfe's *You Can't Go Home Again*, in which Lewis appears as "Lloyd McHarg."

17. Quoted in Jack Alexander, "Rover Girl in Europe," *Saturday Evening Post*, CCXII (May 25, 1940), 116.

18. Fadiman, 8. Cf. also C. F. Crandall. "When Sinclair Lewis

Wrote a Sonnet in 3 Minutes, 50 Seconds," *New York Herald Tribune Books*, XXVIII (Sept. 2, 1951), 4.

19. George Jean Nathan, *The Intimate Notebooks of George Jean Nathan* (New York, 1932), pp. 9-21.

20. W. E. Woodward, "Sinclair Lewis Gets the Job," *Saturday Review of Literature*, XXX (Nov. 1, 1947), 11; Thompson, 46; Frederick F. Manfred, "Sinclair Lewis: A Portrait," *American Scholar*, XXIII (1954), 165. The phrase "psychic trauma" appears in *With Love from Gracie*, p. 45. Mark Schorer, "Two Houses, Two Ways," *New World Writing: 4* (New York, 1953), p. 144, also testifies that Lewis's appearance added to his loneliness in later years by making him avoid people.

21. Dorothy Thompson, "Sinclair Lewis: A Postscript," *Atlantic*, CLXXXVII (June, 1951), 73. Lewis's loneliness is also graphically described in Alexander Manson's, "The Last Days of Sinclair Lewis," *Saturday Evening Post*, CCXXIII (March 31, 1951), 27, 110-12.

22. Constance Rourke, *American Humor* (New York, 1931), pp. 283-86.

23. Lewis's admiration for Garland has been cited by Clemens, 139. Benét, 421, records that in his early stories Lewis imitated Edith Wharton. Also see Kenneth S. Rothwell, "From Society to Babbittry: Lewis' Debt to Edith Wharton," *Journal of the Central Mississippi Valley American Studies Association*, I (Spring, 1960), 32-36.

24. E. M. Forster, "A Cameraman," *Life and Letters*, II (May, 1929), 336-43; reprinted in *Abinger Harvest* (New York, 1936), pp. 129-36.

25. For some of the suggestions regarding the similarity of Lewis and Marquand, I am indebted to J. Donald Adams, "Speaking of Books," *New York Times Book Review* (July 31, 1960), 2.

26. Perry Miller, "The Incorruptible Sinclair Lewis," *Atlantic*, CLXXXVII (April, 1951), 32.

27. James Branch Cabell, *Some of Us, an Essay in Epitaphs* (New York, 1930), pp. 61-73.

28. Most of my material on Dickens, although *not* the comparison of Lewis and Dickens, has been drawn from Monroe Engel, *The Maturity of Dickens* (Harvard University Press, 1959). The quotation appears on page 72.

Chapter Two

1. Lewis's first novel was actually a boy's adventure book called *Hike and the Aeroplane*, published by the Frederick A. Stokes Company in 1912. I have omitted it from the discussion. I have used, except as noted, the editions of Lewis's novels cited in the "Selected Bibliography" of this book.

2. James D. Hart, *The Popular Book* (Oxford University Press, 1950), 223.

3. The best references for Lewis's early novels are John T. Flanagan, "A Long Way to Gopher Prairie: Sinclair Lewis's Apprenticeship," *Southwest Review*, XXXII (Autumn, 1942), 403-13; and Maxwell Geismar, *The Last of the Provincials* (Boston, 1947), 73-83. My discussion covers some of the same ground but is not dependent on theirs except where specifically noted.

4. I am indebted to Harrison Smith's introduction to *Our Mr. Wrenn* (New York, 1951), for some of this material.

5. Quoted in George Leroy White, Jr., *Scandinavian Themes in American Fiction* (University of Pennsylvania Press, 1937), p. 137. White's book contains an extensive account of Lewis's use of characters of Scandinavian origin.

6. Van Doren, *Sinclair Lewis: A Biographical Sketch,* is the general source for the biographical parallels between Lewis and his early heroes. Flanagan, 407, has also noted the importance of travel in Lewis's novels.

7. Geismar, pp. 82-84.

8. *With Love from Gracie,* pp. 153 ff. *et passim.*

9. The quotations, in the order of appearance, are taken from *With Love from Gracie,* pp. 43, 73, 152. Cf. also *Half a Loaf* for details of the courtship.

10. Francis Hackett, "A Stenographer," *New Republic,* X (March 24, 1917), 234.

11. *With Love from Gracie,* p. 109.

12. Lewis expressed his indebtedness to Wells in his essay, "Our Friend, H. G.," reprinted in Maule and Cane, pp. 246-53. Although many critics have commented on the similarities between Wells and Lewis, my chief source here is Arthur B. Coleman, *The Genesis of Social Ideas in Sinclair Lewis* (unpublished doctoral dissertation, New York University, 1954).

13. Coleman, pp. 30-33.

14. *With Love from Gracie,* p. 74. Also see Lewis's letter to Carl Van Doren, reprinted in Maule and Cane, pp. 136-41.

15. The most complete treatment of Lewis's critical reception is William Couch, Jr., *The Emergence, Rise, and Decline of the Reputation of Sinclair Lewis* (unpublished doctoral dissertation, University of Chicago, 1954).

16. The correspondence between Lewis and the firm of Harcourt, Brace, has been published in *From Main Street to Stockholm: Letters of Sinclair Lewis 1919-1930,* edited by Harrison Smith (New York, 1952). The letters to which I refer appear on pp. 15, 18, and 35. I shall hereafter list this source as *Letters.*

Chapter Three

1. For information on the small town I have drawn chiefly upon Max Lerner, *America as a Civilization* (New York, 1957), pp. 148-55; and Lewis Atherton, *Main Street on the Middle Border* (Indiana University Press, 1954).

2. Meredith Nicholson, *The Valley of Democracy* (New York, 1918), pp. 8, 15.

3. Ludwig Lewisohn, *Expression in America* (New York, 1932), p. 502.

4. Sinclair Lewis, "Introduction to Main Street," reprinted in Maule and Cane, pp. 213-17. The quotation is taken from page 214.

5. See *With Love from Gracie*, pp. 88-98.

6. *Half a Loaf*, p. 119.

7. Quoted in Waldo Frank, *Salvos* (New York, 1924), p. 203.

8. Sinclair Lewis, *Main Street* (New York, 1920). A number of unfavorable portraits of small towns had appeared in earlier novels, notably *The Trail of the Hawk* and *Free Air*. Several of his short stories were also uncomplimentary. Cf. especially, "Detour—Roads Rough," *Every Week*, VI (March 30, 1918), 9-10.

9. *With Love from Gracie*, p. 149.

10. James Branch Cabell, *Straws and Prayer Books* (New York, 1924), pp. 50-51. Cabell also advised Lewis to permit Carol's affair with Eric Valborg to reach physical consummation. Lewis refused.

11. Geismar, p. 85.

12. Maule and Cane, p. 217.

13. Charles Breasted, "The 'Sauk-Centricities' of Sinclair Lewis," *Saturday Review of Literature*, XXXVII (Aug. 14, 1954), 8, 33. Yet Lewis had said in a 1920 letter intended for press release, "Carol Kennicott distinctly is not Sinclair Lewis" (*Letters*, p. 45). Such contradictions between public statement and private truth are common throughout Lewis's career.

14. Thompson, 43-44; *With Love from Gracie*, p. 94.

15. Maule and Cane, pp. 140-41.

16. The reception of *Main Street*, its place in the realistic tradition, and the reasons for its success have been widely discussed. I have used the treatments in Hart, pp. 224 ff.; Harlan Hatcher, *Creating the Modern American Novel* (New York, 1935), pp. 109-21; Ima H. Herron, *The Small Town in American Literature* (Duke University Press, 1939), pp. 377-90; and Fred Lewis Pattee, *The New American Literature* (New York, 1930), pp. 329-45.

17. Cobb is quoted in Heywood Broun, "Hewing to the Line," *Woman's Home Companion*, LVIII (Feb., 1931), 26. The other quotations appear in John C. Farrar, ed., *The Literary Spotlight*

(New York, 1924), p. 37; and Carl E. Roberts, *The Literary Renaissance in America* (London, 1923), p. 110.

18. George E. O'Dell, "The American Mind and Main Street," *Standard,* IX (July, 1922), 17-18.

19. Charles L. Hind, *Three Authors and I* (New York, 1922), p. 186.

20. Frank, pp. 203-12; and Ernest Brace, "Cock Robin and Co., Publishers," *Commonweal,* XIII (Dec. 10, 1930), 147-49, also contain excellent discussions of the significance of *Main Street.*

21. *Letters,* p. 59. The other quotations pertaining to Lewis's plan for *Babbitt* and his changed attitude toward magazine writing appear on pp. 36, 51-52. Lewis's prospectus for the novel is printed in Maule and Cane, pp. 21-29.

22. W. E. Woodward, "The World and Sauk Center," *New Yorker,* IX (Jan. 27, 1934), 25; William J. McNally, "Americans We Like: Mr. Babbitt, Meet Sinclair Lewis," *Nation,* CXXV (Sept. 21, 1927), 278-81.

23. Benét, 422.

24. Cf. "If I Were Boss," *Saturday Evening Post,* CLXXXVIII (Jan. 1, 8, 1916), 5 ff., 41 ff; "Honestly If Possible," *Saturday Evening Post,* CLXXXIX (Oct. 14, 1916), 28 ff.; and "For the Zelda Bunch," *McClure's,* XLIX (Oct., 1917), 27 ff., which deal with business competition, shady real-estate practices, and the ruinous effects of standardization on quality. In another story "A Matter of Business," *Harper's,* CXLII (March, 1921), 429 ff., the hero must make a choice between integrity and profit, and in a series of tales published in *Metropolitan* magazine, 1917-1919, Lewis portrayed an unscrupulous advertising and publicity man mockingly named "Lancelot Todd."

25. Coleman has analyzed the influence of Veblen and Mencken on *Babbitt.* My discussion, however, is based on independent investigation.

26. Randolph Bourne, *History of a Literary Radical: And Other Essays,* edited by Van Wyck Brooks (New York, 1920). Cf. especially pp. 107-27, 128-39. The quotations are taken from pp. 131, 132.

27. H. L. Mencken and George Jean Nathan, *The American Credo* (New York, 1920), p. 29. Cf. also pp. 38-43.

28. Frederick J. Hoffman, *The Twenties* (New York, 1955), p. 369.

29. Geismar, pp. 89-96; Lewisohn, p. 511.

30. Willard Thorp, *American Writing in the Twentieth Century* (Harvard University Press, 1960), pp. 120-21. •

31. The statement by Harding is quoted in Hart, p. 236. Cf. also Hoffman, p. 370. In a letter written in Dec., 1920 (*Letters,* p. 57),

Lewis stated that "Babbittry" would become a standard phrase within two years.

32. For the genesis of *Arrowsmith* see Lyon N. Richardson, "*Arrowsmith*: Genesis, Development, Versions," *American Literature*, XXVII (1955), 225-44; and Barbara Grace Spayd's introduction to the Harbrace Modern Classics edition of *Arrowsmith* (New York, 1945).

33. Quoted in Grant Overton, "The Salvation of Sinclair Lewis," *Bookman*, LXI (April, 1925), 184.

34. *Letters*, p. 90. Lewis was at this time thinking of the labor novel.

35. Sinclair Lewis, *Arrowsmith*, Harbrace Modern Classics, p. 3. The relationship of Arrowsmith to the pioneer tradition has been suggested by Lucy L. Hazard, *The Frontier in American Literature* (New York, 1927), pp. 283-85.

36. Cf. *With Love from Gracie*, and *Half a Loaf*, *passim*.

37. Martin Light, *A Study of Characterization in Sinclair Lewis's Fiction* (unpublished doctoral dissertation, University of Illinois, 1960), agrees that Gottlieb is one of Lewis's most successful character creations. Lewis Mumford, "The America of Sinclair Lewis," *Current History*, XXXIII (1931), 531, has written that Gottlieb is a recognizable portrait of Jacques Loeb, as has Upton Sinclair in *Money Writes!* (Long Beach, Calif., 1927), p. 127.

38. In a "Self-Portrait," written in 1927 (Maule and Cane, pp. 45-51) Lewis stated: "All his respect for learning, for integrity, for accuracy, and for the possibilities of human achievement are to be found . . . in his portrait of Professor Max Gottlieb, in *Arrowsmith*. Most of the fellow's capacity for loyalty to love and friendship has gone into Leora in that same novel."

39. David J. Dooley, *The Impact of Satire on Fiction* (unpublished doctoral dissertation, State University of Iowa, 1955), concurs that Lewis is at his best in *Arrowsmith* and discusses the problem of the scientist's responsibility. For a stimulating reappraisal of *Arrowsmith* see T. R. Fyvel, "Martin Arrowsmith and His Habitat," *New Republic*, CXXXIII (July 18, 1955), 16-18, which views it as a central novel in Lewis's career.

40. This is the title of V. L. Parrington's essay on Lewis in *Main Currents in American Thought* (New York, 1927), pp. 360-69.

41. "Be Brisk with Babbitt," *Nation*, CXIX (Oct. 2, 1924), 437. Other installments under the same title appeared in the Oct. 15 and Oct. 29 issues. Lewis's other campaign articles were, "I Return to America," *Nation*, CXVIII (June 4, 1924), 631-32; and "Main Street's Been Paved," *Nation*, CXIX (Sept. 10, 1924), 255-60. For information on the Progressive Movement I am indebted to Richard

Hofstadter, *The Age of Reform* (New York, Vintage Books, 1960), pp. 282-301.

42. These three essays were "An American Views the Huns," *Nation*, CXIX (July 1, 1924), 19-20; "Self-Conscious America," *American Mercury*, VI (Oct., 1925), 129-39; and "Can an Artist Live in America," *Nation*, CXXI (Dec. 9, 1925), 662-63.

43. *The Intimate Notebooks*, p. 16. The quotation from Lewis's letter appears in *Letters*, p. 188. For material relevant to Lewis's Canadian trip and the genesis of *Mantrap*, see Claude Lewis, *Treaty Trip* (University of Minnesota Press, 1959); and D. J. Greene, "With Sinclair Lewis in Darkest Saskatchewan," *Saskatchewan History*, VI (Spring, 1953), 47-52.

44. Lewis's letter rejecting the Pulitzer Prize is printed in *Letters*, p. 213.

45. For information on Lewis's activities in Kansas City, see Samuel Harkness, "Sinclair Lewis's Sunday School Class," *Christian Century*, LXIII (July 29, 1926), 938-39; McNally, 281; *Letters*, pp. 104, 206, 207, 216; and *With Love from Gracie*, p. 301.

46. Couch, pp. 125-26, points out some of the parallels between Lewis's characters, Billy Sunday, and Aimee Semple McPherson. James B. Moore, "The Sources of Elmer Gantry," *New Republic*, CXLVI (Aug. 8, 1960), 17-18, shows the similarities between Gantry, Stidger, and Straton. I have also examined in the Yale Collection Lewis's notebook of clippings about religion. Some critics have speculated that Lewis was indebted to Frederic's *The Damnation of Theron Ware* for some scenes in *Elmer Gantry*. While Lewis knew the earlier book (it is mentioned in both *The Trail of the Hawk* and *Main Street*), I find no substantial evidence that he used it in *Elmer Gantry*.

47. *With Love from Gracie*, p. 325. Mark Schorer, "Sinclair Lewis and the Method of Half-Truths," *Society and Self in the Novel* (Columbia University Press, 1956), pp. 132-34, has also commented on *Elmer Gantry's* sexuality. Schorer's treatment is both an excellent discussion of the novel and an invaluable general reference.

48. L. M. Birkhead, *Is Elmer Gantry True?* (Girard, Kansas, 1928), lists some ninety books and periodicals which Lewis used in the writing of *Elmer Gantry*, most of them books on homilectics, the work of the minister, histories and encyclopedias of religion, etc. The books mentioned in *Elmer Gantry* (New York, 1927), appear on pp. 121, 123, 246.

49. "Sinclair Lewis and the Method of Half-Truths," p. 128.

50. Mencken's influence on *Elmer Gantry* has been so frequently noted that I will not discuss it here. Lewis dedicated the book to him "With Profound Admiration."

51. For the reception of *Elmer Gantry* see Arthur B. Maurice, "The History of Their Books: Sinclair Lewis," *Bookman,* LXIX (March, 1929), 52; "Storm Over Elmer Gantry," *Literary Digest,* XCIII (April 16, 1927), 28-29; and "Tearing Up Dramatized Version of Elmer Gantry," *Literary Digest,* XCV (Nov. 19, 1927), 29.

52. Quoted in *With Love from Gracie,* p. 303. See also Lewis's letter on religion in Maule and Cane, pp. 41-42.

53. "Assails Church Censors," *New York Times,* LXXXVII (Dec. 17, 1937), 14.

54. Kazin, p. 223; Granville Hicks, "Sinclair Lewis and the Good Life," *English Journal,* XXV (April, 1936), 265-73. Breasted, p. 33, has written that Lewis's bitterness over the breakup of his marriage was partly responsible for the savagery of both *Elmer Gantry* and *The Man Who Knew Coolidge.*

55. Edmund Wilson, *A Literary Chronicle: 1920-1950* (New York, 1956), pp. 38-40, suggests a number of points of comparison between Lardner and Lewis, although he prefers Lardner.

56. Sinclair Lewis, *The Man Who Knew Coolidge* (New York, 1928), pp. 19-21.

57. James Branch Cabell, *As I Remember It* (New York, 1935), p. 169, concluded that even after the divorce each "was quite plainly still more than half in love with the other."

58. Yet Pelham Edgar, *The Art of the Novel* (New York, 1933), p. 299, concludes that Lewis is harder on America than James.

59. Geismar, pp. 112-15; Clifton Fadiman, *Party of One* (Cleveland, 1955), pp. 132-35.

60. Leslie A. Fiedler, *Love and Death in the American Novel,* (New York, 1960), p. xi.

61. For an extended discussion of these matters see my article "Sinclair Lewis and the Nobel Prize," *Western Humanities Review,* XIII (Spring, 1959), 163-71.

62. The phrase "new builder" is taken from the award speech by Erik Axel Karlfeldt, a full text of which was printed in *Saturday Review of Literature,* VII (Jan. 10, 1931), 524-25.

63. "The Nobel Prize for Literature," *Publishers' Weekly,* CXVIII (Nov. 8, 1930), 2197.

64. H. L. Binsse and J. J. Trounstine, "Europe Looks at Sinclair Lewis," *Bookman,* LXXII (Jan., 1931), 455. This article, thoroughly hostile to Lewis, also presents the thesis that the prize was an insult to America.

65. Anders Osterling, "The Literary Prize," in H. Schuck, *et al., Nobel: The Man and His Prize* (University of Oklahoma Press, 1950), pp. 123-24. Cf. also Carl Anderson, *The Swedish Acceptance of American Literature* (University of Pennsylvania Press, 1957),

pp. 45-63, which discusses Lewis's reputation in Sweden and states that Lewis, more than any other American writer, there elevated American literature to the status of a "world literature."

66. Quoted in Allen and Irene Cleaton, *Books and Battles* (Boston, 1937), p. 239. Warren Beck, "How Good Is Sinclair Lewis?" *College English,* IX (Jan., 1948), 174, has called the award to Lewis "outrageous."

67. Lewis's acceptance speech for the Nobel Prize has been reprinted in Maule and Cane, pp. 3-17, which is the source for my quotations from the speech.

Chapter Four

1. Cabell, *As I Remember It,* pp. 167-68. Also see *Letters,* pp. 269-301.

2. Stevens, 24; Austin, 200.

3. For more detail on Lewis's labor novel see my article "Sinclair Lewis's Unwritten Novel," *Philological Quarterly,* XXXVII (Oct., 1958), 400-9. Sources not previously cited which also contain valuable material on the labor novel and Lewis's career in the 1930's are Benjamin Stolberg, "Sinclair Lewis," *American Mercury,* LIII (Oct., 1941), 450-60; and Louis Adamic, *My America* (New York, 1938), pp. 96-104.

4. Maule and Cane, pp. 16-17.

5. Sinclair Lewis, *Ann Vickers* (New York, P. F. Collier, n.d.). The original edition was published by Doubleday, Doran, 1933.

6. There is perhaps some biographical parallel here. Lewis may have been alluding both to his first marriage with a woman he portrayed as a destructive inferior (Fran Dodsworth), and his second to an equal, since Dorothy Thompson was already prominent in her own right. Curiously, when the second marriage went awry, it did so for some of the very reasons Lewis offered in *Ann Vickers* as the basis for such a marriage. It should also be noted that a number of the heroine's experiences as an agitator for women's suffrage and as a social worker parallel those of Dorothy Thompson.

7. In his original conception of the novel Lewis intended to make Ora Weagle a co-hero, but then became fascinated with the hotel business and concentrated on it. Cf. Henry S. Canby, "Sinclair Lewis's Art of Work," *Saturday Review of Literature,* X (Feb. 10, 1934), 465.

8. In 1934 Lewis assisted Sidney Howard in dramatizing *Dodsworth* and in the same year wrote *Jayhawker* in collaboration with Lloyd Lewis. In 1936 he collaborated with John C. Moffitt in dramatizing *It Can't Happen Here* and in 1938 wrote a new version by himself. In the same year he wrote *Angela Is Twenty-Two,* which

deals with a romance between an aging man and a younger woman. In addition, Lewis acted in *It Can't Happen Here*, in *Angela Is Twenty-Two*, and in summer stock. He also directed two plays. Lewis, always lonely, enjoyed the youth and cameraderie of the theater. His theatrical activities, his book reviews for *Newsweek* (1937-38), and his frequent speaking engagements kept his name in the news during the same years that his books were receiving increasingly hostile and scanty critical attention. Lewis also taught courses in creative writing at the universities of Wisconsin and Minnesota in the early 1940's.

9. Of the thirteen stories in *Selected Short Stories*, five had been originally published in the *Saturday Evening Post;* three in *Cosmopolitan;* two in *Redbook;* one in the *Century;* one in *Pictorial Review;* and one in *Nation*. In date of publication the stories range from 1917 to 1931.

10. Lloyd Morris, "Sinclair Lewis—His Critics and the Public," *North American Review*, CCXLV (Summer, 1938), 381-90, is the best article on Lewis's career in the 1930's. For the sales figures of Lewis's books I am indebted to "Sinclair Lewis," *Publishers' Weekly*, CLIX (Jan. 27, 1951), 527.

11. F. I. Carpenter, *American Literature and the Dream* (New York, 1955), pp. 116-25, is pertinent to *Work of Art*.

12. An interesting explanation for Lewis's attitude in *The Prodigal Parents* has been advanced by Budd Schulberg, "Lewis: Big Wind from Sauk Centre," *Esquire*, LIV (Dec., 1960), 110-14. Schulberg states that an unhappy experience which Lewis had at Dartmouth, when he was badgered by some students after a lecture, caused him to turn against the younger generation in *The Prodigal Parents*. I find this a stimulating but questionable theory.

13. Cf. Lewis's "Mr. Lorimer and Me," *Nation*, CXXVII (July 25, 1928), 81. The quotation is taken from Lewis's "This Golden Half-Century," Maule and Cane, p. 263. Although it, too, is nostalgic, it is one of Lewis's firmer and more admirable statements of the decade.

14. Printed in Georges Schreiber, *Portraits and Self-Portraits*, (Boston, 1936), p. 61.

15. Lewis told Allen Austin (p. 200) that he had based *It Can't Happen Here* on the rise of Huey Long.

16. Quoted in Don Wharton, "Dorothy Thompson," *Scribners*, CI (May, 1937), 13. Compare pp. 94-95 of *It Can't Happen Here* with this passage. For other sources dealing with Dorothy Thompson's influence on *It Can't Happen Here*, see Smith, 37; Elmer Davis, "Ode to Liberty," *Saturday Review of Literature*, XII (Oct. 19, 1935), 5; and Alexander, 115.

17. Sinclair Lewis, *It Can't Happen Here* (New York, 1935), pp. 20-22.

18. John Middleton Murry, "The Hell It Can't," *Adelphi,* XI (March, 1936), 324.

19. Davis, 5.

20. Both the Beard and Curti comments are quoted in Couch, pp. 190-91.

21. Cf. Joseph Blotner, *The Political Novel* (New York, 1955).

22. Thompson, 42.

23. Betty Stevens, "A Village Radical: His Last American Home," *Venture,* II (Winter, 1957), 42.

Chapter Five

1. Frazier Hunt, *One American* (New York, 1938), pp. 252-53. Hunt is probably the original for the character Ross Ireland in *Dodsworth.*

2. Apropos of *Cass Timberlane,* these biographical parallels might be noted. Cass has been recently divorced from a woman who basks in public life; Lewis's marriage with Dorothy Thompson had ended in 1942. Cass falls in love with a younger woman who leaves him for a gayer and courtlier man closer to her age; Lewis had for a number of years been romantically interested in a younger woman, for whom he had written the play *Angela Is Twenty-Two.* She has been identified as Marcella Powers, of New York City. Cf. "Laureate of the Booboisie," *Time,* XLI (Oct. 8, 1945), 108. The Yale Collection also has a letter from F. P. Heffelfinger to Professor Norman Holmes Pearson, stating that Lewis was angry at the people of Duluth (Grand Republic) for not accepting Marcella Powers (Jinny) socially. For the suggestion of some of the similarities between *Cass Timberlane* and *Main Street,* I am indebted to "Sinclair Lewis: A Comparison," *Atlantic,* CLXXVII (Feb., 1946), 159-60. Other reviewers also noted resemblances.

3. Sinclair Lewis, *Cass Timberlane* (New York, 1945), p. 173.

4. Manfred's essay on Lewis is extremely valuable for an understanding of Lewis's mood in the 1940's. Lewis appears to have grown very sensitive and bitter about women, referring to them as "killers of talent," yet was still capable of great affection and tenderness toward them.

5. Stevens, "A Village Radical: His Last American Home," notes that in collecting material for *Kingsblood Royal* Lewis had access to the files of the NAACP.

6. Cf. Lewis's "A Note About Kingsblood Royal," in Maule and Cane, pp. 36-41.

7. Some of my material in this section is drawn from Leonard Feinberg, *Sinclair Lewis as a Satirist* (unpublished doctoral dissertation, University of Illinois, 1946), pp. 140-52.

8. Maxwell Geismar, "Sinclair Lewis: Forgotten Hero," *Saturday Review*, XLIII (June 25, 1960), 29-30.

9. Coleman, pp. 132-33; Maxwell Geismar, "Young Sinclair Lewis and Old Dos Passos," *American Mercury*, LVI (May, 1943), 624-28.

10. *Gideon Planish* (Cleveland, 1944), p. 426; originally published by Random House, New York, 1943. For an earlier Lewis story which works with some of the same materials as *Gideon Planish*, see "Proper Gander," *Saturday Evening Post*, CCVIII (July 13, 1935), 18-19 ff.

11. During the last several years of his life Lewis made a strong re-identification with his native state. He lived in several Minnesota cities, traveled in the state extensively, studied its history, and used Minnesota locales in three of his last five books. Cf. "Sinclair Lewis's Minnesota Diary," edited by Mark Schorer, *Esquire*, L (Oct., 1958), 160-62; and John T. Flanagan, "The Minnesota Backgrounds of Sinclair Lewis's Fiction," *Minnesota History*, XXXVII (March, 1960), 1-15.

12. Coleman, pp. 146-49, offers quite another interpretation. He sees *The God-Seeker* as a satire on American foreign policy.

13. Mark Schorer, "The World of Sinclair Lewis," *New Republic*, CXXVIII (April 6, 1953), 18.

14. Miller, 34.

15. I am here indebted to Dooley, p. 12.

16. C. C. Hollis, "Sinclair Lewis: Reviver of Character," in Harold C. Gardiner, ed., *Fifty Years of the American Novel* (New York, 1952), pp. 89-106.

17. David Cohn, *The Good Old Days*, with a Foreword by Sinclair Lewis (New York, 1940).

18. Cosmo Hamilton, *People Worth Talking About* (New York, 1933), 279.

19. Herbert Croly, *The Promise of American Life* (New York, 1909), p. 451.

20. Hart, p. 236.

21. In my evaluation of Lewis's place in the 1920's I have drawn from Henry Seidel Canby, *American Memoir* (Boston, 1947), pp. 306-9; Kazin, pp. 206-8, 219; and Arthur Mizener, "Scott Fitzgerald and the 1920's," *Minnesota Review*, I (Jan., 1961), 161-74.

22. Bernard de Voto, *The Literary Fallacy* (Boston, 1944), pp. 95-123; Hatcher, p. 126; H. S. Canby, in *Literary History of the United States* (New York, 1948), p. 1227.

Selected Bibliography

PRIMARY SOURCES

1. Books by Sinclair Lewis

   (These publications are listed chronologically.)

Hike and the Aeroplane. New York: Stokes, 1912. Written under the pseudonym "Tom Graham."

Our Mr. Wrenn. New York: Harper, 1914. Reprinted by Crowell, New York, 1951.

The Trail of the Hawk. New York: Harper, 1915.

The Job. New York: Harper, 1917.

The Innocents. New York: Harper, 1917.

Free Air. New York: Harcourt, Brace and Howe, 1919.

Main Street. New York: Harcourt, Brace and Howe, 1920. Also available in Harbrace Modern Classics.

Babbitt. New York: Harcourt, Brace, 1922. Also in Harbrace Modern Classics.

Arrowsmith. New York: Harcourt, Brace, 1925. Also in Harbrace Modern Classics.

Mantrap. New York: Harcourt, Brace, 1926.

Elmer Gantry. New York: Harcourt, Brace, 1927.

The Man Who Knew Coolidge. New York: Harcourt, Brace, 1928.

Dodsworth. New York: Harcourt, Brace, 1929. Also available in Modern Library edition.

Ann Vickers. Garden City: Doubleday, Doran, 1933.

Work of Art. Garden City: Doubleday, Doran, 1934.

It Can't Happen Here. Garden City: Doubleday, Doran, 1935.

The Prodigal Parents. Garden City: Doubleday, Doran, 1938.

Bethel Merriday. Garden City: Doubleday, Doran, 1940.

Gideon Planish. New York: Random House, 1943.

Cass Timberlane. New York: Random House, 1945.

Kingsblood Royal. New York: Random House, 1947.

The God-Seeker. New York: Random House, 1949.

World So Wide. New York: Random House, 1951.

2. Plays

Hobohemia. Unpublished typed manuscript, in Yale Collection. Written 1919.

Jayhawker. In collaboration with Lloyd Lewis. Garden City: Doubleday, Doran, 1935.

Selected Bibliography

It Can't Happen Here, A New Version. New York: Dramatists **Play** Service, 1938.
Angela Is Twenty-Two. Unpublished typed manuscript, in **Yale** Collection. Written *circa* 1938.

3. Collections

Selected Short Stories. Garden City: Doubleday, Doran, 1935.
From Main Street to Stockholm: Letters of Sinclair Lewis, 1919-1930. Selected and with an introduction by Harrison Smith. New York: Harcourt, Brace, 1952. Contains Lewis's correspondence **with** his publisher.
The Man From Main Street: A Sinclair Lewis Reader. Selected Essays and Other Writings, 1904-1950. Edited by Harry E. Maule and Melville H. Cane. New York: Random House, 1953. Includes most of Lewis's important published essays as **well as** a number of previously unprinted items.

SECONDARY SOURCES

1. Doctoral Dissertations

COLEMAN, ARTHUR B. *The Genesis of Social Ideas in Sinclair Lewis.* New York University, 1954. Studies the influence of Wells, Shaw, Veblen, Mencken, and Garland on Lewis's novels.
COUCH, WILLIAM, JR. *The Emergence, Rise and Decline of the Reputation of Sinclair Lewis.* University of Chicago, 1954. Broader than the title indicates; shows how Lewis's reception was affected by changes in critical taste.
DOOLEY, DAVID J. *The Impact of Satire on Fiction: Studies in Norman Douglas, Sinclair Lewis, Aldous Huxley, Evelyn Waugh, and George Orwell.* State University of Iowa, 1955. Advances thesis that Lewis could not resolve the dilemma of whether to be a novelist or a satirist.
FEINBERG, LEONARD. *Sinclair Lewis as a Satirist.* University of Illinois, 1946. Exhaustive study of satire as a genre and Lewis's satiric techniques.
GREBSTEIN, SHELDON NORMAN. *Sinclair Lewis: American Social Critic.* Michigan State University, 1954. General Study of Lewis's life and literary career.
LIGHT, MARTIN. *A Study of Characterization in Sinclair Lewis's Fiction.* University of Illinois, 1960. Examines Lewis's successes and failures as portrayer of character.
STORCH, WILLY. *Sinclair Lewis und das Amerikanische Kultur und Sprachbild.* Marburg, 1938. Focuses on Lewis as representative

of American civilization and language; contains close analysis of Lewis's style.

WASMUTH, HANS-WERNER. *Slang bei Sinclair Lewis.* Hamburg, 1935. Studies and classifies Lewis's use of slang, viewing it as typical of American English.

2. Books

ADAMIC, LOUIS. *My America.* New York: Harper, 1938; pp. 96-104. Personal reminiscences by one of Lewis's collaborators on labor novel.

ADAMS, J. DONALD. *The Shape of Books to Come.* New York: Viking, 1944; pp. 131-43. Critical evaluation; compares Lewis with Steinbeck and Dos Passos.

ANDERSON, CARL F. *The Swedish Acceptance of American Literature.* Philadelphia: University of Pennsylvania Press, 1957; pp. 45-63. Surveys Lewis's reception in Sweden.

BIRKHEAD, L. M. *Is Elmer Gantry True?* Pamphlet. Girard, Kansas: Haldeman-Julius, 1928. Defends validity of Lewis's satire in *Elmer Gantry;* also has list of Lewis's reading for *Elmer Gantry.*

BOYNTON, PERCY H. *America in Contemporary Fiction.* University of Chicago Press, 1940; pp. 164-84. Concludes Lewis has not lived up to his promise.

CABELL, JAMES BRANCH. *Straws and Prayer Books.* New York: McBride, 1924; pp. 50-51. Lists suggestions Cabell made for *Main Street.*

————. *Some of Us: An Essay in Epitaphs.* New York: McBride, 1930; pp. 61-73. Seminal essay viewing Lewis as creator of goblins.

————. *As I Remember It.* New York: McBride, 1955; pp. 165-71. Expresses disillusionment with Lewis as writer and as person.

CALVERTON, V. F. *The Liberation of American Literature.* New York: Scribner's, 1932; pp. 38-39, 425-33. Hails Lewis as one of emancipators of American fiction.

CANBY, HENRY S. *American Memoir.* Boston: Houghton Mifflin, 1947; pp. 306-9. Estimate of Lewis's historical importance, together with personal reminiscences.

————. In SPILLER, R. E., *et al., Literary History of the United States.* New York: Macmillan, 1948; pp. 1223-28, 1377-88. Cogent analysis of Lewis's career and European reception.

CANTWELL, ROBERT. In COWLEY, MALCOLM, ed. *After the Genteel Tradition.* New York: Norton, 1936; pp. 9-25, 112-26. Introduction sees Lewis as rebel against older literary traditions; later chapter provides general critical estimate.

Selected Bibliography

CARPENTER, FREDERICK I. *American Literature and the Dream.* New York: Philosophical Library, 1955; pp. 116-25. Analyzes causes for Lewis's failure after 1930.

DE VOTO, BERNARD. *The Literary Fallacy.* Boston: Little Brown, 1944; pp. 95-123. Attacks Lewis for criticizing America.

FADIMAN, CLIFTON. *Party of One.* New York: World, 1955; pp. 47-53, 132-35. Comments on Lewis's achievement and personality; compares Lewis with Dickens.

FORSTER, E. M. *Abinger Harvest.* New York: Harcourt, Brace, 1936; pp. 129-36. Discusses Lewis as photographer.

GEISMAR, MAXWELL. *Last of the Provincials.* Boston: Houghton, Mifflin, 1947; pp. 69-150, 364-66. The most thorough and probably the best critical study to date.

GRAY, JAMES. *On Second Thought.* Minneapolis: University of Minnesota Press, 1946; pp. 11-21. Attacks Lewis's superficiality.

HART, JAMES D. *The Popular Book.* New York: Oxford University Press, 1950; pp. 222-45. Shows how Lewis's novels coincided with the mood of the time.

HARTWICK, HARRY. *The Foreground of American Fiction.* New York: American Book, 1934; pp. 250-81. Good general estimate together with biographical information.

HATCHER, HARLAN. *Creating the Modern American Novel.* New York: Farrar and Rinehart, 1935; pp. 109-26. Sets forth factors for success of *Main Street.*

HERRON, IMA H. *The Small Town in American Literature.* Durham, N. C.: Duke University Press, 1939. Traces Lewis's depiction of small towns.

HOFFMAN, FREDERICK J. *The Modern Novel in America.* Chicago: Regnery, 1951; pp. 110-17. Sees Lewis as creator of fantasy.

————. *The Twenties.* New York: Viking, 1955; pp. 364-70. Close analysis of *Babbitt.*

HOLLIS, C. C. In GARDINER, HAROLD C. *Fifty Years of the American Novel.* New York: Scribner's, 1952; pp. 89-106. Discusses Lewis as reviver of Theophrastian Character genre.

HUNT, FRAZIER. *One American.* New York: Simon and Schuster, 1938; pp. 248-55. Illuminating reminiscences of Lewis at the height of his fame by one of his closest friends.

KARSNER, DAVID. *Sixteen Authors to One.* New York: Copeland, 1928; pp. 67-82. Valuable biographical source.

KAZIN, ALFRED. *On Native Grounds.* New York: Reynal and Hitchcock, 1942; pp. 205-26. Places Lewis in tradition of realism.

LEWIS, CLAUDE. *Treaty Trip.* Eds., DONALD GREENE and GEORGE KNOX. Minneapolis: University of Minnesota Press, 1959. Abridgement of journal kept by Lewis's older brother during 1924 Canadian trip.

LEWIS, GRACE HEGGER. *Half a Loaf*. New York: Liveright, 1931. Mrs. Lewis's reply to *Dodsworth*.

————. *With Love From Gracie*. New York: Harcourt, Brace, 1955. Invaluable source of biographical information.

LEWISOHN, LUDWIG. *Expression in America*. New York: Harper, 1932; pp. 492-513. Excellent critical analysis; compares Lewis with Molière and Dickens.

LIPPMANN, WALTER. *Men of Destiny*. New York: Macmillan, 1927; pp. 71-92. Perceptive treatment of Lewis's books of the 1920's.

MICHAUD, REGIS. *The American Novel To-Day*. Boston: Little, Brown, 1931; pp. 129-53. Useful interpretation by a prominent French critic.

MORRIS, LLOYD. *Postscript to Yesterday*. New York: Random House, 1947; pp. 134-42. Estimates Lewis's impact on American thought.

NATHAN, GEORGE JEAN. *The Intimate Notebooks of George Jean Nathan*. New York: Knopf, 1932; pp. 9-21. One of best sources on Lewis's personality and mimic ability.

PARRINGTON, VERNON L. *Main Currents in American Thought*. New York, Harcourt, Brace, 1930; pp. 360-69. Sees Lewis as gadfly to native complacency.

ROURKE, CONSTANCE. *American Humor*. New York: Harcourt, Brace, 1931; pp. 283-86. Places Lewis in American comic tradition.

SCHORER, MARK. "Two Houses, Two Ways," in *New World Writing: Fourth Mentor Selection*. New York: New American Library, 1953; pp. 136-54. Excellent treatment of Lewis's last year of life.

————. *Society and Self in the Novel: English Institute Essays*. New York: Columbia University Press, 1956; pp. 117-44. Perceptive analysis of Lewis's career, with special emphasis on *Elmer Gantry*.

————. *Sinclair Lewis: An American Life*. New York: McGraw-Hill, 1961. This is the "official" biography of Lewis. According to enthusiastic advance reports, it is a lively account which runs to over 800 pages. It will surely be an indispensable reference.

SHERMAN, STUART P. *The Significance of Sinclair Lewis*. New York: Harcourt, Brace, 1922. An early pamphlet, but still valuable for its insights.

TAYLOR, WALTER F. *A History of American Letters*. Boston: American Book, 1936; pp. 382-90. Sensible critical and historical survey.

VAN DOREN, CARL. *Sinclair Lewis: A Biographical Sketch*. With a Bibliography by Harvey Taylor. Garden City: Doubleday, Doran, 1933. Frequently uncritical but still useful source of biographical information.

WEST, REBECCA. *The Strange Necessity*. New York: Doubleday, Doran, 1928; pp. 295-309. Shrewd analysis of *Elmer Gantry*.

Selected Bibliography

WHIPPLE, T. K. *Spokesmen*. New York: Appleton, 1928; pp. 208-29. Remains one of most perceptive discussions of Lewis's worldview.

3. Periodical Articles

ADAMS, J. DONALD. "Speaking of Books," *New York Times Book Review* (July 31, 1960), 2. Compares Lewis and Marquand.

ALEXANDER, JACK. "Rover Girl in Europe," *Saturday Evening Post*, CCXII (May 25, 1940), 20-21 ff. Biographical material on Dorothy Thompson, some of it pertinent to Lewis.

AUSTIN, ALLEN. "An Interview with Sinclair Lewis," *University of Kansas City Review*, XXIV (1958), 199-210. Has useful biographical material, based on 1948 interview.

BABCOCK, C. MERTON. "Americanisms in the Novels of Sinclair Lewis," *American Speech*, XXXV (May, 1960), 110-16. Views Lewis as recorder and contributor to American popular speech.

BACON, LEONARD. "Yale, '09," *Saturday Review of Literature*, XIX (Feb. 4, 1939), 13-14. Reminiscences of Lewis at Yale by a classmate.

BAKER, JOSEPH E. "Sinclair Lewis, Plato and the Regional Escape," *English Journal*, XXVIII (June, 1939), 460-68. Depicts Lewis as a modern counterpart of Plato and Spengler, critic of a decaying culture.

BECK, WARREN. "How Good Is Sinclair Lewis?" *College English*, IX (Jan., 1948), 173-80. Finds Lewis vastly overrated.

BECKER, G. J. "Apostle to the Philistines," *American Scholar*, XXI (Fall, 1952), 423-32. Focuses on Lewis's limitations.

BENÉT, WILLIAM ROSE. "The Earlier Lewis," *Saturday Review of Literature*, X (Jan. 20, 1934), 421-22. Valuable for information on Lewis's college years and early career.

BINSSE, H. L., and TROUNSTINE, J. J. "Europe Looks at Sinclair Lewis," *Bookman*, LXXII (Jan., 1931), 453-57. Advances thesis that Lewis's books added to European misconceptions of American life.

BRACE, ERNEST. "Cock Robin and Co., Publishers," *Commonweal*, XIII (Dec. 10, 1930), 147-49. Analyzes success of *Main Street*.

BREASTED, CHARLES. "The 'Sauk-Centricities' of Sinclair Lewis," *Saturday Review*, XXXVII (Aug., 1954), 7-8, 33-36. Suggests autobiographical factors in Lewis's novels.

BROWN, DEMING. "Sinclair Lewis: the Russian View," *American Literature*, XXV (March, 1953), 1-12. Parallels Lewis's reputation in Russia with changes in Communist Party doctrine.

CALVERTON, V. F. "Sinclair Lewis, the Last of the Literary Liberals," *Modern Monthly*, VIII (March, 1934), 77-86. A prominent Marxist critic of the 1930's attacks Lewis for living in the past.

CLEMENS, CYRIL. "Impressions of Sinclair Lewis, with Some Letters," *Hobbies,* LVI (April, 1951), 138-39. Has information on Lewis's boyhood.

CROCKER, LIONEL. "Sinclair Lewis on Public Speaking," *Quarterly Journal of Speech,* XXI (April, 1935), 232-37. Studies Lewis's satire of public speaking; concludes Lewis uses it to represent hollowness in American life.

FLANAGAN, JOHN T. "A Long Way to Gopher Prairie: Sinclair Lewis' Apprenticeship," *Southwest Review,* XXXII (Fall, 1947), 403-13. Thorough treatment of Lewis's early work.

————. "The Minnesota Backgrounds of Sinclair Lewis' Fiction," *Minnesota History,* XXXVII (March, 1960), 1-15. Detailed survey of Lewis's use of Minnesota as locale.

FYVEL, T. R. "Martin Arrowsmith and His Habitat," *New Republic,* CXXXIII (July 18, 1955), 16-18. Views Lewis as creator of nightmarish, demonic world, but asserts he had great virtues as well as faults.

GAUSS, CHRISTIAN. "Sinclair Lewis vs. His Education," *Saturday Evening Post,* CCIV (Dec. 26, 1931), 20-21 ff. Demonstrates how Lewis's environment and education affected his career.

GEISMAR, MAXWELL. "Sinclair Lewis: Forgotten Hero," *Saturday Review,* XLIII (June 25, 1960), 29-30. Calls for revival of interest in Lewis and reappraisal of his contributions.

GRATTAN, C. HARTLEY. "Sinclair Lewis: The Work of a Lifetime," *New Republic,* CXXV (April 2, 1951), 19-20. Concludes that Lewis was essentially a storyteller.

GREBSTEIN, SHELDON NORMAN. "Sinclair Lewis' Minnesota Boyhood, *Minnesota History,* XXXIV (Autumn, 1954), 85-89. Detailed study of Lewis's Sauk Centre experiences.

————. "The Education of a Rebel: Sinclair Lewis at Yale," *New England Quarterly,* XXVIII (Sept., 1955), 372-82. Studies Lewis's college career and writing.

————. "Sinclair Lewis's Unwritten Novel," *Philological Quarterly,* XXXVII (Oct., 1958), 400-9. Discusses Lewis's labor novel and reasons for his failure to complete it.

————. "Sinclair Lewis and the Nobel Prize," *Western Humanities Review,* XIII (Spring, 1959), 163-71. Studies factors involved in award of Nobel Prize to Lewis, his European reputation, and Prize's effect on his career.

GURKO, LEO and MIRIAM. "The Two Main Streets of Sinclair Lewis," *College English,* IV (Feb., 1943), 288-92. Asserts that satire is essential to Lewis's success.

GUTHRIE, RAMON. "The Labor Novel Sinclair Lewis Never Wrote," *New York Herald Tribune Book Review,* XXVIII (Feb. 10,

1952), 1, 6. Important article on a crucial phase of Lewis's career by a close friend and collaborator.

HICKS, GRANVILLE. "Sinclair Lewis and the Good Life," *English Journal*, XXV (April, 1936), 265-73. Analyzes Lewis's career from viewpoint of his attitude toward rebels.

JOHNSON, GERALD W. "Romance and Mr. Babbitt," *New Republic*, CXXIV (Jan. 29, 1951), 14-15. An excellent short article summarizing Lewis's thought and achievement.

LYNAM, HAZEL PALMER. "The Earliest Lewis," *Saturday Review of Literature*, X (April 14, 1934), 628. Anecdotes of Lewis as a boy in Sauk Centre.

MANFRED, FREDERICK F. "Sinclair Lewis: A Portrait," *American Scholar*, XXIII (1954), 162-84. Invaluable for account of Lewis in the 1940's and for insight into his loneliness and sense of failure.

MANSON, ALEXANDER and CAMP, HELEN. "The Last Days of Sinclair Lewis," *Saturday Evening Post*, CCXXIII (March 31, 1951), 27, 110-12. Poignant account of Lewis' last year alive by his personal secretary and companion.

MCNALLY, WILLIAM J. "Americans We Like: Mr. Babbitt, Meet Sinclair Lewis," *Nation*, CXXV (Sept. 21, 1927), 278-81. Good for material on Lewis's personality, especially its contradictions.

MILLER PERRY. "The Incorruptible Sinclair Lewis," *Atlantic*, CLXXXVII (April, 1951), 30-34. Invaluable personal reminiscences of Lewis and analysis of his career.

MOORE, JAMES BENEDICT. "The Sources of 'Elmer Gantry,'" *New Republic*, CXLIII (Aug. 8, 1960), 6. Traces Lewis's hero to its true-life originals.

MORRIS, LLOYD. "Sinclair Lewis—His Critics and the Public," *North American Review*, CCXLV (Summer, 1938), 381-90. Points out why Lewis continued to engage readers after he had lost critical favor.

MUMFORD, LEWIS. "The America of Sinclair Lewis," *Current History*, XXXIII (1931), 529-33. Eminently sensible, balanced appraisal of Lewis in light of Nobel award.

SCHORER, MARK. "The World of Sinclair Lewis," *New Republic*, CXXVIII (April 6, 1953), 18-20. Compares *Our Mr. Wrenn* and *World So Wide;* also praises Lewis as an essayist.

————. editor. "A Minnesota Diary," *Esquire*, L (Oct., 1958), 160-62. Introduces and reprints excerpts from Lewis's journals in the early 1940's.

SCHULBERG, BUDD. "Lewis: Big Wind from Sauk Centre," *Esquire*, LIV (1960), 110-14. Portrays Lewis in the 1930's; offers an explanation for *The Prodigal Parents*.

SMITH, HARRISON. "Sinclair Lewis: Remembrance of the Past," *Saturday Review of Literature*, XXXIV (Jan. 27, 1951), 7-9, 36-38. Invaluable personal account of Lewis by one of his oldest friends; focuses on Lewis's loneliness.

STEVENS, BETTY. "A Village Radical Goes Home," *Venture*, II (Summer, 1956), 17-26. Record of a 1945 visit with Lewis; contains pertinent biographical material.

————. "A Village Radical: His Last American Home," *Venture*, II (Winter, 1957), 35-48. Continuation of above but about 1947 visit. Has interesting data on Lewis's political views.

STOLBERG, BENJAMIN. "Sinclair Lewis," *American Mercury*, LIII (Oct., 1941), 450-60. Pertinent to Lewis's personality and to labor novel; compares Lewis with Twain.

THOMPSON, DOROTHY. "Sinclair Lewis: A Postscript," *Atlantic*, CLXXXVII (June, 1951), 73-74. Important biographical material by his former wife.

————. "The Boy and Man from Sauk Centre," *Atlantic*, CCVI (Nov., 1960), 39-48. Essential for its insights into Lewis's personality and career.

TINKER, CHAUNCY BREWSTER. "Sinclair Lewis, a Few Reminiscences," *Yale Alumni Magazine* (June, 1952), 10. Memories of Lewis at college and thereafter by a former teacher.

WALKER, FRANKLIN. "Jack London's Use of Sinclair Lewis Plots," *Huntingdon Library Quarterly*, XVII (1953), 59-74. Reprints some of Lewis's plots sold to London.

WARREN, DALE. "Notes on a Genius: Sinclair Lewis at His Best," *Harper's*, CCVIII (Jan., 1954), 61-69. Favorable account of Lewis's personality in the 1930's.

WATERMAN, MARGARET. "Sinclair Lewis as a Teacher," *College English*, XIII (Nov., 1951), 87-90. Reminiscences by a member of Lewis's writing class at the University of Wisconsin.

WOODWARD, W. E. "The World and Sauk Centre," *New Yorker*, IX (Jan. 27, 1934), 24-27; (Feb. 3, 1934), 24-27. Detailed account of Lewis's personality.

————. "Sinclair Lewis gets the Job," *Saturday Review of Literature*, XXX (Nov. 1, 1947), 10-11. Recalls Lewis's employment as reviewer for syndicated book-review column in 1912.

Index

Hart, James D., 37, 38
Hatcher, Harlan, 166
Hemingway, Ernest, 121, 122, 135
Henry, O., 37, 52, 139
Herrick, Robert, 30, 72
Hicks, Granville, 108, 143
Hitler, Adolf, 135, 139, 140, 142
Horace, 165
Howe, Edgar Watson, 72
Howells, William Dean, 30, 59, 120
Hunt, Frazier, 148
Huxley, Thomas Henry, 83

Inherit the Wind, 105
Irving, Washington, 101

James, Henry, *The American,* 114, 116, 175*n*
Joyce, James, 121

Kafka, Franz, 92
Karlfeldt, Erik Axel, 118-19
Kazin, Alfred, 108
Ku Klux Klan, 81, 140, 141

La Follette, Robert M., 26, 96, 97, 142, 146
Lardner, Ring, 108
Lewis, Claude, 21, 22, 97, 167*n*
Lewis, Edwin J., 21, 22, 71
Lewis, Grace Hegger, 22, 27, 47, 48-50, 57, 62, 113, 123
Lewis, Isabel Warner, 71
Lewis, Lloyd, 132
Lewis, Michael, 27
Lewis, Sinclair: ambivalence as a writer, 19-21, 24-26, 50-60, 71-72, 84-85, 112-13, 125-26, 129, 133-39, 160-62, 171*n*; as humorist, 30; as satirist and social critic, 24-25, 53-59, 63-67, 73-85, 89-90, 95, 99-105, 108, 111, 114-16, 128-29, 131, 133, 139-42, 145-46, 148, 150-51, 152-54, 155-57, 158-59, 160; at Yale, 22-24; autobiographical elements in novels, 38, 45, 47, 48-50, 55, 71-72, 75, 86-88, 112-14, 125-26, 176*n*, 178*n*; boyhood in Sauk Centre, 21-22; counter-education as theme

of later novels, 64-66; early writings, 24-25; education as theme of early novels, 38-42, 44-48; effect of Depression on career, 124-25, 128-29, 137-39, 141; labor novel, 85, 122-25, 138; literary significance, 19, 30-32, 72-73, 85, 90-91, 93, 105-6, 117-18, 137-38, 143-44, 154-55, 161-66; membership in Socialist Party, 25, 168*n*; Nobel Prize, 30, 117-23, 175-76*n*; parallels with Dickens, 33-36; personality, 21-23, 26-29; portrayal of sexuality, 101-2, 126-27, 147, 150, 151; portrayal of women, 42, 48-49, 67-68, 70-71, 88-89, 110-12, 114, 125-26, 134, 149, 151, 158, 178*n*; relationship to Progressive Movement and political beliefs, 96-97, 145-46; relationship with father, 21-22, 71, 167-68*n*; reading, 20, 23, 24, 25, 31, 103; rejection of the Pulitzer Prize, 26, 98, 118; similarities to Emerson and Thoreau, 31-32; socialism in early novels, 45, 50, 54, 57-58; socialism in later novels, 145-46; style in early novels, 42-44

WRITINGS OF:

Angela Is Twenty-Two, 176-77*n*, 178*n*
Ann Vickers, 112, 125-20, 131, 147, 148, 176*n*
Arrowsmith, 32, 33, 44, 53, 85-96, 98, 109, 112, 114, 115, 117, 123, 128, 130, 140, 155, 164, 173*n*
Babbitt, 26, 30, 33, 34, 44, 62, 73-85, 86, 88, 89, 91, 95, 96, 98, 100, 101, 108, 109, 110, 114, 115, 117, 118, 119, 121, 128, 131, 133, 137, 141, 142, 152, 155, 157, 163, 164, 165
Bethel Merriday, 43, 112, 129, 134-36, 157, 164
Cass Timberlane, 148-52, 154, 156, 178*n*
Dodsworth, 42, 46, 53, 109-17,